# Schooling and the Rights of Children

## THE NATIONAL SOCIETY
## FOR THE STUDY OF EDUCATION

Series on Contemporary Educational Issues
Kenneth J. Rehage, Series Editor

*The 1975 Titles*

*Reading: Some Points of View*, Samuel Weintraub, Editor
*Systems of Individualized Education*, Harriet Talmage, Editor
*Schooling and the Rights of Children*, Vernon F. Haubrich and
   Michael W. Apple, Editors
*Educational Policy and International Assessment: Implications of
   the IEA Surveys of Achievement*, Alan C. Purves and Daniel U.
   Levine, Editors

The National Society for the Study of Education also publishes Year-books which are distributed by the University of Chicago Press. Inquiries regarding all publications of the Society, as well as inquiries about membership in the Society, may be addressed to the Secretary-Treasurer, 5835 Kimbark Avenue, Chicago, IL 60637. Membership in the Society is open to any who are interested in promoting the investigation and discussion of educational questions.

# Schooling
# and the
# Rights of Children

Edited by

# Vernon F. Haubrich

and

# Michael W. Apple

University of Wisconsin
Madison

McCutchan Publishing Corporation
2526 Grove Street
Berkeley, California 94704

ISBN 0-8211-0755-0
Library of Congress Catalog Card Number 74-24477

# Series Foreword

Issues pertaining to the rights of children in school situations are coming into public view with increasing frequency. The contributors to this volume provide a broad perspective within which those issues may be considered. They note the historical, sociological, psychological, and political forces that have recently brought about a major reassessment of the long-established doctrine of "in loco parentis" and have created a climate in which school authorities are expected to see that constitutional guarantees, including "due process," are observed in dealing with students. The authors conclude that schools must provide a setting in which a process of conflict resolution can be the means of adjudicating issues arising in connection with the extension of rights and liberties of children.

*Schooling and the Rights of Children* is one of the four titles in the 1975 Series on Contemporary Educational Issues published under the auspices of the National Society for the Study of Education. Other titles in the series are:

*Systems of Individualized Education*, edited by Harriet Talmage;

*Reading: Some Points of View*, edited by Samuel Weintraub;

*Educational Policy and International Assessment: Implications of the IEA Surveys of Achievement*, edited by Alan C. Purves and Daniel U. Levine.

The Society is grateful to the editors, Professors Vernon F. Haubrich and Michael W. Apple, and to their associated contributors, for this interesting collection of essays.

*Kenneth J. Rehage*

for the Committee on the Expanded
Publication Program of the
National Society for the Study
of Education

# Preface

The forces surrounding the developing area of children's rights are both historical and contemporary, both psychological and sociological, both philosophical and legal. Intertwined so as to present no clear and simple pattern, but interrelated so as to reinforce one another, are the following:

1. The changing role of the child within the family structure;
2. The changing role of the school in a highly bureaucratized, industrial, technological society;
3. The growing interest of the state in a redefinition of childhood and adolescence based on the increasing interest of the state in talent, achievement, and international competition;
4. The growing political power of youth in America stemming in large part from the length and extent of the Vietnam war as well as the struggle for civil rights.

These forces have forced courts, legislatures, universities, and schools to a position of necessary reassessment and change given the basic political processes related to pressure groups, legislative processes, and legal thinking. In many respects the reconsideration of student and children's rights and their continual downward extension to younger age groups has been a struggle to have the various institutions reconsider the *process* by which authority over children is conceptualized.

The authority employed by schools and other public agencies over children has been one of in loco parentis—standing in the place of the parents. This authority was clearly hierarchical in nature and centered on the view that the experience and age of adults in schools and other agencies gave them a privileged position vis-à-vis children and students. The father's power over his family as well as the school's authority to make rules was not to be questioned, nor was the school that made rules without consulting the student. This basic assumption—that schools do not have to justify the rules they establish—was forced into the areas of due process of law and the equal protection of the laws. It is best illustrated by the fundamental change that took place in the courts between 1959 and 1963. As late as 1959 students who wished a hearing on suspension, or expulsion by college authorities simply had no recourse. Colleges and schools were places where actions by administrators could not be challenged because schools and colleges held that unique position of being in loco parentis. The courts were reluctant then to enter into the area of college and school authority over minors or even over those who had obtained their majority in college. The civil rights movement and the growing dissatisfaction with the arbitrariness of institutional intransigence resulted in a basic shift in policy by the federal courts.

Critical to this new stance was the new reasoning that public schools (colleges in particular) are, indeed, public institutions, and action taken by these agencies falls into the same category as any other publicly supported institution and must contain the basic due process procedures available to all citizens. No longer could schools simply discharge a student for wearing an arm band, long hair, or short skirts. All the safeguards of due process had now to be followed to justify rules, regulations, procedures, and actions.

This shift, from an institution that enjoyed a uniquely protected status acting in the role of the parent, to that of a public agency having to conform to basic constitutional guarantees, is momentous in that teachers, administrators, and related personnel have all been conditioned to behave in exactly the opposite way. It was both understandable and inevitable that this shift of court policy would be followed by the anguish of the displaced authority.

What is now imperative is that relationships of authority be reconstructed so that the tasks of education may go forward. This reconstruction must necessarily take into account several issues that must be joined before some resolution and accommodation can be made. Among those issues that educators need to reassess are:

1. The definition of student rights and the classes into which they fall;
2. The historical process by which the state and courts began to assert a larger interest in the welfare and rights of children;
3. The sociology and psychology of child growth and development and the issues related to questions of responsibility, control, and protection;
4. The legal development of children's rights and the controlling cases that apply to school procedures;
5. The implications of these movements for school policy, administrative behavior, and teaching procedures.

We are indeed in a strange age where the process of bureaucratization and rigidity have created a public institution of schooling that seems to oppose all extensions of children's rights and views these extensions as threats to its own survival, while only a few generations ago the schools were championing their programs against established business and tax groups. Inexorably the schools have become conservative and, in some cases, reactionary. This volume is, consequently, intended to establish a new perspective on the extension of liberties and rights of children within the confines of the public schools. The collective view of the writers is that a process of conflict resolution is necessary and essential to avoid the debilitations of continued battle and struggle over which rights are or are not operative. This is *not* to say that such conflict itself is necessarily negative. Indeed, it may very well be an exceptionally important educative experience for all involved. Our point is, rather, that it is necessary to provide more educationally responsible institutions while the more basic and necessary questioning of the forms of interaction that dominate schools and other institutions in this society also occurs.

This procedure attempts consistently to review the rules, regulations, and procedures of schooling with particular attention to the full participation of all relevant and interested parties. School boards, administrators, teachers, and legislative leaders may have to review fundamental assumptions regarding the nature of authority in public schools. The sharing of power with students is a process that can be threatening or rewarding depending on the outlook and philosophical dispositions of those who hold power. It is threatening if our view of schools remains hierarchical and bureaucratic and exhibits a philosophy of authority that resides at the top. It is rewarding if we view the interest of students, at any level, as legitimated by their actual concerns for particular rights. Indeed, what may well happen is that the school leaders of tomorrow will become skilled negotiators attempting to arbitrate, extend, refine, and develop both a sense of rights and of responsibilities within the framework of the public school system.

This volume is directed toward arriving at a sensible and accommodating position. One would hope for a reformed policy that is more open than closed, more knowledgeable than ignorant, more democratic than authoritarian. But hopes must be accompanied by committed action on a wide variety of fronts—economic, educational, political—for only action based on knowledge can recreate the sense of responsiveness and justice so often missing in major institutions today. As educators, we cannot afford to ignore these missing elements.

This volume grows out of a seminar and study group on "Schooling and the Rights of Children" held at the University of Wisconsin, Madison, during the spring of 1973. Its roots also lie in the activity of a number of the participants as activists in the student rights struggle. Both as members of the university community and as actors in the larger movement to make institutions more responsive and to extend constitutional guarantees to individuals and groups who are denied them in this country, we believe that schools cannot be truly educative in the best sense of the word without being concerned with the rights and forms of justice accorded to their primary clientele—students.

The editors and authors would like to thank their colleagues and the high school students, judges, lawyers, and student advocates who all contributed to the seminar and continually provided stimulation and challenge in grappling with the problem of student rights. Finally, thanks must also go to those individuals whose continued commitment and action have made progress possible in student rights.

*Vernon F. Haubrich*
*Michael W. Apple*

# Contributors

*Michael W. Apple,* Associate Professor of Curriculum and Instruction, University of Wisconsin, Madison

*Thomas Brady,* Doctoral Candidate, University of Wisconsin, Madison

*Bonnie Cook Freeman,* Assistant Professor of Education, University of Texas, Austin

*Vernon F. Haubrich,* Professor of Educational Policy Studies, University of Wisconsin, Madison

*Sharon L. Koenings,* Teacher, Public Schools, Racine, Wisconsin

*Guy Leekley,* Professor of Law, Lewis University, Lockport, Illinois

*Linda M. McNeil,* Doctoral Candidate, University of Wisconsin, Madison

*Paul C. Magnusson,* Assistant Professor of English Education, Reed College

*Patricia K. Naherny*, Doctoral Candidate, University of Wisconsin, Madison

*Steven L. Ober*, Educational Consultant, Station KRON-TV, San Francisco, California

*José Rosario*, Assistant Professor of Education, Inter-American University, Puerto Rico

*Peter J. Sartorius*, Educational Planner, West Michigan Regional Planning Commission, Kalamazoo, Michigan

# Contents

# 1. Morality, Science, and the Use of the Child in History

*Patricia K. Naherny* and *José Rosario*

The present controversy surrounding the issue of extending rights to children is characterized by limited legal precedents, inconclusive and conflicting psychosocial evidence, and the value-laden arguments of several and diverse interest groups. Within this labyrinth, educators, administrators, and other school officials struggle along, seeking consistent and reliable evidence upon which to base decisions in the resolution of the increasing number of student rights "situations." Hard pressed by the practical and political immediacy of these situations, we seldom seriously consider the historical roots of the issue, much less wonder about the historical position of the child himself. Of what use is an understanding of the kind of life a child led in medieval France or the discipline he endured in seventeenth-century New England when dealing with such problems as whether to regulate a student's physical appearance and dress or to permit him free access to his records? A review of the changing conceptions of the child throughout history does not purport to provide solutions to these and other specific dilemmas facing school officials today. Such a review as presented here can, however, be useful in removing the issue of children's rights from the time and place of the 1970s and putting it in a more general historical perspective.

If we view the contemporary concern for the rights of children solely as a phenomenon of recent times and refuse to account for its significant historical underpinnings, we assume that the child has always held the same status as he does now in our society and that parents and society of other ages have had the same attitudes toward and expectations of the child as parents of this age. But historical evidence contradicts this assumption. For example, the ten year old, whose behavior our schools, parents, and courts so carefully watch over and regulate, participated fully in the affairs of adults in the 1500s. There was no thought that a child of that age was either intellectually or physically incapable of performing these tasks. Through study of the variations in attitudes toward and treatment of the child throughout history, one sees clearly that these changes are manifestations of the continual process of redefining the status of the child in society. When viewed in this perspective, the present concern for the rights of children can then be understood as the most recent attempt to define the status of the child in American society. The focus of this concern has until now been the relationship between the child and the family, as exemplified by child labor legislation and the child welfare movement. That the focus has shifted to the relationship between the child and the school reflects in part the growth of the school's involvement in nearly every aspect of the child's life.

This premise concerning the continual redefinition of the status of the child in society forms the thread that joins the two analyses comprising this discussion. The first section, written by Patricia K. Naherny, undertakes a broad look at the Western European child from the fourteenth through the nineteenth centuries to review the development of those conceptions which helped to delineate a special and distinct status for the child. The major thrust of this analysis argues that the definitional nature of children's rights evolves in part from the confluence of dominant philosophical, political, social, and economic variables in a particular time.

The second section, written by José Rosario, narrows the scope of the discussion to direct attention to the child in American society as he was viewed and treated from the beginning of the colonial period to the close of the nineteenth century. It traces the transition in intellectual thought from moralistic views of the child to scientific or psychological views. This analysis demonstrates that certain themes underlying the present relationship between the child and the school have their origins in the earlier moralistic thinking, which contemporary scientific views of childhood have neither disproved nor replaced but rather have actually legitimized.

The present discussion does not pretend to match the definitive works of Aries and other social historians. Although it recognizes and touches upon the inextricable relationship of thought to a social, political, and economic matrix, the treatment is necessarily incomplete. The major purpose has been to put forth those significant historical ideas and themes and to suggest those trends which may affect the direction of the present movement toward the rights of students and children.

## Social Structure and the Use of the Child in the Past: Historical Views of Childhood in Europe

### Overview

Much of the argumentation concerning the rights of children gives the impression that these rights are founded upon an absolute principle of justice or immutable law of child development and exist separately from the rights extended other groups in society. Certain rights, for example, the right to life and other constitutional guarantees, are absolutes and exist equally for children as well as for other groups in American society. With regard to option rights, such as the right to drink alcoholic beverages, however, historical evidence finds no law or principle justifying them, albeit existence of such a law would considerably minimize the problems encountered in deciding what option rights should be extended to children. Historical data indicate, rather, that the rights of children are but one component of a larger framework which also encompasses the rights of adolescents, parents, and the state. Within this framework, the rights defined for one group are dependent upon and related to the rights defined for the other groups, so that shifts or changes in the rights held by children will bring about changes in the rights held by parents or the state. The system of interrelationships that exists between the rights of these individual groups at any particular time is molded by the interplay of several key variables, such as dominant political and philosophical ideologies and existing social and economic conditions.

Evidence for this supposition is found in the analysis of the concepts of childhood that emerged between the fourteenth and the
nineteenth centuries in Western Europe, specifically in France and
England. Through this analysis, we first discover that the concept of
childhood itself, which distinguishes the child as an entity separate
and distinct from the adult, is a relatively modern idea. The brief
examination given to some of the factors influencing the development of the concept is important in demonstrating that certain critical notions we still hold about children are not inherent characteristics of either the child or childhood.

The second part of the analysis reviews certain themes as underlying intellectual thought in the period after the emergence of the
concept and the rationales used in support of specific English welfare
and compulsory education legislation. These themes have undergone
many variations in the last five hundred years, but basically see the
child as man's spiritual and moral salvation; as unique laborer vital to
the economy; as a precursor of the Rational Man; as the living essence of the state of nature and the seed of the Natural Man; and as
"the father of the man."

Initial examination of these themes reveals a unifying concern for
the importance of childhood as preparation for adulthood, a concern
that is a function of the inherent educative aspect of the concept of
childhood. With further analysis it becomes evident that these
themes or "theories" on the importance of childhood are basically
reflections of certain needs of individuals and groups, who seized
upon the idea of childhood as a means toward fulfilling those needs.

This idea of the use of the child as a means toward specific ends
cannot be overemphasized. Even within the boundaries of this particular study, it is strikingly clear that the concern expressed for the
education, care, and rights of the child was more accurately a desire
to attain some political, social, or economic end. While advocating
aesthetic appreciation for the child or a genuine concern for his abuse,
those who held these views really conceived of the child primarily in
light of his usefulness to society. Economic considerations were most
often at the core of this concern. The emergence of the concept of
childhood itself was, in fact, part of this pattern, having evolved in
some degree from the needs created by the development of the modern industrial state.

If the rights of groups in society are definitionally related, then the balance formed by the interrelationships between the rights of these groups should shift occasionally to favor one group over another. And yet, as this review will attempt to show, since the emergence of the concept of childhood, the balance seems never to have been in favor of the child. The concept of childhood and the several refinements of the idea have served to define a status for the child separate and distinct from adults, differentiating expected and appropriate behaviors for the child. These processes of definition and differentiation have usually limited and restricted the child's behavior, thus narrowing his rights as well.

## The Emergence of the Conception of Childhood

According to Aries in *Centuries of Childhood,* an awareness of the child as someone distinct and different from an adult was not an idea generally accepted until the seventeenth century. An individual's life comprised but two broad periods: an extended "infancy," which lasted until six or seven years of age, and "adulthood."[1]

The infant was generally regarded by adults with fear and indifference. The fear grew from the prevailing notion of the infant's bestiality, which no doubt stemmed from general ignorance of the infant and from the pain and death often accompanying childbirth. Although writing from observations made in the late 1800s, Maria Montessori aptly describes this irrational fear: "from the first moment of its arrival among us we are instinctively on our guard against it. With instinctive greed, we hasten to protect whatever we possess . . . . From the moment of a child's birth, the mind of an adult is dominated by this thought: 'Take care the infant does not soil anything or become a nuisance. Watch out. Be on your guard.' "[2]

The child passed quickly from this period of infancy to adulthood, usually discarding his infant's attire at the age of six or seven when he had been completely weaned. While a child, he had remained with his parents, receiving the necessary care and supervision from the family. With the onset of adulthood, he usually left home either to attend school, to apprentice himself to a master of some trade or another household, or to do both. When he came to be viewed as an adult, he shared equally in the activities and responsibilities of the older adults. He was expected to and did work as other adults. He frequented the same places of entertainment, attended the same social gatherings, participated in the same games, and, if he could, read the same books. Today this adult society would seem somewhat puerile, given the free mixing of so many age groups.[3] Yet, while perhaps the mixing made for a less sophisticated society by our standards, it also served to encourage a child to be rather precocious.

The problem of the younger adult's lack of experience was handled by a system of peer group regulation. Students banded together into societies or corporations, in which the older individuals acted as leaders to the neophytes. "Parents did not abandon the child of ten to the hazards of the road and foreign towns; they entrusted him to an older and therefore more experienced student, who was better equipped for a dangerous life."[4] Since there was little parental control—the child did not live at home—and minimal supervision on the part of the school or apprentice master, these older individuals provided instruction in the practical aspects of the world and the discipline necessary to behave in a socially acceptable manner.

High infant mortality rates and the short life span of adults were undoubtably major factors underlying the indifferent attitude toward the infant and the early initiation of the young into the adult world. At this time, people were constantly beset by disease, famine, and war. "As late as 1720 a severe outbreak of the plague in Southeastern France left 40,000 dead out of a total of 90,000 in Marseilles."[5] Infants often did not live more than one or two years after birth; they died from disease, lack of food, and, more generally, medical ignorance and misapplication of basic infant and child care. Even in the early eighteenth century, "only about four in every 100 persons failed to contract smallpox, a hideous illness that afflicted children in the first year or two of life."[6] Because of the high probability of a child's early death, indifference toward the infant protected the parents and family against the constant trauma of loss.

Similarly, the reality of early death for those who survived infancy—life expectancy was only half what we know—required the child to become an adult early so that the family and society would gain some benefits from his existence. Especially for middle- and upper-class parents, the brevity of life necessitated that the child be able to manage adult affairs to ensure the transmittal and continued ownership of all property among direct family members.

Mortality rates do not, however, provide a complete explanation. Until the mid-nineteenth century, when the concept of childhood had already gained widespread acceptance, the mortality rates remained high, with the major cause of death being infanticide.[7] It is obvious that the indifference manifested by this behavior had its roots not in fear of the loss of a child but in the burden presented by too many children.

Of greater significance in explaining the absence of a distinction between the child and adult in preindustrial society is the socioeconomic context in which that society existed. The economy was still basically agrarian; the social structure was feudal in nature and was characterized by communal living. The extended family, a large household of immediate and distant relatives, servants, and continuous stream of guests and visitors, served as the primary unit of social organization. As a result, "children were no different from the adult members of the family in that they were all conceived as component parts of a far larger unit, the extended family, to whose interest those of the interrelated nuclear families of parents and children were subordinated. The promotion of family ambition, the advancement of family interest . . . were seen as the common, all-important social task."[8]

Since the child was considered able to share the responsibilities of older adults and to contribute equally to the benefit of the society and the family, there was no reason to treat him any differently or restrict him from participation in any activities. This communal world view was at the heart of the society's acceptance and approval of the system of apprenticeship and peer group regulation. Since all members of the community contributed equally to its maintenance, parents had no reservations about relinquishing their control over the child to someone else. Because there was no distinction between the behavior permitted the child and the adult, there was no reason to have a system of control imposed from outside by the parent or master.

In sum, the maintenance needs of this particular society were such as to benefit from and foster a view of the child that did not distinguish him from the adult. The need to utilize all the manpower available in promotion of family ends mitigated against such a distinction. As a consequence, children had the same rights as adults.

When urbanization and industrialization changed the socioeconomic structure of the society, the family changed too, emerging ultimately as the modern nuclear family. The functions and the maintenance needs of this private and insular social unit were quite different from those of its antecedent.[9] Thus, the emergence of the concept of childhood can be seen, in part, as the attempt of the family to fulfill those needs, to redefine the status of the child to complement his changed status. The evolution of the concept of childhood was, however, a gradual process. Before it could become firmly entrenched in the thinking of the seventeenth century, the specific ideas that characterized it had to be introduced and accepted. These ideas were the notions of childish innocence and discipline of the child.

The idea of childish innocence was clearly not a part of the thinking that sanctioned the child's participation in all adult activities, including the modern taboos of sex, drinking, and gambling. It was the religious pedagogues of the fifteenth and sixteenth centuries who first introduced and promulgated the idea of innocence. Because the influence of the Church was so extensive, its writings received considerable attention. The Church first took an interest in the child when it recognized the infant had an immortal soul. Prior to this recognition the Church regarded infants with the same indifference as their parents. But even when the soul of the child was recognized, children were subjected to the frightening dogma of the shame and guilt of original sin and the threat of punishment in life after death. Children were not understood to require either more or less moral teaching and penance than adults. They suffered equally with adults the fear of eternal damnation. Parents were admonished to "Take some time daily to speak a little to your children one by one about their miserable condition by nature. They are not too little to die, not too little to go to hell."[10]

Eventually the interests of Christian philosophers and educators turned to the child, claiming him to be innocent, and thus requiring special attention and procedures in his upbringing. The motive is clear enough. If the child were innocent, protection and nurturance of that state would keep him free of vice and corruption until manhood, and the spiritual salvation of man on earth would be more easily achieved. Aries argues that, as a consequence of this new belief, two new sets of responsibilities and correlate behaviors were imposed upon adults: the first was that of the protection of the child from the evils of life; the second was the strengthening of the child's character and reason. With regard to his protection, these new responsibilities now required that the child never be left alone. He was to be protected from sexual knowledge. Special books and toys specifically for children's use were created to assure this end. Language and manners used in his presence were formalized and moderated.

Perhaps the greatest change for both adults and children concerned the second responsibility, that of strengthening the child's character and reason. To accomplish this goal and also to harden the child's body and soul against the physical and spiritual trials of the world, the child was to be subjected to a discipline imposed upon him by his parent, master, or teacher. Now, he was not only considered innocent, but weak as well.[11] He was, in addition, no longer allowed to be responsible for his own actions and thus to engage in self or peer group regulation. The critical change was not in the type of discipline used, that is, corporal punishment. The comrades of the "societies" frequently beat one another. The most important change then was that children no longer regulated themselves. The institutionalization of a systemized method of discipline on the part of adults against children served to separate children from adults.[12] In this move to "protect" children and strengthen their character, the freedoms and privileges children had known were restricted and denied.

## The Themes of Childhood

With the introduction and acceptance of the ideas of the child's innocence and spiritual and physical weakness, the concept of childhood was well on the way to becoming firmly established in contemporary thought. At this point, several themes or theories regarding childhood began to appear. Some of these views were more widely favored than others, but each had an influence on the implementation of policies and programs concerned with the treatment of children.

The writings of Locke and Mill provide the best-known examples of childhood viewed as a means to developing the Rational Man. This view articulates most clearly one of the current responsibilities of adults to children: the strengthening of the child's character and reason. It is a view springing from the rationalist and deterministic philosophy of that century, a philosophy that was developed in response to the social chaos of the day. The triumph of man and order over his imperfect and problem-ridden institutions through the application of reason was the promise of this philosophy. Careful training of the child was seen as the way to developing the Rational Man.

Thus, "the child was to be trained out of his childish ways into the moral and rational perfection of regulated manhood . . . ."[13] Basic to this view was Locke's postulate that the mind at birth was a tabula rasa and that learning was impressions made on this blank tablet as received through the senses. It denied the innate nature, corrupt or otherwise, of the child, thus making it possible to mold the child as desired. Mill expanded this idea, the thrust of his works being the development of the good citizen.

In reaction against the position concerning the Rational Man, a new view of childhood emerged, at least in intellectual circles. It was the view of the natural child. This new perspective was part of the broader romantic philosophy of feeling and sensibility that evolved in the eighteenth century in opposition to the rationalist world view. The adherents of the romantic philosophy believed the rationalists failed to solve or even systematically to order the many social problems of the day. The failure of reason and order stemmed from its lack of concern for the individual. A partial solution was seen in a return to an appreciation and use of the moral aspect of man and the renewal of interest in the social nature of man as well. Rousseau, for example, espoused the view of the child as the seed from which Natural Man would develop. This new type of adult would know and understand the new sensibility emphasized by the romantic philosophy and ultimately would be able to influence the direction of events in the society surrounding him. Coveney, in his historical analysis of children in literature, finds that the two major characteristics of this view of childhood were the removal of the child from the area of guilt and shame associated with original sin ("there is no original sin in the human heart, the how and why of the entrance of every vice can be traced")[14] and the rejection of the idea that children are little adults with whom one can reason.[15]

The child's innocence was basic to this belief that the child was in a state closest to nature, a state still untainted by the evils of the world. His inability to reason and understand as an adult was related to a rather new idea, that these faculties were developed over time and that specific parts of these processes and functions become operative only at definite times or ages. Proper protection of the child's innocence and nurturance of his development required the provision of a special and controlled environment. The importance of the controlled environment was a concept first introduced by Locke and other rationalists. Rousseau incorporates the concept in his theory, describing in *Emile* the basic principles of this environment, which were based on the ideas that learning must take place through experience, through the senses, and according to specific ages.

Rousseau's ideas concerning childhood, particularly the idea of developmental growth and education, had more influence on the child development theories of the late nineteenth and early twentieth centuries[16] than on the thinking or beliefs of contemporary educators. It did serve, however, to influence many eighteenth- and nineteenth-century writers and poets whose descriptions of the child are the ones we think of in recalling the image of the child in that age.

The social, political, and intellectual chaos created in part by the Industrial and French Revolutions upset not only established social and economic structures, but created an identity crisis for many artists as well. The upheaval made it especially necessary for writers such as Blake, Coleridge, and Wordsworth to find some theme or topic that would help to make relevant their chosen livelihood. In their struggle to find a place for themselves and to make some sense of the turmoil, they seized upon Rousseau's romantic view of childhood, embellishing it as it suited their personal psychology or interpretation. In the opinion of Coveney, childhood became the focus of the search for stability and a sense of continuity. "The child could serve as a symbol of the dissatisfaction with society . . . . In a world given increasingly to utilitarian values and the Machine, the child could become the symbol of Nature set against the forces abroad in society actively de-naturing humanity . . . . In childhood lay the perfect image of insecurity and isolation, of fear and bewilderment and potential violation."[17]

This search for stability and continuity on the part of eighteenth- and nineteenth-century writers is explained by Sennett as a search for a "purified identity in the face of major societal disorder . . . . The effect of this defensive pattern is to create in people a desire for a purification of the terms in which they see themselves in relation to others. The enterprise involved is an attempt to build an image or identity that coheres, is unified, and filters out threats in social experience."[18] As modern man has centered upon a myth of a "purified community," a closed solidarity with like individuals of our urban society, to ward off unwanted and threatening encounters with the chaos of the real world, the writers of this age chose the child, with his new characteristics of innocence and weakness, as the image with which to defend and insulate themselves against the disorder created by current social upheavals.

An awareness of the physical abuse and squalid living conditions endured by many children soon made this rose-colored view of childhood unviable. Consequently, many writers, Blake and Dickens, for example, addressed themselves in their poems and novels to the contradiction existing between the popularly held view of a child's innocence and the way some children actually lived, thereby chastising the modern industrial society for its continued and constant violation of the child's natural state. These writings were partially responsible for, or influential in, the enactment of English child welfare legislation and, ultimately, the set of acts that created their complex system of compulsory education.

## Poor Laws, Factory Acts, and the Education Act of 1870

The Poor Laws were a series of laws enacted by the English between 1535 and 1601 to deal with the problem of a growing and increasingly troublesome poor population. The stresses and strains of a society in economic and social transition and beset by the costs of foreign wars and material disaster produced large groups of uprooted agrarian families, displaced and unemployed industrial workers, and idle soldiers and sailors. These people frightened the legislators, who feared for the stability of the state, and burdened the state with added expenses.

Until this time private charity supposedly had taken care of the poor, but now their numbers had increased to the point where private charity could no longer handle the situation. The solution was to put the children of these groups to work to pay for the burden they caused. Child labor was still a generally supported social goal. During the Middle Ages, as we have seen, it was a crucial part of the economic system and social structure. But even the new view of childhood supported this ideal of child labor. On the one hand, it reduced idleness, which was considered "the greatest abomination, the source of debauchery and beggary!"[19] On the other hand, it hardened the child's body and soul. Thus, child labor satisfied the two obligations of protecting the child from the evils of the world and strengthening his character and reason, while at the same time it reduced the swelling vagrant and criminal adult population. In 1536, therefore, "The authorities of every parish were authorized to take healthy, idle begging children between the ages of 5 and 14 and apprentice them to masters in husbandry or other crafts to be taught, 'by which they may get their livings when they shall come of age.' "[20] Implementation of such an order required taking the child away from his parents and "vicious" environment and administering punishment such as flogging or imprisonment when children failed to comply. Maintenance and training of the child were supported initially by contribution, but later local compulsory poor rates took up the burden.[21] This first act applied only to vagrant children, but subsequent legislation included all children whose parents were thought incapable of maintaining them, the result being the establishment of workhouses.[22] The use of the workhouse in this manner, supported by the wages the children's labor brought on the open market, became quite a popular idea, extensively influencing policymaking and legislation until the nineteenth century. It received support from individuals such as Locke and other rationalists, who saw the benefit of these schools in training poor children for hard work from infancy and in providing a controlled environment away from the contamination of the paupers and beggars.[23]

Establishing the idea of "vocational education" for the poor, however, was not the only important aspect of these laws. Of equal significance was the introduction of the principle of state intervention. "Where parental rights clashed with the security of the State and the welfare of the child as in the vagrant and criminal sections of the community, they were to be overridden. And in principle the State accepted the responsibility for securing proper treatment and training of children by those into whose care the law had entrusted them."[24] Prior to this time the state interfered little in the relationship between parent and child. The rights of parents and family over their children were held sacrosanct. The breakdown of this system of control created many problems for the state, which it felt could be solved by regulation of the lives of poor children. Thus, using the rationale of concern for the child, the state accepted the obligation of protecting him and, in doing so, extended its rights over the child. New obligations toward the child were also imposed upon the poor parent. In order to retain their rights to the child, they were obligated to care for and treat him in certain ways. Their rights with regard to the child were restricted, as were the rights of the child.

Whatever freedoms he had known during his vagrant life under the supervision of a lax parent were now restricted by state demands for certain kinds of behavior. We are not implying here that the poor child lived a good life, that he did not require some care and protection. To do so would be to succumb to the same nostalgia of the romantic writers during that period. We are suggesting, however, that during the period where no government obligation of protection existed, the child enjoyed certain freedom of behavior, which the state, using the rationale of concern for his welfare, restricted in order to implement a social goal—the reduction of the welfare rolls.

Although now the vagrant and uncared for child was required by law to enter an apprenticeship, this compulsory apprenticeship, initially, was not very different from the widespread and accepted practice discussed previously of early apprenticeship of children of all classes. Thus it need not necessarily be viewed as cruel or unconcerned treatment.

In 1563 the informal medieval system of apprenticeship was institutionalized by the Statute of Artificers, "which made a seven-year apprenticeship compulsory for all who wished to take up an industrial craft."[25] The effect of this law was to funnel the children of the emerging middle-class into these positions, leaving only dead-end factory jobs to the poor children. "As local people often disliked industry, and a certain social obloquy met the parents of mill children, it became customary to import children from town workhouses and orphanages. The long established, but decaying custom of long apprenticeship was revived, although in fact, little training was necessary."[26]

In actuality, then, no viable training was given the orphaned or work-house child. The numbers of vagrant and unemployed adults and children continued to increase in the towns and cities. In addition, children still in the custody of their parents, the respectable poor, were also being forced to work under factory conditions harmful to health and general well-being. These facts were the impetus for the child labor reform movement, which began with an attempt to regulate children's work in factories.

Much of the attention given to child labor was no doubt due to the influence of social reformers and philanthropists imbued with the spirit of the French Revolution and the work of the romantic writers. Although the words of these reformers provided the necessary emotional fervor to encourage the passage of reform legislation, the most influential factor was still the supposed increase in the poor population and the economic and political threat that increase posed for the state. There was little hope of training poor children for the better industrial or commercial jobs; they were excluded from these jobs by the children of the middle class. Yet they had to be kept employed and off the streets to minimize contact with the evils of pauperism. Charity schools supported by private contribution of private citizens had been established for this purpose. Attendance at these schools was minimal, however, and education was limited to moral concerns.

The most tenable solution seemed to have been the requirement that the state provide some form of instruction for these children. The result was the passage of the Factory Acts, 1802-1867. These acts attempted to limit and designate the hours children worked and to require that they receive some instruction, usually a half day. The laws reaffirmed the state's responsibility for the care and protection of children and introduced the concept of the state's responsibility for securing some form of instruction for the poor and laboring children. The state again had accepted another obligation, in principle at least, thus extending its rights over the child, limiting and restricting a little more the rights of both the parent and child.

In reality, however, the acts were not very successful. The first act applied only to apprenticed poor, and subsequent acts, although more extensive in coverage, did not meet with compliance. Not all industries were regulated, and, since parents gained more from their child's labor than from his education, the child simply worked in unregulated industries. Though the Factory Act of 1833 established a force of factory inspectors, they had little control over the educational provisions of the law. "The Act of 1844 was the most successful, but it applied to only certain factories and to children between eight and thirteen years . . . . By 1867 the Factory Acts extended to cover most children in industry, but they did not cover the whole child population."[27]

The failure to enforce the acts was due to several factors, from industrialists' pressure for cheap labor to moralists' claims of the benefit of long hours on children's well-being. Most important, perhaps, was the issue of parents' rights. Although the principle that state's rights superseded those of the parents with regard to the vagrant or unsupported child had already been established by the Poor Laws, there was much antipathy against extending the principle to include parents and children of the respectable poor. "It was generally felt that the rights of parents over their children should not be violated as the industry of the child was regarded as essential to family life, as it was necessary for industrial prosperity."[28]

The failure of these acts to achieve in large measure their goals —regulating the hours children worked and providing them with instruction—led to the enactment of the Education Act of 1870, the first legal requirement that schools be provided for children whose parents did not pay a fee above a certain minimal amount and that children between the ages of five and thirteen be required to attend.[29]

In the debates preceding the passage of this act, support again came from the humanitarians who saw education of poor children as a right both of the children and the parents. "It was due to the children of this country—it was due to the state, and it was due to themselves, to provide that the children of the working classes should not grow up to manhood ignorant of the principles, a knowledge of which would enable and induce them to support the institutions of this country in peace and in war."[30] Others, reacting in fear to the political disruption of the French Revolution, argued that education of poor children would keep them peaceful citizens, thus preserving the order of the state. "We have lavished immense sums on the poor which we have every reason to think have constantly tended to aggravate their misery. But in their education and in the circulation of those important political truths that most nearly concern them, which are perhaps the only means in our power of really raising their conditions, and of making them happier men and more peaceful subjects we have been miserably deficient."[31]

Although all these arguments were in part responsible for the acceptability of the Education Act of 1870, the overriding stimulus came from the economic burden imposed by the large number of poor children. The taxpayers of local districts were not happy with the rates they had to pay in support of poor children. The state had spent more money on aid to the charity schools than seemed justified by the attendance or overall results,[32] that is, reduction of the poor population. Musgrove points out that, in addition, investigators in the 1860s had found not only a decline in the proportion of children attending school but a decline in the proportion at work.[33]

From this information, it would be easy for legislators to assume that the unaccounted for children were swarming the streets and engaging in mischief and other undesirable enterprises. Although the arguments outlined above in opposition to state-enforced education were still being used, the pressure to do something more about the education of the poor child was overwhelming. Thus the Education Act of 1870 was adopted. The original intent of the legislation was that the schools provided would only be used by the poor since separation of the social classes in schooling was still held to be a necessity by all but the most radical reformers. But, again because of economic reasons—the rising costs of education for middle- and upper-class families—compulsory education of children not receiving another form of instruction would eventually be extended to include all children.

The English child labor and welfare legislation of the nineteenth century is often viewed as the triumph of philanthropic reformers over the inhumanitarianism of the laissez-faire philosophers. It was, admittedly, an integral part of a network of social legislation dealing with workers' rights and benefits. But, while we cannot ignore or underrate the effect this very real concern for the human rights of the child had upon the thinking of the times and actions taken by legislators, we must also understand this concern as the philosophical justification for treating the child as a means toward achieving socially and economically desirable ends. To be specific, the ascendancy of humanitarian thought in this period provided additional support to the old rationalist view of the child, a view advocating that control and order would come to society through the proper upbringing of the child in a controlled and reasoned environment. As we have seen, the practical application of this view resulted in compulsory employment and education for the poor child. Thus, the new philanthropic concern for the rights of children actually promoted a treatment of the child that further restricted the freedoms we had known before.

## Trends and Implications

In sum, we have attempted to show that the concept of childhood and the dominant historical themes concerning the nature of childhood are not irrefutable facts, but are ideas that have emerged as part of the process of defining the status of the child within a context of

a particular society. Two examples illustrate how the process of redefinition produces interrelated changes in the rights held by children, parents, and the state. First, the concept in which no distinction was made between child and adult evolved into one in which
the permitted behaviors and activities of the child were increasingly
differentiated from those of the adult. Second, the child welfare
movement has gone through a significant evolution. Both of these
developments have produced changes that are heavily influenced by
the combination of philosophical and political ideologies within a
specific socioeconomic context. The definitional nature of the rights
of children was used by the adults of the societies from the fifteenth
through the nineteenth centuries to accomplish certain goals, primarily economic, in such a way that the definition and differentiation of the child's status served to restrict the rights of the child and
the parent and extend those held by the state.

In the past, although claims for the rights of children have been
put forth, the process of redefining the status of the child has seemed
to be a movement toward placing greater restrictions upon his rights
in relation to other groups in society. This is not, of course, intrinsic
to the process, and perhaps the present claims for rights on the part
of students can be seen as an attempt to define the status of the child
on a more equal footing with the status defined for other groups.
Since the school, as a fairly independent arm of the state, has exercised the greatest control over the child in our society, the institution
of the school, rather than the family, has been the arena selected for
the settlement of the conflict in rights among children, parents, and
the state.

In light of the historical evidence presented here, therefore, it
would seem critical for school officials and educators to consider the
definitional nature of the rights of children when deciding what
rights to extend to students. This requires an understanding of the
issue of students rights in relation to the significant thoughts, events,
and concerns of our society and a recognition that changes in these
rights will also effect changes for adolescents, parents, and the state.
Decisions about what rights to extend to both students and children
cannot be, nor should they be, based upon unquestioned and precon-
ceived notions of the nature and capabilities of, say, the ten year old.
Rather, these decisions should, in part, flow from the tenor of the
times and will reflect the school's flexibility in responding to forces

dominant in the society around it. Unlike those individuals of our modern culture described by Sennett who foster a myth of stability to avoid dealing with the disruptions of change, we must accept change in the society and allow both the status and rights held by students to be redefined as part of this change.

## From Morality to Science: Toward an Understanding of Childhood in America's Past

### Overview

In contemporary American society, though certainly not a unique case by any means, we tend to think and speak about the child in "scientific" terms.[34] Psychology, for example, generates the models to which we appeal to legitimate whatever notions we now have about childhood. This mode of thinking and speaking about the child is not, of course, a historical constant that remains as dominant today as it has in the past. Actually, it was not until the latter part of the nineteenth century and the emergence of the scientific study of the child that Americans began with greater consistency to think and speak about childhood in scientific terms. Until then this scientific attitude concerning the child had been simply inconceivable. Although Americans had predominantly defined childhood in strictly moral terms throughout the seventeenth, eighteenth, and the first three quarters of the nineteenth centuries, this view gradually changed. During this period, commonplace notions about childhood were deeply grounded in Calvinist theology. The spirits of the Enlightenment in the eighteenth century and of Darwinism in the second half of the nineteenth century apparently combined to clear the way, challenge, and ultimately replace the moral set of notions most Americans associated with the child.

It will be shown in this section of the chapter just how American society changed from one modal scheme of thinking and speaking about childhood—the moral—to another—the scientific. There will be no attempt to explain this change; there will, rather, be a descriptive analysis of the intellectual aspect of the process. Although explanatory suggestions may seep through, the primary concern will be to describe the historical change in the thought and language associated with discussions of childhood. Considerable attention will also be given to the relationship between this change and child nurture practices. The discussion will begin with the colonial period and end with the close of the nineteenth century.

## The Puritan Context

Any discussion regarding the views of childhood during the colonial period must take into consideration the theological views of a variety of Christian sects: Puritans, Baptists, Quakers, Anglicans, and Catholics. These sects shared a common core of beliefs and values, for example, a supernatural explanation of the cosmos. They also believed in the sovereignty of God, in the origin of the universe as a divine creation, and in divine intervention in natural and human affairs. They adhered strongly to the view of man as a being stained by original sin. Finally, with the exception of the Puritans for whom salvation could never be considered a certainty, they cherished the thought of individual salvation in the afterlife.

The Puritans with their Calvinist theology came in time to dominate the mind of colonial America and as a result did more to shape colonial religious thought and practice than any other sect. The distinguishing features of Puritan theology were the doctrines of divine decrees, total depravity, human helplessness, and irresistible grace. As the dominant system, Puritanism provides the starting point for any discussion of the nature of the child.

## The Puritans and the Child

The Puritans tended to think of the child in purely moral terms, and their actions consistently reflected this view. First, a deep concern for the moral good of their children figured largely in the flight to the New World. Morgan demonstrates that strong among the reasons why the Puritans came to New England "was the urge to perpetuate pure religion among their children."[35] Both in England and later in Holland, the Puritans found "manifold corruptions" and the "danger to degenerate and be corrupted." Their moral quest was so prized by the Puritans that the New England ministers were successful in constructing a myth around it. As Morgan states, "by the latter half of the seventeenth century it had become an accepted tradition that the founders of New England had left the old world for the sake of their children."[36]

The Puritans apparently fled to the New World "to protect their children from profanity" because they felt that here Eden was awaiting them. But their hopes were dashed, for soon they found themselves and their children in the midst of an "unregenerate milieu." This time, however, the circumstances were unlike those in Europe; the Puritans were now in the position of exercising the political power necessary to curb the wicked behavior of their sinful foes. But, much to their disappointment, though sin was duly and severely punished, their actions proved too weak in countering effectively the forces of wickedness, corruption, and degeneracy. No civil action, however severe, could now eliminate the presence of the unregenerate in the New World. But impassioned by their vision of the holy life, the authorities of New England continued their aggressive crusade against sin, emphatically directing Puritan parents to keep children "from ill company as much as may be . . . ."[37] "When the ministers instructed parents about the government of their children," writes Morgan, "they always emphasized the importance of keeping them away from wicked companions."[38]

The Puritans' preoccupation with protecting their children from the unregenerate was closely related to a religious doctrine propagated by the New England churches, a doctrine of "human depravity" which literally set down the ruling conception of the child. According to this doctrine, which lasted, incidentally, well into the mid-nineteenth century, the soul of man was irrevocably stained by original sin.[39] Other sects shared this view, but the critical difference was its extension to include the whole nature of man as a "worthless worm," a "poor nothing creature," a "filthy nothing," a "half-devil," and a "guilty wretch."[40] Human depravity was conceived as total, and man was not only naturally wicked but totally helpless. As Jonathan Edwards put it in his sermon "The Justice of God in the Damnation of Sinners," men were corrupt "in every part, in all their faculties, and all the principles of their nature, their understandings, and wills; and in all their dispositions and affections, their heads, their hearts . . . ."[41] In this sinful and wicked state of helplessness, the Puritans believed, man could only wait for God, his true savior, to come and wrench him from the depths of sin. Only a sovereign God had the merciful power to "elect" who would be saved and who would be damned.

Since there were no separate tenets in Puritan theology specifically dealing with the nature of the child as unique and different from that of adults, the doctrine of human depravity applied just as strongly to children as to adults.[42] As Fleming states in his study concerning the place of children in the life and thought of the New England churches, the doctrine of total depravity "classified the child with the unregenerate, and insisted upon a similarity of experience on the part of children and adults."[43] It is not surprising, therefore, to find Jonathan Edwards describing children as "young vipers." "As innocent as children seem to be to us," he wrote, "yet, if they are out of Christ, they are not so in God's sight, but are young vipers, and are infinitely more hateful than vipers, and are in a most miserable condition, as well as grown persons."[44] It was generally assumed, therefore, that the "Connate Corruption in fallen Man, disposeth him to evil Society; and children early discover the Naughtiness of their hearts in this regard, by associating themselves, with such as are lewd . . . ."[45] Though the doctrine of election prevented Puritan parents from assisting children in their religious turmoil by assuring them of eventual salvation, they could, however, restrain them from mingling with wickedness. By so doing, they could at least reduce their chances of being damned. As long as the children were kept within the bounds of Puritan "tribalism," the possibility of salvation, though by no means certain, could at least be guarded and kept open.

Besides having constantly to protect the child, those who thought of him in purely moral terms had to accept other related implications, such as those centered around child nurture per se. Puritan parents were expected to raise an obedient and reverent child, and children were expected to respond accordingly. Should a parent be found negligent in these duties, he was called upon by a court of law to correct the matter. In extreme cases, where the parent was deemed incapable of correcting the problem, the child was sent to another home. If children, because of parental neglect, were disobedient or irreverent toward parents, they, of course, were not found responsible, but simply given over to the care of another Puritan home, usually designated as a foster home. Should a child be found disobedient or irreverent without apparent reason, he or she could expect to be severely punished irrespective of age. In this case, however, children over sixteen were the most severely punished. As an illustration, the following statute was in force in New Plymouth:

If any Childe or Children above sixteen years old, and of competent understanding, shall Curse or Smite their Natural Father or Mother; he or they shall be put to Death, unless it can be sufficiently testified that the Parents have been Un-christianly negligent in the Education of such Children, or so provoked them by extreme and cruel Correction, that they have been forced thereunto, to preserve themselves for Death or Maiming.[46]

This should not strike us as extremely tyrannical, since the Puritans believed that "by the laws of God an incorrigibly disobedient child deserved death."[47] Parents, of course, had to make certain that this would never occur, and the best way to ensure themselves of this was to begin acquainting their children with the Puritan catechism as early as possible.

Though Puritan children were considered ignorant and evil, they could, nevertheless, be enlightened through proper discipline and religious instruction. This instructional process need not account for such a modern notion as a "child's personality" characterized by inherent desirable qualities. Not only did psychological categories not have any meaning in relation to the Puritan mode of life, but the doctrine of total depravity negated any notions that attributed desir-able qualities to the child. Religious instruction was specifically de-signed to help the child overcome his evil tendencies. It was generally believed that after a rigorous process of religious discipline and in-struction the child would be able to transcend his evil nature and exercise his reason.

The method of instruction followed a strict and rigid pattern that was antithetical to the personal views of the child, which were, the Puritans believed, bound to be heretical.[48] There was absolutely no other recourse for the child but to memorize his catechism as pre-sented and without alterations. Yet, the child was expected not only to learn his catechism by rote, but also to understand its meaning. Parents were instructed to have their children "not only to say their Catechismes but to understand their Catechismes; and be well grounded in all the principles of religion; by a sound solid knowledge and beleife of them, that soe they not forget it; and be never the better for it."[49] But even understanding was not sufficient. The in-tent was to have the child's "*Affections*, and *Practices* con-formed to what they understand . . . when we are catechising our *Children*, we are *Delivering* unto them a *Form* of *Doctrine*; and we should contrive all the Charms imaginable, that their *Hearts* and *Lives* may be *Moulded* into that *Form*."[50] The parents, the schools, and the churches all worked in unison to mold the child into this Puritan form.

For the Puritan parents, discipline was essential if the child's moral development was to follow its proper course. The kind of discipline was, of course, a matter of parental decision. Many parents took to the rod since it was considered "Better whipt, than Damn'd." But the use of the rod to discipline a child was advised as a last resort. Kindness, wisdom, moderation, and affection were considered vastly superior as ways of getting children back on their proper course.[51] The principles followed by Cotton Mather with his own children are a case in point:

The *first Chastisement*, which I inflict for an ordinary fault, is, to lett the child see and hear me in an Astonishement, and hardly able to believe that the child could do so *base* a thing, but believing that they will never do it again.

I would never come, to give a child a *Blow*; except in case of *Obstinancy:* or some gross Enormity.

To be chased for a while out of *my Presence*, I would make to be look'd upon, as the sorest Punishment in the family . . . .

The *slavish* way of *Education*, carried on with raving and kicking and scourging (in *Schools* as well as *Families*,) tis abominable; and a dreadful judgment of God upon the world. [52]

It is clear that even though Puritan parents were left to decide on the matter of discipline, they were strongly advised to exercise intelligence and persuasion in rearing their children.

There is one final and interesting point to be made with respect to discipline. Discipline in the Puritan home was considered so important that parents usually placed their children in other homes for fear "of spoiling them by too great affection."[53] Morgan argues that this Puritan custom of placing children in other homes existed in England in the sixteenth century because it was believed that the child learned better manners in a home other than his own. There is no reason to believe that the Puritans believed differently regarding the practice. "Psychologically," Morgan states, "this separation of parents and children may have had a sound foundation."[54] The children left home during a period in their lives when a spirit of independence was just setting in and discipline became much more difficult to administer. It made a great deal of sense, therefore, to transfer the disciplinary function to an unfamiliar master, especially so when these relationships were governed by a legal contract the terms of which clearly specified that the master now controlled all of the servant's time and energies.[55] The servant could act only with the master's permission. Naturally, the contract was enforceable in a court of law. Thus, the master-servant arrangement made it possible for Puritan parents to continue their affectionate relationship with their children without the fear of raising an undisciplined child.

## Calvinist Views of the Child in Decline

There seems to be little doubt that Calvinist ideas and, by implication, the nurturing practices with respect to the child prevailed throughout the seventeenth and eighteenth centuries.[56] As Wishy observes, "by 1800 Calvinist views of the child and of human destiny under God's stern judgment had demonstrated remarkable staying power."[57] Yet, we must not overlook the fact that throughout the eighteenth century orthodox Calvinist thought in general underwent considerable change. This change came about through the appealing influence of Enlightenment ideas imported from Europe to America. The effect that the new ideas of Diderot, Rousseau, Locke, Montesquieu, and other Enlightenment thinkers had on the colonial mind was quite significant. The vibrations were potent enough, in fact, to cause a fissure in Calvinist theology that resulted in the formulation of a more liberal position. Among the laity, this change in theological thought had its effect.[58] And there is no question that it also had a lasting impact on the Calvinist views of childhood.

There is no way of knowing at what point the Enlightenment notion of the child as inherently pure and innocent, as attributed to Locke and Rousseau, began to be accepted. But there are indications that by the late eighteenth century the notion had received significant attention. Nowhere was this more visible than in the American family. That family had already experienced considerable change, so much so, in fact, that during the 1780s it was attacked for its licentiousness and lax discipline.[59] The attack came from a "Protestant Counter-Reformation" which placed the blame on Enlightenment notions of the child.[60] The resurgence of Calvinist thought in the 1780s became so pervasive and influential that between the late eighteenth century and the first three quarters of the nineteenth century criticism centering on child-rearing practices in the American home began to increase. As a result, the 1830s and the decades following witnessed a moral crusade composed of diverse elements of the American populace, among whom were Protestant theologians of different persuasions, members of diverse professions, and interested citizens, primarily concerned with generating new principles of Christian nurture that when applied would help redeem the child both from the bosom of Calvinist orthodoxy and the maladies thought to be endangering the American Republic. The attempt was not so much to eradicate the still extant moral views of the child but to reform them. Yet, the mild call for reform was at least an indication that the Enlightenment had left its mark.

Although they were eventually bypassed, there were forces acting against the reformation of Calvinist views of the child. Many Americans, of course, still supported strongly the orthodox interpretation of the child. The American Tract Society, for example, as representative of Calvinist orthodoxy, issued numerous publications for children emphasizing the lives of wicked boys and girls whose salvation rested in the hands of a fearful but merciful God. Publications such as *Memoir of Henry Obookiah* and *The Youth's Companion* stressed how piety yielded rewards but wickedness brought punishment.

Besides the American Tract Society, there was the conservative writer on the child, Dr. Heman Humphrey, president of Amherst College, who appealed to the same orthodox Calvinist tradition. In his book *Domestic Education*,[61] Humphrey criticized the laxness of parental discipline and suggested the exercise of absolute power as the only way to control undisciplined children. He advised fathers to have the child under control by the age of four months. All children, Humphrey emphasized, were to be controlled until the age of twenty-one, and any child staying at home beyond this age was to be treated as a minor. Although Humphrey believed that no parent could significantly alter the God-given nature of the child, a reflection of his continuing belief in the doctrine of total depravity, he still advised parents to demand filial piety. The critical thing for parents to remember here was that they had to start the child's moral training early, before the age of two. Humphrey was thoroughly convinced that by this age a child, if properly nurtured according to sound Christian principles, was capable of having a sense of right and wrong.

The neoorthodoxy represented by the American Tract Society and Humphrey could not withstand the counterforce set in motion a generation before and the inspirational source of the liberal and enlightened opposition of the nineteenth century which sought a more benign status for the child. Among the most vocal exponents of this enlightened opposition, there was, first, Lyman Beecher, who argued that the Calvinist doctrine of election or predestination did not necessarily imply damnation of children. The child, Beecher argued, could expect to be punished by God. But whether or not the punishment would equal damnation no mortal could ever know; only God possessed such knowledge.[62] Second, there was Jacob Abbott, a former colleague of Humphrey at Amherst, who was by 1840 arguing that the critical factors to consider when thinking about the moral development of the child were not so much those related to his natural essence as those related to his immediate, personal environment. Third, there was Horace Bushnell, who in his revolutionary *Views of Christian Nurture* developed a novel set of principles on Christian nurture to counteract the child's tendencies toward depravity.[63] The child could be saved, thought Bushnell, only if wickedness was attacked during infancy. Finally, there was Lydia H. Sigourney, who in her *Letters to Mothers* argued in the same manner as Rousseau that the critical problem facing mothers was how to rear a child without damaging his good nature.[64] Sigourney believed that the solution to the problem depended chiefly on the realization that the child was incapable of conforming to adult standards. In sum, the views of Beecher, Abbott, Bushnell, and Sigourney had one primary objective: to circumvent the notion of infant depravity.[65]

But there was more to the enlightened opposition of the first half of the nineteenth century than the ideas represented by the above reformers. At about the same time that these reformers were forming a theological alternative to the Calvinist notion of infant depravity, writers like Dr. William Dewees, Dr. P. H. Chavasse, Andrew Combe, the phrenologist Orson S. Fowler, and Mrs. Sarah Hole, editor of the *Ladies' Magazine* and later of *Godey's Lady's Book*, were contributing to a growing body of literature emphasizing the distinct needs of the child.[66] All of these writers were convinced that they had really discovered the laws of nurture and that strict adherence to these laws would result in a sound moral character. They argued, for example, that physical health was inextricably related to spiritual conditions. Dietary prescriptions were commonly justified on the grounds that faulty diets were directly related to faulty characters.

Paying particular attention to the child's unique physiology and psychology, these writers advised parents on such matters as the child's feeding, clothing, and play. Along with this advice came the insistence that the mother exercise complete control over affairs related to the rearing of the child. These writers, as well as a changing economic order, did much to generate a popular consciousness of the distinctive needs of the child. It was mainly because of their efforts and those of the Christian reformers that by the 1850s there existed a public feeling against the Calvinist idea that the child was innately sinful and wicked. Though still viewed within a moral framework, the child was no longer conceived as a "young viper" but as a "plot of fertile ground which could be successfully cultivated if only good seed were sowed in it."[67]

As a result of this change, most Americans exhibited a less repressive attitude toward children. Though still adhering to the Puritan ideal of the obedient and reverent child, Americans yielded to the advice of the enlightened opposition to avoid corporal punishment and to resort to reason, love, gentleness, persuasion, and good example while pursuing this ideal. Parents seemed satisfied and convinced that the new call for greater Christian liberty for the child did not necessarily mean the end to the long-held ideal of child obedience and reverence. To their satisfaction, the enlightened opposition was supplying them with the unquestionable assurance that their ideas and methods were both theoretically and practically sound. And if any American parent still remained skeptical and felt insecure about the new views of the child, he could rest assured that what was being called for in practice was being constantly reinforced through children's literature.[68]

In the children's books of Jacob Abbott, S. G. Goodrich, and T. S. Arthur, for example, the perfect child was being portrayed as one who lived up to the moral principles learned from the parents. The heroes of such stories as *Rollo in Europe, The Bobbin Boy, John Halifax, The Gentleman, Bosses and their Boys, The Duties of Masters and Apprentices,* and *Waste Not Want Not* symbolized the principles of justice, truth, patience, industry, and obedience. But these heroes were not presented as mere symbols; they were treated as genuine persons who consistently proved that they could live up to their ideals by mastering worldly trials and tribulations. Throughout the children's literature, human life was painted in pessimistic colors as a condition infested with a moral cancer whose cure of Christian morality the hero was responsible for providing. As readers of these stories, American children were seriously expected to take heed and imitate the heroes.

## Darwinism and the New Views of the Child

Following the Civil War, views concerning the child that had been developed some sixty-odd years before continued to expand in a scientific direction. By the time the war began, most enlightened writers had come very close to formulating a notion of the child as a being capable at birth of infinite possibilities. What prevented these writers from formally proposing such a radical notion was their persistent reliance on a supernatural doctrine, however modified, to explain the nature of the child; thus they repeatedly rejected the adequacy of a naturalistic framework as a viable and heuristic alternative. Because of their allegiance to a Christian cosmology—a cosmology losing considerable appeal in light of the new advances in astronomy, physics, and geology—they found it exceedingly difficult to support with any theoretical consistency a naturalistic scheme that seemed to repudiate basic Christian tenets. The task became much easier after the appearance of Darwin's *Origin of Species* in that the power of Darwinian thought so blurred the Christian view of man's relationship to nature and the universe in general that by 1870 only an appeal to naturalism could restore the focus. For Jacob Abbott, for example, this was certainly the case. In his *Gentle Measures in the Management and Training of Children*, published in 1871, Abbott combined the new ideas concerning the child developed before the Civil War with the new revolutionary ideas of Darwin to create a vision and interpretation of the child, however close to Christian theology it remained, that foreshadowed what was to come in the later decades of the nineteenth century. In *Gentle Measures*, then, we can discern the truly first nascent indications of a radical shift away from a moral framework as an interpretive scheme of the nature of the child. Without question, the revolutionary ideas developed in *Gentle Measures* offer the first assuring signs of a strong movement toward scientific notions of the child.

Because of the importance of this volume, several observations should be made concerning it. To begin with, Abbott relied heavily on the disclosures of mid-nineteenth-century science. There are, for example, more references to the discoveries of physics, chemistry, biology, and other scientific disciplines than there are to more antiquated theological doctrines. Abbott emphasized throughout that any form of moral training specifically designed for the child could not afford to ignore physiological as well as neurological and environmental factors. He claimed, for instance, that because of physiological and neurological differences, the child tended to make moral judgments that were different from those of the adult. In addition, while arguing that a child's state of sin was a direct consequence of improper moral training rather than an innate and depraved essence, Abbott further claimed that the morally immature and delinquent behavior of children could be traced to learning difficulties affected by his immediate moral milieu.[69] In sum, Abbott suggested that the religious life of the child be guided by a set of simple propositions. Wishy has summarized them as follows:

1. Religious training, like all training, takes time.
2. Trust in God's help.
3. Act as though your will counted even if it is really God's will that is needed.
4. Use only the appropriate means of influence.
5. Parents must set examples.
6. Avoid complex theology and read the Bible to touch the heart; emotions thus aroused will later blossom into right thoughts.
7. Avoid terror and distress.
8. Don't tell children they are sinners; it creates an unbridgeable gulf between them and ministers.
9. If used at all to stimulate piety, rewards and punishments should be employed sparingly.
10. Follow Jesus Christ in emphasizing future goodness and happiness rather than past errors.[70]

True to the old ideal, Abbott did not abandon the traditional faith to belief in an obedient and reverent child. But now that the nature of the child was scientifically explained, the administration of discipline became a complex problem indeed. Yet, it seems that Abbott did not view it as such. His new views of the child notwithstanding, he continued to recognize the absolute character of parental authority, advocating corporal punishment to uphold it whenever necessary. Abbott did agree, however, that corporal punishment could be entirely avoided if other gentler forms of discipline were consistently, deliberately, and kindly administered:

If the penalty annexed to the transgression is made as much as possible the necessary and natural consequence of it, and is insisted upon calmly, deliberately, and with inflexible decision, but without irritation, without reproaches, almost without any indications even of displeasure, but it is, on the contrary, lightened as much as possible by sympathy and kindness, and by taking the most indulgent views and admitting the most palliating considerations in respect to the nature of the offense, the result will certainly be the establishment of the authority of the parent or guardian on firm and permanent basis. [71]

During the decades following the publication of *Gentle Measures*, the systematic employment of a scientific framework to interpret the nature of the child became the norm rather than the exception. The study of the child became a scientific and specialized concern worthy of professional pursuit; such systematic study was conducted, for instance, at the university level. At Clark University, in particular, the work directed by G. Stanley Hall received such wide respectability and recognition that it soon served as the foundation for all subsequent study related to the child. As president of Clark, Hall secured both scientific rigor and status for child study. He made certain, for example, that the research at Clark was in the area of psychology, specifically genetic psychology. The results of this research were then made public through *Pedagogical Seminary*, a publication founded by Hall in 1891. Through his many efforts Hall established Clark as the cradle of child study in America. Lewis Terman and Arnold Gesell were among those who attended that university to learn Hall's so-called "new science." Whether it was "science" or not remains an open question, but one cannot deny that Hall and his disciples compiled an extensive amount of data on the emotional, physical, and physiological growth of the child. The methodology employed was that of thinking of the child as a biological organism that could be easily observed in its natural environment. This methodology not only established a viable principle for the scientific investigation of the child, but it divested the child of any theological significance. [72]

By 1900 the new interpretation of the nature of the child as biologically natural and morally neutral had had far-reaching consequences. [73] The notion of infant depravity was by now almost defunct, as were the more liberal notions of the child as intrinsically divine or innocent. Such morally grounded notions simply seemed inappropriate at a time when the child was no longer viewed as being under the spell of some supernatural essence, whether of evil or innocence. Finally, the pioneering work of E. L. Thorndike, John Dewey, and William James gave final testimony to the proposition that the long-held traditional categories of will, interest, desire, energy, imagination, and temperament were strictly psychological categories devoid of any moral content.

For the parents, the new views posed a problem, and they were expertly advised on how to treat it. There seemed to be no apparent reason as to why a happier and freer child could not be obedient and reverent as well. Since the problem was now only a matter of getting acquainted with the new scientific ideas about the child, parents were continuously advised to read authoritative texts. The suggested reading was coupled with the advice that parents promote a freer atmosphere in the home. They were called upon to strike a perfect balance between obedience and individuality by avoiding excessive restraint and overtraining. Kate Douglas Wiggin, a strong exponent of these views, in her *Children's Rights* clearly defined the desired objective: the building of a strong Christian character without eliminating childhood pleasures.[74] She asserted that childhood was a unique period of life and that the only sensible and right thing a parent could do was to recognize it and yield to its demands.[75] She further asserted that parents only needed to provide the right environmental conditions for growth if they desired a morally disciplined child. Wiggin warned parents, however, that although the right environmental conditions might be present, children could not be expected to respond consistently to their moral expectations. She felt that children, if left to themselves, would always choose the good, which they fully understood and found attractive.

The abandonment of a moral framework to legitimate certain commonplace views of the child resulted in more than a new interpretation of him. It also led to a more permissive attitude toward children; the reason for this seems clear: children were no longer viewed as innately sinful. This new attitude did not necessarily entail a corollary renunciation of moral concerns. On the contrary, these new ideas now served as a dependable guide to follow when assessing the moral possibilities of the child. Besides the cases alluded to already, we should also mention that it was to the new views of childhood that the "Child Savers," Louise Bowen, Ellen Henrotin, Mrs. Potter Palmer, Mrs. Perry Smith, Julia Lathrop, Lucy Flower, Altat Hulett, Dr. Sarah Hackett Smith, Mrs. Andrew McLeish, Florence Kelly, and Jane Addams, appealed to correct the moral plight of urban children.[76] But judging from what Anthony Platt demonstrates, one finds that the employment of scientific notions of the child to legitimate moral programs tends to have worse consequences than could be previously anticipated.

## Conclusion

This discussion began with the premise that the dominant mode of thinking and speaking about the child in contemporary American life could be categorized as "scientific." It then went on to give the premise historical significance by tracing its emergence. The discussion demonstrated much more than simply a significant shift from one way of viewing the child to another; it showed that a serious commitment to a given view of the child necessarily entails a specific course of action. Concepts have built-in obligations. The Puritans' commitment to a theological view of the child, for example, called for a stringent set of religious practices and obligations. The child was expected to subdue his natural inclinations and adhere to a strict moral code. A commitment to a modified theological view of the child, the view of, say, Lydia H. Sigourney, in the early nineteenth century, required a much more relaxed orientation toward the child. The child was now freed of the didacticism that characterized the seventeenth and eighteenth centuries. Finally, a commitment to a "scientific" view of the child in the late nineteenth century demanded yet greater freedom for him and minimal concern for his moral destiny. Wiggin's position that the parents yield to the demands of the child offers the most radical example.

Those concerned with the complex issue of children's rights cannot afford to ignore this "scientific view." It is commonplace to view the child within a scientific framework. In a society where science has become such an important facet of life, this is understandable. There exists the danger, however, that such a view will oversimplify the issue involved (a problem discussed in Chapter 3 of this volume). Adhering to a scientific view of the child, some educators tend to marshal "merely" psychological data either in support of or against children's claims for rights, without, of course, giving thought to the obvious limitations of the data. One way to avoid this dilemma is to point out the limitations in appealing to psychology and to suggest that scientific data from a multiplicity of disciplines be brought to bear on the issue. Although this approach seems plausible, it continues to give tacit support to a scientific notion of the child. It goes even further by strengthening that view and giving support to the naive assumption that scientific data alone can resolve problems relating to children's rights. History suggests that something more fundamental is required. It suggests that we bring the scientific conception of the child to a level of critical awareness so that we can consciously see its latent implications. We need to focus on these implications because the internal logic of such a conception tends toward a supposedly neutral treatment of the question of children's rights. But what is essentially a political and ethical question ought not to be totally reduced to a scientific question. We must be free to recognize that the question of children's rights involves a libertarian principle, one with a built-in ethic extending to all members of a democratic community, including the child. Herbert Spencer wrote in 1850:

Concerning the extension of the law of equal freedom to children, we must therefore say, that equity commands it, and that expediency recommends it. We find the rights of children to be deducible from the same axiom and by the same argument as the rights of adults; whilst denial of them involves us in perplexities out of which there seems to be no escape. The association of filial subservience and barbarism—the evident kinship of filial subservience to social and martial slavery—and the fact that filial subservience declines with the advance of civilization, suggest that such subservience is bad. The viciousness of a coercive treatment of children is further proved by its utter failure to accomplish the chief end of moral education—the culture of the sympathies; by its tendency to excite feelings of antagonism and hate; and by the check which it necessarily puts upon the development of the all-important faculty of self-control.[77]

Thus, while the scientific vision of the child was indeed helpful in providing a certain amount of freedom that children had not enjoyed before, it may well be the case that this scientific view itself may now need to be reconstructed. For, as Habermas[78] has noted, there are constitutive cognitive interests guiding the scientific models that dominate our discourse. These interests include a search for technical control and certainty in confronting the complexity of human interaction. Thus, the commonsense thought and language we now employ to place the child within our universe of meaning may tend to work against the extension of the law of equal freedom to this same child. Are we prepared to reflect on and critically examine this commonsense thought and language? If we are, the struggle for children's rights may at last be placed within its proper framework and may be combined with the struggle for rights by so many groups and classes in our society.

# Notes

1. Philippe Aries, *Centuries of Childhood: A Social History of the Family* (New York: Random House, 1962), 128.
2. Maria Montessori, *The Secret of Childhood* (Notre Dame, Ind.: Fides Publishing Co., 1966), 28.
3. Aries, *op. cit.*, 154.
4. *Ibid.*, 250.
5. William L. Langer, "Checks on Population Growth, 1750-1850," *Scientific American* 226 (February 1972): 93.
6. *Ibid.*
7. *Ibid.*, 96.
8. Ivy Pinchbeck and Margaret Hewitt, *Children in English Society*, Vol. I, *From Tudor Times to the Eighteenth Century* (Toronto: University of Toronto Press, 1969), 13.
9. See Aries, *op. cit.*, for further discussion concerning the modern family's effect on childhood.
10. Janeway quoted in Peter Coveney, *The Image of Childhood* (Baltimore: Penguin Books, 1967), 44.
11. Aries, *op. cit.*, 119.
12. *Ibid.*, 262.
13. Coveney, *op. cit.*, 40.
14. Rousseau quoted *ibid.*, 44.
15. *Ibid.*, 46.
16. See Ellen Key, *The Century of the Child* (New York: G. P. Putnam's Sons, 1909), for an early discussion of children's rights, education, and protection, as well as works by Montessori.
17. Coveney, *op. cit.*, 31.
18. Richard Sennett, *The Uses of Disorder* (New York: Random House, 1970), 9.
19. Quoted in J. T. Ward, *The Factory Movement, 1830-1855* (New York: St. Martin's Press, 1962), 16.
20. Pinchbeck and Hewitt, *op. cit.*, 95.
21. *Ibid.*, 97.
22. *Ibid.*, 146-68.
23. John S. Brubacher, *A History of the Problems of Education* (New York: McGraw-Hill, 1947), 34.
24. Pinchbeck and Hewitt, *op. cit.*, 98.
25. *Ibid.*, 224.
26. Ward, *op. cit.*, 15.
27. Eric E. Rich, *The Education Act of 1870* (London: Longmans, Green and Co., 1970), 21.
28. Pinchbeck and Hewitt, *op. cit.*, 51.
29. *Ibid.*, 89-93.
30. Hume quoted in Rich, *op. cit.*, 79.

31. Malthus quoted in Brubacher, *op. cit.*, 34.

32. Rich, *op. cit.*, 10.

33. Frank Musgrove, *Youth and the Social Order* (New York: Humanities Press, 1964), 75.

34. By this I mean, of course, that when speaking or thinking about the child we usually, in the final analysis, appeal to scientific principles for support. Usually, and often unfortunately, it is a matter of appealing to psychological principles grounded in some kind of empirical evidence.

35. See Edmund S. Morgan, *The Puritan Family* (New York: Harper and Row, 1966).

36. *Ibid.*, 168.

37. *Ibid.*, 172.

38. *Ibid.*

39. See Sanford Fleming, *Children and Puritanism* (New York: Arno Press and the New York Times, 1969), 54-55.

40. *Ibid.*, 55.

41. Quoted in Merle Curti, *The Growth of American Thought*, 2d ed. (New York: Harper and Brothers, 1943), 60.

42. Fleming attributes this to the fact that children were regarded as "little adults." There is enough historical evidence to suggest that this was in fact the case. John Demos, for example, demonstrates that "Childhood as such was barely recognized in the period spanned by Plymouth Colony. There was little sense that children might somehow be a special group, with their own needs and interests and capacities." Although it was certainly not the case for children under six or seven years old, older children dressed like their parents. Boys normally dressed in breeches, shirt, and doublet, while girls normally wore a cap, chemise, bodice, petticoat, and skirt. Children under six or seven were normally dressed in a long robe that opened down the front. It seems that childhood as such lasted for about seven years. For a more detailed discussion regarding the status of the child in colonial America, see Fleming, *op. cit.*; John Demos, *A Little Commonwealth: Family Life in Plymouth Colony* (New York: Oxford University Press, 1971); Morgan, *op. cit.*; Philip J. Greven, Jr., "Family Structure in Seventeenth-Century Andover, Massachusetts," *William and Mary Quarterly*, 3d Ser., 23 (April 1966): 234-56. Also, for a comparative view of similar practices in Europe during the same period, see Aries, *op. cit.*

43. Fleming, *op. cit.*, 59.

44. Quoted *ibid.*

45. Quoted in Morgan, *op. cit.*, 172.

46. Quoted in Demos, *op. cit.*, 100. As Demos clearly points out, parents appealed to the courts only as a last resort. More often than not, parents tried to settle their domestic disputes privately.

47. Morgan, *op. cit.*, 78.

48. Some allowance was made, however, for religious precocity. See Fleming, *op. cit.*, Chapter XIV.

49. Quoted in Morgan, *op. cit.*, 98-99.

50. Quoted *ibid.*, 100.

51. As we shall see later, it is interesting that this attitude toward children is the attitude parents were generally advised to exhibit throughout the period considered here.

52. Quoted in Morgan, *op. cit.*, 105.

53. *Ibid.*, 77. For a similar practice in Europe during the medieval period, see Aries, *op. cit.*, 365.

54. Morgan, *op. cit.*, 78.

55. For a more detailed discussion on the variations of these master-servant arrangements, see *ibid.*, 109-32, and Demos, *op. cit.*, 107-17.

56. The Great Awakening (1734) and the Evangelical Awakening and the Revival Period (1790) did much to keep these ideas alive.

57. See Bernard Wishy, *The Child and the Republic: The Dawn of Modern American Child Nurture* (Philadelphia: University of Pennsylvania Press, 1968), 12. Most of the comments in the next part of the present discussion derive from this work and Robert Sunley, "Early Nineteenth-Century American Literature on Child Rearing," in *Childhood in Contemporary Cultures,* ed. Margaret Mead and Martha Wolfenstein (Chicago: University of Chicago Press, 1955), 150-67. As far as I know, these two treatments and Elaine V. Damis, "The History of Child-Rearing Advice in America from 1800-1940," unpublished honor's thesis, Radcliffe College, 1960, are the only ones to date that attempt to analyze the nurture material of the nineteenth century. For a different but related treatment of this material, see Kirk Jeffrey, "The Family as Utopian Retreat from the City: Nineteenth-Century Contribution," in *The Family, Communes, and Utopian Societies* (New York: Harper and Row, 1972), 21-41.

58. See Curti, *op. cit.*, 103-210.

59. For precise indications as to how the family structure had been changing over two centuries, see Philip J. Greven, *Four Generations* (Ithaca, N.Y.: Cornell University Press, 1970).

60. Wishy, *op. cit.*, 12.

61. Heman Humphrey, *Domestic Education* (Amherst, Mass.: J. S. and C. Adams, 1840).

62. Wishy, *op. cit.*, 22. Notice that Beecher's theological views and the other views to be discussed are extremely moderate when compared with the rationalist views of an earlier generation. Calvinist theology minus the extreme deistic influences remained the source of appeal for the enlightened writers of the nineteenth century.

63. For Abbott, see *ibid.*, 87. Horace Bushnell, *Views on Christian Nurture* (Hartford, Conn.: E. Hunt, 1847). For an excellent portrait of Bushnell, see Fleming, *op. cit.*, Chapter XVI.

64. Lydia H. Sigourney, *Letters to Mothers* (New York: Harper and Brothers, 1846).

65. Wishy, *op. cit.*, 23. One must also note here that the efforts of these notable figures were supplemented by those of the Swedenborgians and others specifically concerned with children's rights. It is interesting that during the nineteenth century this concern was not too contagious. Although the concern seems to have lasted well into the late nineteenth century, Wishy points out that

"the informal movement for children's rights was a minor enthusiasm, even more variegated and occasional than many of the more familiar crusades of the time." For an inside look at this movement, see Paul Siogvolk, "The Rights of Children," *Knickerbocker* 38 (June 1852): 489-90; S. M. Wilcox, "Legal Rights of Children," *Circulars of Information of the Bureau of Education,* No. 3 (Washington, D.C.: Government Printing Office, 1880); Kate Douglas Wiggin, *Children's Rights* (Boston: Houghton, Mifflin, and Co., 1892).

66. Although the concerns of this group of reformers remained fundamentally moral, their contributions represent a tendency toward a scientific outlook and away from the moral framework as an interpretive scheme. Their approach had a scientific cast, though perhaps it was pseudoscientific. Their work reflects, moreover, the first attempts to look toward science as a source of legitimation. Although science in America had had a long history before this, it had not yet been recognized as an organizing principle of life. See, for example, Morton Gabriel White, *Science and Sentiment in America: Philosophical Thought from Jonathan Edwards to John Dewey* (New York: Oxford University Press, 1972).

67. Wishy, *op. cit.,* 34.

68. According to Wishy, there seems to be an element of irony in all this. That is, a comparison of the "literature *for* the child with books *about* children at the same time reveals a difference in tone. While parents were urged to become more realistic about the child's needs and to abandon preaching and over-didactic moral and religious instruction, the children were not themselves allowed to enjoy any significant freedom from moralism and homily in their books." This clearly points to the still dominant view of the child as a moral agent.

69. Notice how close this view is to the Enlightenment view that man's nature is fundamentally shaped by his environment. It was, of course, left to Darwin to give it scientific legitimacy.

70. Wishy, *op. cit.,* 89.

71. Quoted *ibid.,* 102.

72. Although Hall was perhaps the most important figure responsible for popularizing the child study movement, he was by no means the first to express an interest in this area. Before Hall picked up the banner, the American Social Science Association had made some attempts to institutionalize child study. For a more detailed picture of the place of Hall in the child study movement, see *Health, Growth, and Heredity: G. Stanley Hall on Natural Education,* ed. Charles E. Stickland and Charles Burgess (New York: Teachers College Press, 1965).

73. Although Richard Hofstadter, *Anti-Intellectualism in American Life* (New York: Alfred A. Knopf, 1963), 363, has observed that the conception of the child during the late nineteenth century tended to be romantic and primitivist rather than post-Darwinian, it remains that the interpretation of the child during this period was grounded in a form of naturalism. Whether the conception of the child was romantic or primitivist is not very important at this point.

74. Wiggin's emphasis on childhood pleasures marked a further step toward recognition that the child has different and unique pleasures which could be isolated as strictly his own in a sensual way.

75. Wiggin was taking a somewhat radical position here when she stated that a parent should yield to the demands of the child. Many conservative writers viewed this proposition as a real threat to the parent's absolute authority.

76. See Anthony Platt, *The Child Savers: The Invention of Delinquency* (Chicago: University of Chicago Press, 1969).

77. *Herbert Spencer on Education,* ed. Andreas M. Kazamias (New York: Teachers College Press, 1966), 92.

78. Jürgen Habermas, *Toward a Rational Society,* tr. Jeremy J. Shapiro (Boston: Beacon Press, 1970).

# 2. Student Rights and the Social Context of Schooling

*Linda M. McNeil*

Litigation in questions of school authority and student behavior is not new, nor unique to the 1960s and 1970s.[1] Student rights as a public issue, however, is clearly a phenomenon of recent times. For schooling to be educative, students and educators must be more than adversaries. Yet, as we shall see, the needs of educators and students not only tend to contradict each other; the differences can become mutually reinforcing unless some way of mediating them is devised. The codification of student rights can be viewed as such a mediating mechanism. Student rights as seen with this perspective is the subject of the following discussion.

To deal with the student rights issue, we must examine the social conditions that have not only given rise to it but make its resolution so difficult. Such explanations lie deeper than epigrammatic generalizations about a permissive society or an uncaring teaching profession. They encompass instead a broad historical context in which have emerged an intensification of the institutionalization of schooling, a widespread awareness of youth as a distinct and increasingly politicized segment of the population, and a general attention to human rights. The pressures that these phenomena have placed on the educational system have made the school unable to deal with the needs these same social forces have created in the young. Briefly stated, increasing job specialization, especially at technical and management levels, has created a demand for more people with secondary and college education. The diploma or degree has become the key in determining a young person's range of future options. He has a critical stake, therefore, in what goes on in school; he wants to be assured that what happens to him there is fair and is based on a consideration of his needs and his particular circumstances.

To cope with the growing numbers of students who stay in school longer, the schools have become larger, more organized, more bureaucratic. In order to provide a wider variety of course offerings, to encompass an assortment of student services, indeed, to "educate" as many students as possible, administrators have often found that the constraints of larger numbers of students upon administrative policy have tended to increase standardization of content and student evaluation and to obscure the needs of individual students.

One effect of rapid social change has been the conflict between the needs of students and those of educational institutions. Amid a flux of values and patterns of living, a young person is encouraged to "get to know" himself, "to find a place" for himself, to establish some kind of individuality amid social upheaval and crisis events. The school would seem to be a logical place for descriptive and analytical study of the present society and for the discussion of meaningful choices of life style within that society. But schools, tied to capital outlays and tradition, change much more slowly than the world around them. In the search for institutional survival, school personnel have usually opted for avoidance of controversy in favor of an innocuous curriculum presenting consensus slogans about "American ideals,"[2] treading the fine line between various political factions within the community whose alienation or open conflict would threaten the school's tax base.

The discrepancies between what school personnel need in order to keep schools running smoothly and what students need from schools arise then out of many of the same pressures. In the 1960s there was not only a widening gap between the needs of students and of educational institutions, but there were also events that precipitated direct encounters between students and school personnel over those discrepancies. When, for example, students pressed their teachers to invite speakers in to talk about voter registration drives in Mississippi, they soon discovered their schools had limited definitions of free speech, and, even more important, their schools had few if any procedures for handling student grievances in such matters. Issues of substance soon grow into issues of due process, especially where formal grievance procedures were minimal, arbitrary, or aimed more toward the smooth running of the school than toward protecting the student.

Students have come to question not just administrative decisions, but the very legitimacy of the procedures by which these policies are derived. Compelled by law to attend school, and dependent on favorable school records for their entry into the job market in a consumer culture, many students have begun to demand that their education be based on concern for the student rather than on economic or political expediency or tradition. While administrators might agree with this principle, they must answer to people and institutions beyond themselves. Their rules and policies reflect this. In fact, they in turn question the legitimacy of students to assert demands in the first place.

It is out of this conflict over what is legitimate that the issue of rights arises. Students, "caught" in the social and economic milieu, act in certain ways; administrators, equally "caught" in the same social context, respond in opposition. The following discussion will explore this dilemma, some sources and implications, and possible resolution in the codifying of student rights.

## Youth in a Technological Society: Discovering the System

### *Youth as a Social Category*

There is no lack of attempts to account for what have come to be known as the youth subculture and student movement of the past decade. Global summaries are dangerous at best because of the vast diversity of factors—regional, biographical, financial, military, political, educational, racial—whose interplay has generated a new consciousness of youth as a distinct group in the culture, and of the concomitant politicization of American youth in unprecedented numbers. There may, however, be much to be gained from sketching a general picture of youth's changing place in society and of specific events that precipitated collective response to these changes.

Technological change has greatly affected the young. The explosion of technological knowledge has increased specialization throughout the economy, proliferating job choices and requiring more sophisticated training to fill the kinds of jobs being created. Unlike their parents, who by their late teens were highly dispersed into the economy, many young people today are delayed by their formal education from entering the job market, and thus "the adult world."

The same technology that has given many an imperative to seek higher learning has tended to produce machines to replace much unskilled and semiskilled labor. Chances for employment have dwindled for youth among black and other minorities for whom the paths of educational and economic mobility have been traditionally blocked. Black youth during the 1960s consistently constituted the largest group of the unemployed, which was another factor contributing to the separation of youth as a distinct segment of society.[3]

The role of youth in families illustrates the separateness of that group in our culture. Some writers claim that the democratization of the American family has placed increased pressures on children to assert their preferences, though at the same time their extended age of dependence precludes real autonomy.[4] Children often engage in activities designed specifically for them, while other members of the family pursue activities suited to their own age.[5] An incredible number of personal choices confront the young person in an industrial society: place of residence, occupation, spouse, parenthood, place and type of education, patterns of consumption and political activity. These urgent and critical choices must be made during years of rapid physiological development and psychological maturation. Adolescence has traditionally been the period during which a person wrestled with the conflict between his own need for independence and his love for his family. Youth then becomes the time for working out one's relationship to the larger society.[6] Making choices of spouse or occupation would be difficult enough within the framework of cohesive, traditional community values, but the modern pluralistic society offers no generally accepted hierarchy of values as criteria against which to measure decisions amid a virtual supermarket of choices.[7] The actual exercise of choice in these areas becomes even more difficult for the many young people who find that "unlimited opportunity" is for them limited very definitely by their social class, sex, race, level of schooling, or previous school tracking.

Kenneth Keniston uses the word "alienation" to characterize the great personal turmoil that engulfs a young person faced with many choices but with little sense of direction for making them. Alienation not only implies a feeling of estrangement from one's culture, but also the utter inability to make commitments that would be a link to that culture. As a general rather than an isolated phenomenon, alienation may dispose youth to empathize with others who feel estranged from the social order, such as blacks and poor people. Alienation can also increase reliance on peers for values, as though only others in similar circumstances are qualified to understand and give advice.

One further observation about the youth subculture of the 1960s is critical to an understanding of student rights. A glance at the sources of youth's symbols—black Africa, the Orient, Marxism and Maoism, fundamentalist religions, rock music, and drugs—reveals an interesting fact about schools: their decreasing role as the major source of information. While the content of school curricula may traditionally be thought of as an "official model" of knowledge to be transmitted to the younger generation, it is clear that this content must now compete with independent sources of information.[8] The same media that capitalize on the dress and protest of youth have in large measure been responsible for supplying American children with information previously inaccessible except through years of direct experience or membership in a social, political, or intellectual elite. Children are instantly relayed news of geographically remote countries, documentary accounts of American political and military involvements, new visual forms and musical expressions, and discussion of topics far beyond the range of usual classroom content. Moreover, they also see conflict. Textbooks traditionally have portrayed, or one might say caricatured, American governmental procedures and institutions as two-dimensional organization charts of order and consensus.[9] Many of the young readily acknowledge internalizing not only the information obtained through media, but the sense of immediacy conveyed by television, immediacy they relate to their own expectations about the world and immediacy they can exploit to convey their own messages of protest.

To summarize briefly, youth as a social category has developed in

an economic context that delays the entrance of youth into the adult
occupational structure and in a cultural context wherein young
people must choose not only virtually every aspect of their future
lives, but must do so without reference to any clear, universally
authoritative value system. The subculture of the young of the past
few years reflects not only this delayed suspension between childhood and adult status, but attempts to create a style of living that
meets the needs of that suspended existence. If biological adolescence could be said to make youth vulnerable to societal changes
that have tended to separate them into a distinct group, that separation may be said to have made young people more collectively the
victim of the political, and especially military, events that took place
in the sixties.

## *Politicization*

Youth's emergence as a distinct group can have two contrasting
effects: to insulate them from events in the "real world" (as clichés
portray the big football game rock 'n' roll fun of students during the
fifties); or to provide a base for mobilizing them in collective response to contemporary events. America in the 1960s became, of
course, an arena for the latter. The politicization of many youth
during this decade arose from events they could not ignore because
such events directly affected youth as a group.

Many parents and educators have shaken their heads at student
protest, asking: "Why don't they just take advantage of their opportunity to get an education and forget about politics until they graduate? They have plenty of time for that later." Events affecting
youth in the past decade were not, for the young, to be com-
partmentalized into "education," or "politics," or "ethics." Most of
the crucial issues—Vietnam, civil rights, school reform—dealt directly
with the authority that institutions could exercise over their daily
lives. For this reason, the issues became acutely personal, cutting
across such mutually exclusive categories. The question of institutional authority is a political question, and like other groups in the
society, youth have begun to respond to the matter of institutional
authority in the language of rights, that is, of claims against the
arbitrary actions of those institutions.

To see how this emphasis on rights emerged, it will be helpful to
recall some of the dominant issues of the student movement. Briefly

outlined, the politicization of youth during the 1960s generally began with issues of substance—racial discrimination and the civil rights movement, free speech, and peace—and moved to issues of procedure—grievances, legal rights, redress—because response to youthful protest over substantive matters usually took the form of legal mechanisms.

Throughout the movement three themes have predominated: peace, civil rights, and school reform. Each of these movements had a history prior to the post-Sputnik era, but their emergence as issues concerning youth and their intermeshing in a call for general societal reform are new to that history. In the United States, decades of groundwork for civil rights had been laid by court cases brought by the American Civil Liberties Union, the National Association for the Advancement of Colored People, and others. Worldwide, laborers' rights had been long disputed and variously resolved. The rights of women had been an issue in many countries. McCarthyism had crystallized the issue of free speech for many Americans, and World War II had engendered international organizations to try to codify or expand documents of rights for many different groups, from refugees and prisoners of war, to wartime civilians and international travelers. Indeed, what one observer terms a growing consciousness of rights in Western industrial nations[10] is a consciousness borne of a series of concrete events and struggles.

Of these, it was the civil rights movement that first involved young people in a major way in matters of politics and set the stage for later student protest of the Vietnam war and school policies.[11] When great numbers of students, mainly from northern campuses, began going south to join blacks in lunch counter sit-ins, freedom rides, and voter registration drives, they found themselves in direct opposition to established institutions of authority: elected officials, owners of businesses that catered to "whites only," and even local police and sheriff departments. The jolting effect of discovering that the people in positions of social esteem and legal authority were the same ones violating court orders and constitutional liberties was a surprise from which the young have not since recovered. Indeed, similar shocks repeatedly marked escalation of the Vietnam war and other political crises. School tests have generally supported myths of heroism and virtue among elected officials and economic leaders. The myths of consensus and virtue could not withstand the actuality of institutional racism and of flagrant violations of the law committed or supported by local legal structures.

Through the civil rights movement, students became acquainted with the legal system and with the language and process of law.[12] Bailey notes that the civil rights movement showed students that protest could be directed against existing laws and, furthermore, that it could work. Probably most important was the fact that students met lawyers whose work in constitutional questions of civil rights and whose sympathies would make them readily available to assist students when protest eventually turned toward the schools themselves.

The most enduring outcome of the early civil rights movement was undoubtedly the politicization of many young people. To be politicized means not only to be made aware of politics but to see oneself—individually or collectively—in terms of political relationships, that is, in relationships of power. Power in this "free country" is, in theory, distributed and balanced and held in check by the mechanisms established by the Constitution, with the most basic freedoms, those of religion, speech, and assembly, being held inalienable by the individual. Power to act "freely" is, in actuality, highly contingent upon one's economic resources, social position, racial heritage, or age.

Questions of power arise in the day-to-day lives of people, and they lead to further questions about the legitimacy of authority and about the rights of individuals. A student hassled by a sheriff while registering black voters in Alabama reacts; "What right does he have to say who can vote and who can't?" The question was asked in dozens of ways: "What right does General Hershey (or Lyndon Johnson or Richard Nixon) have to tell me I must go to Asia to kill other people?" "What right does the dean have to expel me for publishing this underground paper?" "What right does the principal have to tell me how to wear my hair?" Whatever words the question contained, its real message was to raise to public awareness the issue of the relationship of individuals to institutions in their society: What rights does an individual have? On what basis does a school justify what happens to its students? What limitations on institutional authority exist?

For youth to become politicized, then, is for them to raise questions about the sources and limits of power held by individuals and by institutions. The first part of this question has just been stated: Who has what justification for doing what to whom? A second part of the question emerged during the crisis events of the decade: How do the institutions of power seem to be related? Or, put another way, How does one institution in our society seem to provide the justification for what another can do? The slogan became "the system," which refers to the complex interconnections between institutions of power that emerged to unite what otherwise might have been many separate, disjointed efforts at reform. Awareness of a "system" had profound ramifications, not only in extending the common ground underlying disparate protests, but in underscoring the great difficulty with which any significant social change could occur, since for even one institution to be drastically reformed would mean many others would have to be also. The politicization begun by the civil rights movement was reinforced by the Vietnam war, which brought to the surface links between many institutions affecting youth.

Many of the links among the targets of young protesters had been obvious. Schools were known to be tied to the military through ROTC and recruiter programs, to industry through sponsored scholarships and endowed research. But, as time went on, other links became more apparent. With regard to civil rights, the military drafted a greater proportion of men from minority groups and promoted fewer of them to officer levels. To many blacks, killing Asians became complicity with whites against other nonwhites. The schools were also linked to discrimination. Most universities hired few blacks; blacks and other minority groups of all levels found themselves omitted from the study of American history and letters, though their role had been prominent. Universities were accused in some cities of being slum lords or of using eminent domain to destroy neighborhoods in the interest of acquiring cheap lands. Furthermore, black students and others became more vocal in protesting the discriminatory funding and hiring practices in ghetto schools and the prevalence of tracking minority and impoverished students into noncollege-preparatory curricula.

The school's role in relation to the military was revealed to be complex, increasingly so with the escalation of the Vietnam war. Many university students found their schools were of little use as a base for criticizing the war because faculties depended on military

contracts to supplement university budgets and because the university itself might own corporate stock in companies producing lethal
war materials. School records were a crucial part of any man's draft
file, and his selective service classification after the mid-sixties depended directly on his academic standing. A poor high school record
would probably result in a 1-A classification because it greatly reduced chances of college admission and a student deferment.

While most activism on university campuses focused at first on
national or or international issues, student protest in high schools
aimed primarily at school rules and policies.[13] It is true that many
younger students first became involved in political activities or dress
styles of the youth subculture by adopting the styles of college students. But this emulation itself often precipitated response by school
officials that illustrates the ties of the public schools to the other
institutions of the community, notably the system of justice. Students who experimented with drugs often found that an arrest after
school hours could bring punishment from the school, and students
who had nothing to do with drugs found their lockers being searched
by police or school staff along with those of everyone else in hunts
for incriminating evidence.[14]

Students who protested such actions may have found that their
protest was not taken seriously; they were still technically viewed as
children by many school people, and thus their behavior was attributed to outside agitators[15] or to the powerfully suggestive activities of
university students given news coverage. Even so, Bailey records that
85 percent of those schools studied by the Syracuse University Policy Institute experienced some kind of disruption in the three years
preceding 1970. What the study, or similar ones cited by Bailey, does
not reveal, is how each "disrupter" was dealt with.[16] It is at this
point that the links between the public school and the "system"
become most clear. As a component of the system of justice dealing
with juveniles, the compulsory attendance law, the school furnishes
records, testing data, and testimony by school personnel when they
are requested to do so by a juvenile judge. The attendance records,
upon which are noted disciplinary suspension and expulsion, are
weighed heavily in the dispositions of "offenders."[17]

On both the high school and university levels, then, students encountered links between the schools and the social system. The
young learned that the world described in their textbooks does not

always, or even usually, match the world they live in. They were having to experience and try to make sense of social upheaval for which their school had not prepared them. Their response to the inequities and inadequacies of schooling took many forms. Many dropped out or played the "grades game" in order to have a chance at something better. Some set up "free high schools" or special projects during after-school hours to discuss matters not included in the school curriculum. Others have pressured for changes within the school, for added courses, for altered student conduct codes, for student input into policymaking and the development of curricula. Still others have viewed the inadequacies of schools as basically systemic, that is, as inherent in the present structure, and have attempted to change that structure. One way of doing this is to bring out into the open the relationship between the individual and the school by spelling out the rights of students. While demanding a bill of rights may be seen as a basically conservative tactic, because it assumes the perpetuation of the institution, it may alter the locus of power within that institution by defining the rights of individuals and by stating explicitly what justifications may be used for the abrogation of any of those rights.

Thus, while students may discover varied solutions for their grievances, documents concerning student rights may be helpful in answering specifically the question of legitimacy raised so often by events of the past decade. But before the efficacy of codified rights to mediate between students and schools can be fully explored, it will be necessary to examine some of the institutional characteristics of schools in order to get closer to the basis of the conflict to be resolved.

## Schools as Institutions

As an institution, each school is a composite of its own economic history. It also reflects a history of political pressures and an accretion of traditions in addition to its current goals and practices, which are rooted in education theory. Thus, the rationale for what goes on in schools, and for what to students may appear arbitrary and capricious decisions, is derived from a complex relationship of factors of which "purely educational" considerations are merely a part. Examples of the influence of some institutional constraints on school life may illuminate, first, the nature of authority and rules in schools and, second, reasons for the apparent slowness with which schools adapt to the needs of their students who live in times of rapid social change and dislocation. These constraints may be economic, political, or traditional.

## Economic Constraints

Economic pressures on schools are visible, controversial, and always central to administrative concern. They are based on two main factors: scarcity, or having to work within limits set by something other than maximum needs; and lack of control over resources. Public schooling must compete with other public goods for the tax dollar, and in many residential communities the tax base is shrinking or at best inadequate to meet demands for all public services required by the citizens. That schools do not generate their own funding has several important ramifications. First is the need to be thrifty about what is allocated, to be able to give an accounting to justify expenditures. "Accountability" as a slogan refers to the attempt to make these justifications in terms of a cost-benefit model, even though schooling per se is not merely an economic activity. Whether or not stated in terms of this model, the justifications usually must demonstrate that expenditures serve the greatest numbers of students. Efficiency becomes a chief criterion for educational policy; much school reform has, in fact, centered around making schools do more efficiently what they have been trying to do all along.[18]

Goals of efficiency have several effects. First, many aspects of schooling are standardized in order to deal with large numbers of students. To ascertain student "needs" and "aptitudes," commercially produced standardized tests are administered for determining pupil placement and giving teachers instant background information on their dozens of pupils. Materials supposedly programmed for individual instruction are usually geared more for efficient use of time (that is, a student can proceed at his own rate) than for individuality of personality. Teachers rely on standard texts for instruction of large groups and can even buy packages of lesson plans and teaching objectives as well as short-answer tests, all designed to fit certain statistical "norms" rather than the individual students in a specific situation. This can lead to ad hoc curriculum planning and can even make students in one state dependent on what textbook publishers think will be marketable in a more populous state.

Economic factors also have an important historical effect within the school. Quite often the supplies in a school, and in fact the very architecture itself, reflect whatever was available or in fashion during some previous time. This is crucial to any understanding of school authority and rules because it reveals the lack of autonomy of any agency that cannot generate its own resources. Unlike an industry or business which has several means of refinancing in order to modernize, the schools do not have the luxury of "operating at a loss" for this year's class in order to get more graduates into good jobs or colleges five years from now. Change takes place much more slowly in schools and must build on existing and often mutually contradictory furnishings and supplies rather than totally revamp in order to meet new societal developments.

The making of rules within the school often reflects the same economic realities. Architectural limitations are notoriously a source of rules. Hall passes in many schools are required because there is literally no place a student can go since all available space is being used. Or outmoded acoustics may amplify hall noise rather than absorb it, and so, again, no one is allowed in the halls. This lack of private space becomes critical since students, at a communicative and active time in their lives, must often sit in crowded rooms for several hours, near their friends but prohibited from speaking with them except during structured class discussion.[19]

### Political Constraints

Political pressures are tied to economic ones since the school is either supported by taxes directly or indirectly through tax exemptions. In political terms, school policies reflect not only their statutory basis and applicable legislation and court decisions but also informal, political pressures by citizens. This pressure alone illuminates many school practices, especially where traditions of in loco parentis have encouraged the setting of explicit rules to which the schools could point in order to justify punishment, especially when that punishment is selective. Also, compulsory education laws give schools control over who exits but little control over who enters, short of severe labeling as "uneducably retarded." Since much tax support is calculated on the basis of daily pupil attendance, the school is caught in the trap of wanting students to attend but not necessarily having adequate resources for them if they all do. The issue of attendance is also important in the making of rules, since compulsory schooling makes truancy an offense subject to expulsion, possible court hearings, and even institutionalization in a "correctional facility." This becomes a political issue in that it is often the very poor children or those from minority neighborhoods who are "truant," and the truancy often results because the school curricula have little relation to their needs.

Dependence on the taxpayer is an additional factor in the making of much school policy. Often curriculum content is designed to be so bland as to be offensive to no one in the community;[20] thus many issues of social conflict may be omitted even though students are aware of them outside the school. The importance of the school's image in the community can lead to undue influence by school personnel on the number of students entering college or acquiring scholarships. When the school's image is suspect, school personnel may hope for low visibility; dress codes, reluctance to add new courses or allow an "open campus" or permit presentation of political issues in school publications may arise from a fear of offending taxpayers or of inviting questions about other school policies. One great irony in the attempt to maintain a favorable image is that many educators have for years acknowledged and even attempted to correct the very inequities and defects in school content and procedures that students have recently so vigorously pointed out. These inadequacies have often even been the basis for requests for additional funding. But as school staff they have the dual tasks of asking for funds or discretion to alleviate deficiencies and, in order to gain them, of having to give evidence that, overall, the school is doing well. If it is not, their jobs may be threatened; if it is embroiled in controversy, the principal may risk losing funds for innovative programs to "quieter" schools within the system.

One other political influence is of great importance in sketching a background for the treatment of student rights. Many educational policies and even reforms reflect changes in the political life of the nation rather than just changes in educational theory.[21] Examples are numerous, but among the most evident are the impact of Sputnik on curricula in the sciences and foreign languages and the perceived need to inculcate "American" values of a consensus nature during times of peak immigration or cold war. Desegregation has been more a response to the larger civil rights movement than to studied correlations between student well-being and the integration of schools. The student movement itself is an example of political pressure that has altered school policies, in some cases toward the desired goals, and in others against them. Similarly, the unionization and professionalization of teachers have placed political and economic pressures on schools. While many of these pressures aim at what might be termed reform (higher qualifications for hiring and retaining teachers, reduction of class size), others have limited administrative flexibility in granting to students or local citizens participation in developing school policies.

### Constraints of Tradition

Many school policies cannot be easily traced to specific political pressures or economic factors, but receive their legitimacy on the basis of what might be termed "tradition." A rule of activity became a part of the school in some previous day and has taken on a life of its own; a unit of study persists in the curriculum (*Silas Marner* is an infamous example) because it has "always" been there. If a student feels he cannot for religious or moral reasons participate in a recitation of the Pledge of Allegiance, he may find himself up against not a moral or political argument (at least not at first), but the response that "American children have always said the Pledge," and therefore so should he. Because many school newspapers were begun when the school was much more a center of community life, they included mainly announcements of school events and social activity. For students now to wish them to deal with subjects of national or international interest is to define the term "community" in ways that contradict its traditional usage.

Also, local tradition usually dictates what is considered "political." We have seen that the word "political" refers to power relationships. Each group in a pluralistic culture views its own ideas as commonsensical and the ideas of others as questionable, controversial, or political, that is, as somehow different from common sense. By custom, position, or numerical majority, a group may press its own opinions upon others by saying divergent views are too controversial, too potentially disruptive to be heard. The schools offer clear examples of this. For years the American Legion post in many communities has supplied schools with Veterans Day speakers whose partisan speeches are not labeled political even though a contrasting position on the same subject in a speech by a civil rights lawyer would be considered too political and too controversial to present in the school. This difference in definition becomes critical when students view certain rules as political, that is, as relating to issues of power and therefore rights, while administrators regard the same rules as merely efficient means of establishing routine and order where so many people are gathered under one roof.

Teachers and students are themselves defined in some ways by tradition. "Teaching" is often defined as "what teachers do," meaning what they have always done.[22] When a teacher first begins to raise politically sensitive issues in faculty meetings or to revise curricula to deal with controversy, he or she may be called "unprofessional," or "unteacherlike," by colleagues. For students to demand a part in lesson planning or to call for the right to evaluate their teachers or have input into their own school records is similarly to overstep the bounds of being a student. This helps explain the question "Why don't they concentrate on getting an education and stay out of politics?" "Politics" has not traditionally been thought of as being what a student is all about.

The defining of the role according to its past tradition applies to administrators in a way that is probably the key to this discussion of institutional rules and individual rights. Administrative policies are usually a combination of rules and personal discretion. Rules are established to cover the routine, the usual; discretion is employed to handle specific cases to which explicit rules may not apply or may not allow for all relevant details to be considered. To the student, "rules" may mean undue standardization of the treatment of students within the school; "discretion" may, on the other hand, appear to be favoritism or vengeance. But to the administrator, such a combination of policy is crucial for the exercise of what has traditionally been the chief duty of school administrators, the smooth running of the school, especially because they are dealing with growing children and often wish to take into account the child's degree of maturity when dealing with his "infractions."

One last observation about the traditional role of an administrator bears mention: school problems have, in the past, been dealt with within the school. A survey of court cases involving disputes between school authorities and students reveals that most judges have tended to reinforce the role of the administrator as a keeper of order and have thus decided most cases on the basis of whether a particular action by students disrupted the school rather than on the basis of the substance of the student's "disruption."[23]　　One objective of students has been to call into question this ultimate goal of orderliness by suggesting that some things that go on in schools should not only be disrupted but should be revised or discarded because of their harm to students or their lack of educative value.

The rules and evaluation procedures and regulations of a school are a way of shaping its reality, and thus the child's educational environment. We have seen that in the making of these policies the school's present staff is merely the latest in a series of contributors from inside the school system and outside it as well. The message of the student movement has been that the magnitude of the "system" on which school policy is based does not relieve present school personnel of responsibility for practices that seem to infringe upon individual rights. Instead, these students wish to make this previously compiled history of school policies problematic, that is, to open them up to question. They feel that what goes on in schools should be based on what is good for the student, what is relevant to the changing and confusing world in which he or she lives, and what is helpful for the teacher-student community. To legitimate school policy on other grounds is to sacrifice the educational tasks of schooling to institutional contingencies.

## Codifying Student Rights

The challenge to the legitimacy of school policies and policy-making can take many forms. Because of the societal context of movements for rights for other groups, and because of the place of the school in the juvenile justice system by virtue of the compulsory attendance laws, one of the challenges has been in the form of assertions about rights.

The student movement has served to raise serious doubts in the minds of educators about what they can and cannot do to and for young people. Even principals who make the same decisions they have always made, and in much the same way, now do so with the awareness that at some point a student may ask them to justify these decisions. The old authoritarian model that depicts a principal beating a student and telling him "it's for your own good," or "this is to show you to stay in your place," is clearly derived from in loco parentis values. The authority figure has rights and can grant privileges to subordinates who gain them by merit.

Such a pattern might have had some validity in a community where agreement existed among parents about what was worthwhile for children. But in the social context where the school administrator is not autonomous but accountable to other institutions and conflicting community groups, there exists no central "authority" on which to base "authoritarian" policies. In the larger society, this pluralism is dealt with by reversing the locus of rights and justifications: a constitutional framework guarantees rights to the individual, and any institution that infringes upon them must bear the burden of justifying the infringement. For example, in the case of a search through a person's property for crime-related evidence, it is the searcher who must provide justification for a search warrant. The individual is otherwise assumed to be entitled to his privacy, just as he is assumed to be innocent until a prosecutor proves his guilt to a jury.

Because of their largely dependent status as the "domain" of parents, the schools, and the state, children in this country have in many ways been outside this constitutional framework. Rights to constitutional protection have generally applied only to adults and not to children except through their parents. Those who would advocate building into the school structure the concept of student rights argue that to deny children rights is anachronistic. The evolution of a youth segment of the population, the high degree of political awareness of many young people, the compulsory nature of schooling, the lasting effect of the school record in the life of the young person—all point to a need to change overtly and structurally what has already changed tacitly (that is, the decreasing role of the school as "official model" of information or source of values) in the relationship between schools and children.

One might ask why any explicit codification of student rights would be necessary. Several reasons seem clear after our look at the position of youth in the culture and our analysis of the institution of schools. As discussed by Calkins, Lukenbill, and Mateer,[24] the establishment of rights is a trade-off between the needs of institutions or social groups and of individuals. As we have seen, the concept of school existing to serve the needs of the young is *only* an ideal today in bureaucratic school systems where many other considerations also enter into school policy. The contingencies of institutional management can swamp the individual case, especially when the institution is a public one and the individual is a child. The only way for an individual to win in a power struggle against an institution is either to join with others in disrupting it (which some students have resorted to in order to force school personnel to discuss grievances) or to have the protection of legal sanctions.

The courts are seen at present as guardians of the right of students (and of other individuals). While the courts will continue to have an important role to play, and while the decisions in cases involving students have proved interesting, they reflect the inadequacy of relying solely on litigation to protect an individual. Litigation is slow, costly, and complicated. Geographical variation in similar cases creates ambiguity (see Chapter 6). In a curious way litigation places the burden of proof on the individual because an individual must initiate suit to protest illegal, discriminatory, or abusive treatment. So long as no one litigates an issue, such as school regulation of student smoking or hair styles, school administrations can continue to impose restrictions.

Waiting for litigation, then, would seem to benefit school personnel. As students find administrative procedures (outwaiting the courts, keeping administrative hold on all problems) to be ineffective, however, they resort to direct confrontation or resistance through strikes or subterfuge. Little or no flexibility remains for resolving serious conflict without either undermining administrative authority or merely exacerbating conflict.

What is needed is a mechanism by which to deal with the dilemma of both students and administrators. One such mechanism could be a bill of student rights, which would prevent further erosion of administrative authority when it is needed, while at the same time it would protect individual students against arbitrary use of that authority. As a mediating mechanism, bills of student rights would have several implications for what goes on in schools. First, acceptance of a bill of student rights is an acknowledgment that much of the conflict among administrators, teachers, and students is systemic, that is, it is a part of the reality of the structural nature of large-scale institutions in a democratic society. This leads beyond simplistic notions of personality conflicts or villain theories on either side.

Second, in order for such a bill of student rights to be developed in a community, students and school personnel must talk with each other, both contributing to the codifying process. This communication between the two sides brings the practices of schooling into public view. (See Chapter 5.) For students, teachers, administrators, and parents to join in drafting and adopting a bill of rights involves a discussion of substantive issues about the nature of schools, the limits of authority, the place of the student in the legal system. Thus the very process of making statements regarding student rights contradicts the traditional administrative handling of student grievances "within the school." It builds in a mechanism beyond the administrator to which students may appeal.

Adopting bills of student rights is also a way of guaranteeing that what happens to students will not depend on the level of activism of any particular year's class or on the sympathies of any one teacher or administrator. Since a written bill of rights would incorporate an amendment process, it would transcend rapid turnover of student body populations and less rapid but very real turnover of faculty and principals.

We have said that the main difficulty between students and school personnel is that they have very different rationales for what they expect from students and schools. They legitimate their behavior on conflicting bases. One function of a codification of student rights can be to establish a common ground for discussion. If substantive issues are frequently to turn into issues of due process, then having that process spelled out for both students and administrators would seem helpful, especially when the process would bear a relationship to the legal workings of the nation as a whole. As Selznick discusses,[25] the handling of grievances within nongovernmental organizations such as industries has traditionally been based on internal rules pertinent to the organization and its power structure. But he points out that workers increasingly are taking their grievances into the courts, going outside the internal administrative hierarchy to get protection for rights that subordinate positions within the organization might preclude.[26] As workers appeal to the legal system of the larger community, industrial managers are becoming more cognizant of the need to include adjudicative considerations, that is, matters of individual rights, in their traditionally goal-oriented administrative decisions. For their part, workers are demanding that consideration of basic constitutional rights (free speech, political participation, racial justice, privacy) be added to customary wage and benefit clauses in contracts. Bills that explicitly define student rights might be considered as parallel to the trend in many sectors of the society to correlate public and private law and thus extend constitutional guarantees into more institutional contexts.

In summary, the political events and social changes of the 1960s became an arena in which the conflicts between students and schools took on political significance. It is possible that the implementation of bills of student rights can provide a new arena for the working out of some of these conflicts. None of the issues raised by the student movement will have easy solutions. Indeed, codifying student rights may raise even more questions—questions concerning the rights and obligations of teachers, administrators, and parents. Statements of rights of due process raise questions about vaguer claims of a right to a "decent" or "quality" education. If schooling is to be more than obtaining the proper credentials, certainly these larger issues will have to be dealt with.

## Notes

1. *Lander* v. *Seaver*, a case in 1859 involving a student who was punished for calling his teacher a bad name after school hours, is cited in E. Edmund Reutter, Jr., *Legal Aspects of Control of Student Activities by Public School Authorities* (Topeka, Kansas: National Organization on Legal Problems of Education, 1970).

2. Michael W. Apple, "The Hidden Curriculum and the Nature of Conflict," *Interchange* 2 (Spring 1971): 27-40.

3. Richard Flacks, *Youth and Social Change* (Chicago: Markham Publishing, 1971), includes the establishment of a large peacetime standing army as another factor segmenting youth from the larger society. While this is true, the relevance of youth in the military to the youth subculture was probably minimal until the commitment of American troops to South Vietnam.

4. Among others, Philip Slater, *The Pursuit of Loneliness: American Culture at the Breaking Point* (Boston: Beacon Press, 1970).

5. James S. Coleman *et al., Youth: Transition to Adulthood,* Report of the President's Science Advisory Committee (Chicago: University of Chicago Press, 1974).

6. Jurgen Herbst, "High School and Youth in America," in *Educational and Social Structure in the Twentieth Century,* ed. Walter Laqueur and George Mosse (New York: Harper and Row, 1967), 165-82.

7. For a discussion of the breakdown of societal value systems, and the concurrent emergence of privatization of values and meaning, see Thomas Luckmann, *The Invisible Religion* (New York: Macmillan, 1967); also related are Clifford Geertz, "Ideology as a Cultural System," in *Ideology and Discontent,*

ed. David E. Apter (New York: Free Press, 1964), 47-76; and Nigel Harris, *Beliefs in Society: Problems of Ideology* (London: Watts, 1968).

8. The discussion by Luckmann, *op. cit.*, of the church as an "official model" supplanted by institutional specialization and social diversity offers a striking parallel to the changing role of the school.

9. For a fuller analysis of the absence of conflict in school curricula, see Apple, *op. cit.*

10. Jürgen Habermas, *Toward a Rational Society*, tr. Jeremy J. Shapiro (Boston: Beacon Press, 1970).

11. Student activism in politics prior to the sixties was generally of low visibility, typified by student government within the school or student clubs, or, for a few, participation in issues facing the general public. Children who marched in the 1950s to protest America's commitment to making and testing nuclear weapons usually did so with their parents. Such "youth" issues as mandatory ROTC saw some early opposition at Berkeley and other campuses, but the response was localized, as described in Seymour Lipset and Sheldon S. Wolin, *The Berkeley Student Revolt: Facts and Interpretations* (New York: Doubleday, 1965).

12. Stephen K. Bailey, *Disruption in Urban Public Secondary Schools* (Washington, D.C.: National Association of Secondary School Principals, 1971).

13. *Ibid.*; *How Old Will You Be in 1984?* ed. Diane Divoky (New York: Discus Books, 1969).

14. While the student rights issue was in elementary schools also a result of "modeling" older students' actions, the most profound influence on children's rights at this level was the mere raising of the issue of rights so that parents protested or initiated litigation on behalf of their children. Prior to the 1960s, student rights at the elementary school level centered on racial discrimination, infringement on religious beliefs by school practices or curricula (biology as offensive to some Christian Scientists, the Pledge of Allegiance to Jehovah's Witnesses), or corporal punishment. Later the issue broadened to include limits on behavior modification techniques, drugs administered by school personnel, the use of standardized testing.

15. Committee on Internal Security, "SDS Plans for America's High Schools," House of Representatives, Ninety-first Congress (Washington, D.C.: Government Printing Office, 1969).

16. Administrators' dilemmas over handling student protest probably stemmed in part from the fact that "deviance" in a school had traditionally been seen as individual misbehavior against accepted rules rather than as collective activism against the rules and their legitimacy. Because such "deviance" had customarily been handled as an in-school problem, and perhaps because to confront larger substantive issues would appear to undermine their authority, administrators preferred to keep conflict within the realm of administrative procedure. This will become clearer upon reading the cases discussed in Chapter 6 herein and the implications drawn in Chapter 7. For example, a principal who wished to stop students from wearing arm bands as a protest against the Vietnam war would want to do so on the basis of administrative policy, that is, the need to avoid

disruption of the school, rather than on the basis of the rightness or wrongness of the students' beliefs about the war. To pursue the second course would be to open up the issue to nonadministrative frames of reference (political strategy, personal morality, and so on), each of which would have its own referent authority quite apart from the principal's administrative authority. To decide the matter on nonadministrative grounds would not only abridge the principal's prerogatives in this instance, but would set a precedent which, if followed, would threaten any attempts to legitimate rules on the basis of administrative goals.

17. In discussions with lawyers, social workers, police, a judge, and others who work with juveniles in relation to the law, the authors of this book repeatedly encountered in descriptions of juvenile justice procedures references to the school experience and to the information provided by schools to courts. A critical analysis is needed of the school as a component of the juvenile justice system in this country.

18. The basis of efficiency criteria in a factory model of schooling is treated by Herbert M. Kliebard, "Bureaucracy and Modern Curriculum Theory," in *Freedom, Bureaucracy and Schooling*, ed. Vernon Haubrich (Washington, D.C.: Association for Supervision and Curriculum Development, 1971), 74-93. Implications of the model are discussed in Michael W. Apple, "The Adequacy of Systems Management Procedures in Education," *Journal of Educational Research* 60 (September 1972): 10-18; and in Linda M. McNeil, "School Rules and the Production Model: Some Implications for Administration," paper for Public Schools Title III Human Relations Inservice Programs, Madison, Wisconsin, 1974.

19. Philip W. Jackson, *Life in Classrooms* (New York: Holt, Rinehart and Winston, 1968); Jules Henry, *On Education* (New York: Random House, 1966, 1971); Mary Alice White, "The View from the Pupil's Desk," in *The Experience of Schooling*, ed. Melvin Silberman (New York: Holt, Rinehart and Winston, 1971), 337-45; and others document the many classroom practices that seem to ignore the social and biological development of children, and the resultant problems of disorder, apathy, and acquiescence.

20. Apple, "Hidden Curriculum."

21. Clarence Karier, "Testing for Order and Control in the Corporate Liberal State," *Educational Theory* 22 (Spring 1972): 154-80.

22. Peter Berger and Thomas Luckmann, *The Social Construction of Reality* (New York: Doubleday, 1966); Michael W. Apple, "Common-Sense Categories and Curriculum Thought," paper presented at the conference "Toward the Reconstruction of the Curriculum Field," Philadelphia, May 10-11, 1973.

23. Reutter, *op. cit.*; Carol Ziegler, *Struggle in the Schools: Constitutional Protection for Public High School Students*, Woodrow Wilson Association Monograph in Public Affairs, No. 1 (Princeton, N.J.: Princeton University Press, 1970).

24. Carl K. Calkins, Ronald W. Lukenbill, and William J. Mateer, "Children's Rights: An Introductory Sociological Overview," *Peabody Journal of Education* 50 (January 1973): 89-109.

25. Philip Selznick, *Law, Society and Industrial Justice* (New York: Russell Sage Foundation, 1969).

26. Alvin Gouldner, *Patterns of Industrial Bureaucracy* (New York: Free Press, 1957), also deals with the problems of subordinate-superior relationships in an egalitarian society.

# 3. Social-Psychological Concepts and the Rights of Children

*Peter J. Sartorius*

Adolescents have a very rocky insecure time. Grown-ups treat them like children, and yet expect them to act like adults. They give them orders like little animals, then expect them to react like mature, and always rational, self-assured persons of legal stature. It is a difficult, lost, vacillating time!

Anonymous, *Go Ask Alice (The Story of a Runaway Girl)*

When we consider the granting of rights to children, our deliberations are frequently bogged down by questions of ability to accept one's responsibility and the capacity to make "good" judgments. Children's rights are, in effect, determined (implicitly or explicitly) by notions of maturity. A person's maturity may be considered differently at different times during his growth. Social and emotional maturity, for instance, are not necessarily concomitants of physical maturity at any given moment. How then can we appeal to maturity as a viable criterion for the conferring of rights, when the concept at its most specific is vague? To bypass this obstacle, we have tended to look toward psychological paradigms to make the concept of maturity more precise and, consequently, more useful in nonarbitrary determinations of rights. The most notable of these are psychological taxonomies that characterize maturity in terms of the development of successive age-stages, marking hierarchical cognitive and moral structures, but it is my view that maturity, though involving transitions and phases, is not thoroughly explained by psychological principles and developmental constructs. Sociocultural history and individual experience are, at least, coequal determinants of the degree and the rate of an individual's growth into maturity. The determination of maturity should be seen in terms of the individual in situ, while moral and scientific principles should not be conceived as self-contained; rather they are bound up with and modified by the content of human experience. Principles should, moreover, be comprehended in relation to concrete sociocultural traditions.[1] We may assert, therefore, that the concepts of childhood and rights are not to be regarded as empirical or moral absolutes, but as phenomena in context and thus are subject to change in their general and specific meanings. Age-grade and age-stage distinctions are then inadequate benchmarks of maturity, and as these classifications are used in psychological testing and as often in pedagogical judgments, administrative decisions, and court deliberations, they are misleadingly precise.

The underlying point is that the questions of extending rights to children is more fundamentally conceived as an ethical rather than a psychological issue. This is not to say that psychological input is irrelevant to the granting of certain types of rights, driving an automobile, for example, in contrast to, say, the right of free speech. Those responsible for making judgments and decisions about rights must be mindful of a broad context for the interpretation of maturity. I feel, in summary, that a greater understanding and more information than are provided by psychological theory and data are necessary to make reasonable judgments and good decisions in cases of rights.

## "Childhood" and "Rights"

Anthropologist Claude Levi-Strauss has said that "psychology presupposes cosmology."[2] Operational definitions of the child have historically been subsumed under a broad reality: the definitional conceptions peculiar to a given era. The seventeenth and eighteenth centuries, for example, viewed the child within the moral framework of Christian theology. The child was father to the man, representative of both his fallen grace and his possibilities for moral salvation.

As scientific thought gained prominence in the nineteenth century, the emphasis on the child's moral state gave way to the naturalistic interest in the biological development of the child (hence, the Darwinian-Spencerian notion that "ontogeny recapitulates phylogeny"). It is not my purpose to trace changing conceptions of childhood in the course of Western intellectual history, but to point out that both conceptualizations are historically continuous, both are embedded in contemporary views of childhood, both are perhaps necessary, but neither in itself is sufficient for the purposes of examining the issue of juvenile rights. Each epochal conception of childhood reflects the truth and temper of the times, but truth itself is a historical notion— cumulative and relative to the point of view of the research and knowledge at hand. Thus, I do not mean to imply that aspects of morality and ontogeny are irrelevant to contemporary thought on the subject of childhood, but I am suggesting that the tendency to think of childhood in terms of a univocally defined status, whether moral or biological, is a misapprehension. I would submit, alternatively, that childhood is properly understood as a phenomenon, having substantive meaning in space, time, and place, and, as such, moral, psychological, sociological, and developmental considerations are all relevant, while none provides a definitive disclosure model.

Let us examine briefly the notion of rights that corresponds to the notion of childhood sketched above. It should be clear that the question is not so much whether or not children possess certain rights in the Rousseauistic sense. Children are entitled to the same inalienable rights as adults, specifically in relation to the Fourteenth Amendment rights to due process—this by virtue of their ontological status as persons. Fortas' opinion in the *Tinker* case[3] settles this point. We are, rather, concerned with rights in the pragmatic-contextual sense: claims to rights relating to certain legal protections and to certain goods and services from society at large. Rights or claims to rights of this sort are perhaps more properly seen as privileges of citizenship, accorded to persons on the basis of their relative status within the particular cultural system. These rights are commonly referred to in the literature as "welfare rights" and are distinguished from "human rights."[4] Welfare rights have to do with sociopolitical claims to collect certain goods and services that the claimant feels ought to be provided him by society. Welfare rights are statutory and "alienable" (that is, changeable). They are, in short, contingent rights, traditionally conferred on the basis of age, sex, and other qualifying conditions, and they refer to cultural values, normative assumptions, and to one's relative state of dependency. Human rights, in contrast, refer to rights of free action and due process, which have ontological status in relation to the Constitution.[5] Such rights do not have to be earned; rather a claimant merely has to demonstrate his membership in the group that, according to rule, has these rights. In the case of human rights, then, and by virtue of the Tinker decision, a child has only to show that he is a member of the class "persons" to qualify for these rights. In summary, the notion of rights as used here, like the notion of childhood, is a phenomenological and not an ontological concept. Welfare rights are contingent upon cultural-historical values and norms; thus, the legitimacy of claims to them is relative to the sociotemporal location or context of such claims.

A significant implication of the *Tinker* decision is that the constitutionally guaranteed human rights of children justify their claims to welfare rights generally accorded to and reserved for adults. The import of the decision is, therefore, that it acknowledges the right of a child to make claims to those rights and privileges heretofore denied him on the basis of his status as a minor. This does not imply, however, that any particular claim must necessarily be acknowledged, nor that any specific welfare right must necessarily be accorded to juvenile claimants. It means simply that children have the right to press their specific claims to welfare rights granted to adults (either by statute or by convention) and that any such claims must be adjudicated in accordance with the constitutional guarantees of due process of law. We may conclude, then, that questions of a person's relative level of maturity and his intellectual, physical, or emotional capacities are irrelevant to questions of human rights, and, thus, the right to make a claim and to due process are guaranteed to children. Relative maturity may be considered relevant in the disposition of children's claims to certain welfare rights, such as to drive a car or to drink liquor, though not to their human (option) right to make such claims. Hence we may consider one's level of maturity a necessary but not a sufficient condition for the granting or denying of certain welfare rights.[6] In any given case, however, the decision to grant or deny a particular welfare right to a particular minor individual is ultimately a function of the judicial elements directly involved in the case (that is, the judge and/or jury). In this sense, the individual dispositions of judges and the respective community values prevailing at the time must be seen as intervening factors or mitigating circumstances in specific children's rights cases. It cannot be otherwise, until or unless unsatisfied claims are pressed to high appellate levels, up to and including the U.S. Supreme Court.

As in other societies, welfare rights are determined largely on the basis of traditional age and sex distinctions, but it seems clear that, as a society becomes increasingly diversified and industrialized, individual experience becomes more segmented and specialized. The traditional age-sex distinctions become less valid, and consequently more arbitrary, and there are increasingly ardent challenges to them. In this context, then, the various trustees of welfare rights—parents, educators, judges, legislators—have been searching for more definitive ways of determining when, how, and where to grant these rights. In the last few decades we have relied on levels of educational attainment as indicators of an individual's preparedness for adult responsibilities and privileges. Traditional age-sex distinctions were refined to age-grade distinctions, based on the assumption that productivity is a sufficient measure of maturity and that the attainment of successive grade levels is an adequate indication of one's progression from a nonproductive to a productive status in society. Other forms of productivity such as the ability to work or to produce children may, of course, also be acknowledged as evidence of maturity under certain conditions, but the chief determinants are still age (laws governing work and marriage, for example, specify age) and educational attainment level (for example, a system of officially sanctioned credentials).

Even if we assume that productivity is a measure of maturity, this would not seem adequate as the sole determining criterion of rights. It is becoming increasingly apparent, moreover, that age-grade distinctions cannot be relied upon for determining an individual's real productivity, let alone his level of maturity. Classifying a person as a low achiever or underachiever does not characterize all his physical and cognitive capacities, but only those analytic verbal abilities relative to the norms of school achievement. Where the rights of juveniles are concerned, we must look for additional criteria. The trend has recently been to look toward research in child development for consistent concepts and definitive criteria. Psychological age-stage distinctions have already replaced age-grade distinctions for many educators, and there is considerable enthusiasm over the possibility that developmental norms may provide suitable distinctions for adjudicating cases involving children's rights. We feel, however, that such enthusiasm is certainly premature, if not misguided.

## Growth and Dependency

As has been said, the growth of the child into an adult is not simply a matter of moral training, nor is it strictly a biological transformation, though it does include both. Here we shall understand growth and maturity as the dynamic interaction over time among three types of factors: ontogenetic, individual personality, and contextual or field factors. The first includes biological development, among which are the development of perceptual, cognitive structures and the capacity for moral reasoning. The second encompasses emotional development and motivation. The third comprises the sociohistorical milieu, cultural demands, standards, and expectations. We might say, more precisely, that the idea of growth from childhood to adulthood, as this transformation relates to notions of rights and responsibilities, is a multidirectional function of biological maturity, access to information, intensity of individual experience, and exposure to global concerns. Conceptions of childhood and adolescence and attitudes toward maturity should therefore be viewed equally in terms of experience as well as aging, which means that we must be cognizant not only of biological development but also of the qualitative aspects of acculturation into family and community life and of the socialization process taking place within such larger institutions as the schools. This is important because reliance on age-stage norms ignores educational space and time, that is, the context and content of individual experience. Studies by anthropologists such as Margaret Mead have uncovered correlations between developmental processes and adult institutionalized behavior.[7] Such studies of age patterning disclose the multiple imprint of a few broad values (each with its special age, sex, and other distinctions) through a complex pattern of experiences to which a growing person is subjected in any culture. The point is that so long as individual diversity and culture change are viewed as conceptually constant, developmental universals cannot adequately capture the nature of the process of change we call "maturation." Yet, theories of personality development (including moral development) strongly reflect universal developmental assumptions. Peck and Havighurst, for example, regard their five character types as successive developmental stages.[8] It is therefore assumed that preschool children are incapable of the highest type and that the middle types are associated with middle to late childhood. Those who fall below normative types are deemed to have become immobile at earlier developmental stages. Kohlberg's theory of moral development follows a similar line of reasoning.

Some psychological, sociological, and anthropological studies, however, challenge developmental assumptions about the invariant relations between infantile experience and adult personality,[9] and about the invariability and irreversibility of successive stages.[10] In commenting upon the developmental theory as a reliable basis for understanding personality (character/moral) development, Goodman writes that the Peck and Havighurst

... theory is untenable in light of much evidence .... It does not square with a vast body of anthropological reporting, nor with common-place observation and experience. Margaret Mead speaks for the anthropologists when she says that cross-cultural variation is so great as to "make any idea of general stages appear useless." ... the young child/adult discrepancy is surely a matter not of kind, but of degree. To state, or even to imply, that children of preschool age are capable of no more than amorality or expediency is to perform a quite remarkable trick. It involves either mutilating the facts to make them fit the Procrustean bed of theory or performing some sleight-of-hand that causes inconvenient facts to disappear. The result, in either case, is distortion of a sort by no means peculiar to Peck and Havighurst. Numerous others (Lawrence Kohlberg, for example) following in the footsteps of Freud and more particularly, of J. M. Baldwin and of J. Piaget, have accepted uncritically the age/stage assumptions set forth long ago by these authorities. But we are now seeing a significant decline in adherence to propositions resting heavily on the truth-by-assertion method of verification, or on data drawn only from the United States or another Western society.[11]

The implication, then, is not so much that developmental processes are judicially arbitrary, but that they do not empirically account for a number of dimensions relevant to moral and physical growth. As such, developmental concepts are unreliable as universal assumptions and thus are not appropriate as a basis for the determination of welfare rights.

Psychological characteristics of children and adolescents are not to be seen as defining categories; nor should we hypothesize causal links between observable characteristics and developmental concepts—at least for the purpose of defining juvenile rights. Maturity interpreted in terms of a few selected developmental phenomena and expressed in terms of statistical norms is grossly arbitrary and systematically unjust in the determination of individual rights for two major reasons: first, some developmental processes are neither universal nor perfectly reliable; second, a statistical mean is not itself a fact of observation, but merely a convenient way of expressing the central tendency in a distribution of actual (observed) characteristics in aggregate. The use of developmental concepts within a statistical framework reifies the individual in a way not appropriate for considerations of rights. If we are going to grant certain rights on the basis of maturity then we must recognize it as a holistic, qualitative concept—a continuous process—reflecting dynamic tensions among an individual's developing biological structures and competencies, his personal experience and sensitivity, and the pervasive sociocultural pressures of his particular milieu. Relationships between developmental learning sequences and personality (or character/moral) development are at best probabilistic, suggesting that progress may be made by discovering the empirical limits in predictions of personality development. Such limits will, presumably, vary both with the identity and complexity of the particular aspect of the developmental process being predicted and with the number and identity of the independent variables on which the prediction is based. We have identified the nature of these independent variables generally as having to do with aspects of the sociocultural context. We shall now try to discover something about their specific natures.

It should be stressed that the growth of a child is dependent, perhaps more than anything else, upon the significant others, such as parents and relatives, peers, and teachers, who control his life and set guidelines for his experience. A child relies primarily on these people for the provision of his physical, psychological, and emotional needs. The point to consider is that maturation is a continuous process that marks a relative transition from child to adult status, the definition or recognition of which is a function of an individual's various states of dependency—physical, psychological, and emotional. These states of dependency relate to the provision of needs in separate but overlapping areas of growth: biological development (material needs),

cognitive development, learning (increasing information and reper-
toire), personality and motivational development (affection, guidance, inculcation of values, behavior norms). All of these areas may
have age-stage implications to some degree (biological growth, cognitive development, moral reasoning), yet taken together they cannot
be said to be completely dependent on age-stage. Field factors such
as access to information and intensity of experience constitute covar-
iants in the growth of the child, and these factors may be encouraged
or discouraged by controlling individuals, institutions, and the overall
social configuration of a given child's life.

Psychological concepts of childhood and maturity focus on the
developmental needs of the growing individual from the standpoint
of a Freudian concept of ego. Stage theorists such as Erikson, Piaget,
and Kohlberg assert that the ego becomes increasingly defined with
age, governed by a regular sequence of universal biological states.
Cultural relativists such as Lewin and Kimball,[12] on the other hand,
emphasize that maturational changes unfold as adaptations to one's
specific cultural environment. Whatever the emphasis, certain developmental phenomena are apparent in the transition from childhood
to adulthood: first, the search for individual identity and self-definition; second, the search for enduring values from adult society; third,
the search for role models, that is the search for one's proper location in the social order, with its concomitant responsibilities, by
reference to significant others (including peers as well as adults);
fourth, the securing of independence; fifth, the securing of recognition. The argument between stage theorists and cultural relativists
centers on whether these phenomena accompany the gradual succes-
sion of biological structures or whether they occur abruptly at critical periods of cultural pressure. Regardless of their theoretical bias,
most theorists tend to agree that these phenomena are a product of
interaction between innate physical capacity and environmental
influences. "Stages" of emotional-psychological development, in
other words, should not be seen as abstractions, but as meaningful in
the context of individual experience.

Within a person's environment are social structures which, together with the development of biological-psychological structures,
affect qualitative advances in the maturation process. The idea of
special identity in the sense of role behavior and in the context of
controlling institutions is an important example of such social

structures. From the practical standpoint the above transitional phenomena involve the adoption of various roles; an individual's perception and appropriation of relevant roles are instrumental for the acknowledgment of maturity. Thus, a crucial consideration in the determination of maturity or adult status in any society (most particularly in a diverse one) is the degree to which its accepted roles are clearly delineated and unambiguously communicated to its members. In addition to clarity these roles must manifestly express cultural-historical continuity: that is, with respect to role viability, the needs and expectations of society must complement those of the individual. If this is not the case, the process of recognizing, understanding, and adopting roles will be problematic. Maturity is not determinate in any fixed sense, as is often inferred on the basis of psychological stage theory; variables pertaining to general social structure and to individual social experience are at least equally significant with developing biological-psychological structures in the determination of relative levels of maturity.

## Role Clarity

It is becoming increasingly attractive for educators and jurists to look toward age-grade and age-stage definitions in considerations of maturity and juvenile rights. We have argued that the extension of psychological concepts beyond adduceable empirical and epistemological limits is, at best, a dubious enterprise. Let us then consider the idea of role clarity as a way of achieving a broader context for the idea of maturity.

In a practical sense individual psychology may be subsumed under the functional aspects of the social context. Hence the concept of role behavior is directly relevant to normative standards and expectations as well as to the evaluation of the actual performance of individuals within society. To be a functioning member of society is to assume any number of roles within it; the number and nature of these roles relate to the variety of social institutions embraced by the society from the family up to the most inclusive governmental structures. A structurally complex society has more differential roles and a greater potential for overlapping domains, role incompatibility, and ambiguity. Thus it is important for the society to lay bare its criteria for role eligibility and the performance expectations for any given role (while societal role definitions must be compatible with human needs). In the context of rights the critical question regarding role expectations is the relation between the needs of the social system and the needs and rights of the individual. The nature and degree of the rights of any particular group (or class) balance between societal needs and human needs.[13] The consequences of incompatibility are generally characterized in psychological parlance: in the case of inadequate role definition, "alienation"; in the case of inappropriate or unclear performance expectations, "deviancy."

With this in mind, let us now turn specifically to the status of children. The role and concurrent rights of children can be expressed historically in terms of two polar ideologies.[14] On the one hand childhood has been seen as a conceptual means of "rationalizing, controlling and exploiting children" for the purposes of industrializing societies; on the other, children are seen as a special class, held in awe, to be protected and carefully nurtured as a natural resource. The first extreme has promoted the excessive use of cheap child labor; the second has resulted in treatment that "can be stiflingly sentimental and can be used to keep children out of practical life, so that they are ignorant and retarded."[15] Both attitudes reify the child, their respective roles reflecting the needs and demands of others. With respect to rights, the operational and organizational demands of the social system have been the sole determinants of the roles of children and consequently have overridden the actualization of their human rights.

Psychology is relevant to role behavior, and we have already mentioned some of the psychological functions of role clarity for the transition from child to adult—for self-definition, for gleaning enduring adult values, for locating oneself in society and identifying responsibilities, for independence, and for recognition. Psychologists of diverse theoretical biases tend to agree implicitly on one point: that confusions about roles and values contribute to emotional instability, impede emotional growth, and, thus, retard the maturation process. Lewin, for example, characterizes the adolescent as "marginal," pointing to changing personal biology and shifting group identification as the major contributors to adolescent insecurity; he suggests that discrepancies between child and adult values and prolonged uncertain status result in emotional suffering.[16] Several studies have related socially disruptive behavior among youth (delinquency, use of drugs, recklessness) to identity factors that suggest the lack of clear delineation between childhood and adulthood (for example, early feminine dependence and absenteeism of the father).[17] Erikson asserts that his adolescent stage ("identity" or "role confusion") involves establishing an ego identity consistent with sex roles, mores, vocational expectations, and future orientation of the particular culture. Furthermore, the adolescent must receive unambiguous signals from his milieu in order to distinguish between what is acceptable and rewarded and what is repudiated and punished.[18] Cultural relativists (or "environmentalists" or "transactionalists") argue that clear perception of consistent and continuous roles helps to prevent difficulty in the transition from childhood to adulthood. Stage theorists assert that the clear perception of roles at each successive age-stage aids a smooth transition to the next stage.

Regardless of the psychological theory one prefers, two separate but related points must be emphasized. First, role behavior is an extremely important factor for growth and maturation insofar as maturity depends on continuity between personal (psychological) and social identity; in this respect, clarity of roles is of paramount concern. Second, lack of clarity of roles and role contradictions contribute to the vagaries surrounding the idea of maturity—for both children and adults. In this regard, the tendency of our institutional framework to prolong the dependency of the child on adult society, an attitude for which psychological theory is a frequent rationale, merely adds to the problems of ambiguity in role expectations and performance.

As we have suggested, psychological data and disclosure models, while helpful as heuristic tools for understanding psychological processes, do not offer substantive solutions to the real problems of coming of age. Assuming that children want adult status, they must be able to recognize "adultizing" roles and interpret them unambiguously. And if they successfully adopt these roles, they must also be acknowledged by the society—by the bestowal of the functional rights and privileges of adulthood. The procedure seems simple enough, but the problem is whether or not these "adultizing" roles are clearly delineated, clearly communicated, and, finally, whether they are commensurate with popular needs and expectations. A brief discussion of the anthropological rites of passage or initiatory experiences seems relevant to the problem of role clarity and the transition to adulthood since the historical and traditional functions of such rites have been to provide clear operational distinctions between the status of a child and that of an adult.

Every culture establishes certain institutional patterns and rituals, supported by emotional and intellectual (informational) preparation to mark a child's entrance into adulthood. In traditional literature these patterns and rituals are called rites of passage. Aside from birthdays, rites of passage are probably the most significant of life's passages. Many cultures formalize their significance with explicit and elaborate ceremonial rituals; for others, the transformation is marked less abruptly by a number of formalizing ceremonies. Needless to say, rites vary in nature from place to place, as well as from time to time. All rites of passage, whether abrupt or incremental, have, however, certain characteristics in common: they ascribe adult role responsibilities to a preadult; initiates are divested of characteristics of youth and invested with those of adulthood, with the explicit aim of effecting changes in values, motivation, and social roles; continuity with previous generations is stressed as traditional values and lore are transmitted to the young; and the neophyte adult is invested with new authority and privileges (rights).[19] Regardless of the duration of the rites of passage, the period can be described as one of cultural compression:

The individual is "compressed" into the cultural mode decisively and finally at this period of time in most human cultures. It may be that the compression occurs as a climax to a more or less gradual series of educational experiences in terms of intensity and difficulty, or it may be as in the case of [tribal cultures] that there is an abrupt transformation at this time. In any event, most initiatory rites are characterized by isolation and separation from familiar things and people, and emphasize the dramatic aspects of information giving and getting. The atmosphere is sacred. Strangers are used as instructors rather than familiar friendly people. Rigid rules for the conduct of the individual and for the conduct of the educational experience as a whole are maintained. [20]

In traditional, preindustrial societies, rites of passage are few and simple: they are occasions for dramatic ceremony, marking the unequivocal, if abrupt, status change from child to adult. The simple, traditional way of life is relatively constant from one generation to the next, so that the clarity of adult role expectations and consequent responsibilities and privileges present no special problem. The simple tribal ceremony marking adulthood is paralleled in complex, industrialized societies by several less overt, but often equally ceremonious occasions, each related to a different activity system.[21] For example, confirmation and Bar Mitzvah relate to the religious system; army induction and voting have to do with the political system; graduation is connected to the educational system; acquisition of occupational identity such as apprenticeship, rookie-ship, or the attainment of occupational licenses pertain to the eco-nomic-work system; marriage marks entry into the family system. There are, in addition, several lesser milestones such as the legal age to obtain a driver's license or the legal drinking age. All are subject to more or less institutionalized physical and mental ordeals, tests of competence, and, in some instances, organized hazing. At the same time, they are usually accompanied by relevant instruction, profes-sional secrets, codes of ethics, and so forth. The principal difference then between stable and complex societies is the number of activity systems requiring role-specific behavior and, consequently, the number of adult identities one is permitted or required to assume. Whereas stable cultures provide clear, consistent information con-cerning roles,[22] it becomes very important for an individual in com-plex cultures to know in which activity systems he qualifies as mature and to what extent any particular benchmark contributes to his adulthood in a general sense.

It is no wonder that a highly specialized, complex culture such as ours attempts to embrace stage theory to structure the relationship between the growing child and the manifold rites of passage required in our culture. In the application of stage theory it is asserted that children acquire cultural concepts within parameters set by universal age-stage sequences; thus the structural concepts that specify com-petencies and judgmental attitudes are accompanied by necessary and biologically determined critical periods of adjustment.[23] Hence, society need only build social structures that support the individual's passage from one age-stage to another. The environmentalist (or cul-tural relativist) view presents problematic implications with regard to the responsibility of society for providing the social conditions neces-sary for smooth role transition. The relativistic view implies that society can eliminate qualitative differences between age-stages by focusing on the cultural provisions for biological and social matura-tion processes. The relevant point for our purpose is that psychologi-cal theory, whether developmental or environmental, stresses continuity, in terms of both invariant stage sequence and consistent cultural messages. It may be that continuity between individual societal needs, between role definitions and role expectations, however interpreted, is a necessary developmental condition for the smooth transition from childhood to adulthood.

An understanding of biologically determined developmental sequences is necessary but not sufficient to determine maturity in the context of the determination of rights. Put another way, there is more to maturity than is dreamed of in our psychology. In this connection, we must note the dual function of rites of passage: notifying society of a change in role and status and instilling in the initiates the values and beliefs that will make the new role congenial. The several rites of passage, singly or in various combinations, must signal functional adult status in a definitive way; there must be continuity among activity systems, such that a holistic meaning of adulthood is clearly recognized by the young and unequivocally acknowledged by the society. In addition to psychological research this requires extensive analysis of the interrelationships among biological, psychological, sociological, and anthropological structures. A few anthropologists who have been doing this kind of research have looked at sequential conditioning processes in societies whose role transitions are discontinuous and have suggested that the individual pays a "great psychic cost" for the lack of such ritual conditioning.[24] Yet the effectiveness of various kinds of rites of passage, under various circumstances, in transforming motivation is not known. Experimental and field research are badly needed in this area.

## Discontinuity

Discontinuity is a rare occurrence in stable cultures. Such societies are highly integrated, are homogeneous with respect to values, customs, and expectations, and are generally characterized by a simple division of labor. Cultural patterns are unequivocal to the members of the society, and, consequently, a high degree of continuity with respect to values and roles exists among individual members and successive generations. A single, abrupt rite of passage is thus sufficient to communicate the meaning, status, and privileges of adulthood.

Contemporary American culture, however, is diverse and highly specialized, manifesting discontinuities with respect to the clarity of roles and rites of passage. We shall discuss the nature of this discontinuity in terms of, first, role ambiguity and, second, role conflict.

Physical development may be readily understood by reference to biological changes, but emotional and social maturity are largely dependent upon experience, acquired competencies, and the willingness to adopt responsibilities commensurate with the role of an adult. In our society maturity or adulthood is differentially related to various activity systems. Thus, adulthood in a holistic sense is never clear, but relative to a particular activity system. The degree of one's maturity is always open to question: benchmarks are accorded with age or experience as one advances along elaborated status hierarchies within each activity system. Hence, when we talk of the rights of juveniles to make life choices in the various activity systems as opposed to their readiness to make such decisions, we more often refer to broad sociocultural norms than to the actual circumstances of the particular individual. For instance, if one's graduation marks the ceremonial discharge from the in loco parentis jurisdiction of the educational system (and thus adulthood with respect to this particular activity system), one should be in a position to assert rights and make choices previously denied. Yet graduation seems merely to mark entry into a new activity system (college or graduate school or the world of work) where new competency tests, and new rites of passage await the initiate. The ceremonial rites themselves are not particularly meaningful with respect to clarity of adult roles, and are in fact contradictory, since the possibility that a young person may be mature enough to make crucial choices before his graduation is conceptually precluded.

Transition from the status of child to that of adult obviously involves personal identity changes. It is crucial to the process of identity change, however, that the new identities be recognized and accepted by others, and that those making the changes conceive of themselves as actually having new identities. Concomitant requirements for changes in social identity accompany those for personal identity, but a youth can only variously relate new social identity to adulthood, depending on the particular activity system he is involved in at any particular time. Since there is little continuity among activity systems with respect to role criteria, it becomes difficult for the youth to locate himself in the overall social order.

The notion of attaining achievement levels in various activity systems is far too ambiguous to serve as the basis for conferring adult rights and privileges, particularly when this system confounds rather than clarifies adult role definitions and expectations.

The notion of role conflict is related to role ambiguity. In American society little continuity exists between the behavior patterns expected of and by adults and those expected of and by youth. Much of this is due to incongruities in values between the generations on questions of morality, authority, politics, interpersonal relationships, and so on.[25] Sex education is a good example: parents want their children to receive adequate sex education and are concerned that they understand various birth control methods, and yet they do not want birth control devices dispensed to minors. Goodman points out that American society systematically evades moral issues by turning them into empirical problems with technical solutions.[26] Youth perceive an overriding commitment to expediency and compromise even though this weakens the ethical fabric of individual experience; hence they protest, escape, and create an alternative life style that seems consistent with the ostensible values of a democratic society.[27]

In addition, adult society understands little of the nature of intergenerational change in group character in a fast-moving technological society. Though mediated by processes of child development, intergenerational change in character comes about by way of cultural changes that first affect postinfantile experience.[28] Change is much more highly compressed in an advanced technological society; thus, changes in group character are not necessarily generational, but are a function of time. Such factors as enhanced exposure to global concerns, intensity of experience, and pervasiveness of the mass media make children generally more competent and sensitive at earlier ages than their generational antecedents. While conformity to the group values of previous generations has been a traditional socialization function, the generation of the sixties is more committed to diversity than to replicating uniformity. The resultant effect with regard to rights has been that individual rights (or, in this case, children's rights) are conceived as antithetical to the group obligations of adult society.

One further issue should be raised in connection with role conflict. Complex societies often consist of heterogeneous groups or classes, with corresponding alternative sets of values and world views. Though broad role definitions may overlap in a societal sense, often the role perceptions and expectations of different groups or classes—racial, ethnic, religious, socioeconomic—are incompatible with each other and the cultural mainstream. Hence, discontinuities exist along the lines of major demographic categories (including women and children), resulting in role conflicts of a general (relative to society at large) as well as a specific (relative to the various activity systems within society) nature. Ambiguity and conflict over role expectations are tremendously costly to society in terms of organizational efficiency, authority structure, and open disruption, to the various subgroups in terms of mobility and discrimination (de facto or de jure), and to the individual in terms of alienation, frustration, and anxiety. Children, in this sense, may constitute a class by virtue of their dependency on adult society. Thus, the role difficulties associated with entrance into adult status may have some similarity to the difficulties encountered by minority groups attempting to enter the mainstream or to colonized nations attempting to gain independence. In any case, the point is that role ambiguity and role conflict in no small way account for the impossibility of defining children's rights in any absolute or fixed sense.

## Exacerbating Conditions

> I remember all those thousands of hours
> that I spent in grade school watching the clock,
> waiting for recess or lunch or to go home.
> Waiting: for anything but school.
> My teachers could easily have ridden with Jesse James
> for all the time they stole from me.
> Richard Brautigan, *The Memoirs of Jesse James*

The concept of adolescence in American culture represents a contemporary substitute for tribal rites of passage. It implies an extended period of gradual transition to adult status, cumulative growth through knowledge, wisdom, and emotional stability, and, finally, a protracted period of dependency which is deemed necessary in order for the entire transformation process to take place. All of our institutions, in fact, are geared to delay the adult role. The American concept of the nuclear family is characteristically protective and child centered (see Chapters 1 and 2). Children and youth are discouraged, if not prohibited, from participating in the social realities of life, with the rationale and rhetoric of preserving childhood as a carefree, fun-loving period to be nostalgically cherished in adult life. Consequently children and adolescents are afforded little opportunity for real social action, for political commitment, and for exploring new roles. They are systematically denied or precluded from the very experiences that contribute to their growth and maturity.[29]

The essence of our era is in the diversity that an advanced heterogeneous culture provides. Conformity, uniformity, and passivity are the thrust of adult (and institutional) socialization efforts and are the core of society's normative categories for the analysis of behavior. Individual expression, if it does not conform to traditional values and beliefs, finds no affirmative support. In such instances, self-actualization becomes problematic: "What is immeasurably destructive is the kind of conformity that abandons the experience of the individual in order to usurp a tradition to which [the adolescent] does not belong and to express a view of life foreign to his experience and, on his lips, phony."[30] Not only does the rigid adherence to and preservation of traditional political and social ideas (J. Edgar Hoover's definition of national security, incidentally)[31] stultify youth and stunt growth into adulthood, but the pervasiveness of this attitude toward socialization has implications for society's machinery for evaluating and changing its systems.

One principal means by which children are kept isolated from the adult world is by protracted economic dependency on adult society. Friedenberg likens the economic position of youth to that of colonized peoples: "Like a dependent native, the teenager is encouraged to be economically irresponsible because his sources of income are undependable and do not derive from his personal qualities."[32] Friedenberg argues that the whole society has a stake in the economic dependency of children: the schools for their custodial care, labor to keep them off the tight labor market, business to keep the teenage fad and junk market booming. Since children have no serious economic status (except as a resource for adult society), it is difficult for them to develop personal and responsible patterns of economic behavior. Children are, in general, regarded as beneficiaries of the philanthropy of adult society, by virtue of their economic idleness.[33]

The problem of adolescent dependency is compounded by the scarcity of traditional jobs for youth, such as delivery boy, messenger, and elevator operator. Teenagers have no legitimate role outside their status as high school student, and it is becoming increasingly apparent that high school does not serve the developmental needs of certain segments of the youth population. It is, in fact, dysfunctional in this regard. Many young people find themselves in a double bind: high school affords them no independence, no responsibility, and no income, while dropping out means long periods of unemployment and dead-end unskilled or semiskilled jobs. They are, accordingly, encouraged to stay in school; yet it is ironic that dropping out may be the most rational decision a particular youth can make, from the standpoint of his personal needs and development.

The situation is especially problematic for lower-class youth. In large class-stratified societies such as ours, rites of passage for these youth are likely to be fewer and simpler. It would seem, therefore, that adult status would be clearer for them, at least within class boundaries. Yet members of lower socioeconomic classes are not likely to advance far through the status hierarchies of the various activity systems, so that formal maturity in the sense of role clarity is seldom achieved. It would seem to follow that when juveniles are allowed more control over their life choices, the children of the poor will be the last to receive such acknowledgment; for, in general, they are seen as relatively low achievers and thus are subject to extended jurisdiction by adult society.

High school represents an extended puberty rite (though without any sex role esoterica) in the sense that the educational function of the schools is to inculcate in the young the relevant societal values, knowledge, and skills that prepare them for adult roles. The social function of the schools, as we have indicated, contradicts the educational function: it is designed to prolong adolescence and delay entry into the adult world. High schools, in effect, suspend young people between the ideals of childhood and the responsibilities of adulthood. The very concept of high school, in this sense, symbolizes and actualizes the timelessness, the "nowheresville," and the vagaries of adolescence for many teenagers. Let us examine, in some closer detail, the efficacy of the high school as a preparatory rite of passage. From the viewpoint of the psychological-developmental needs mentioned earlier, high school is only partially successful for certain segments of the youth population, notably the poor, the culturally and racially different, and some elements of white middle-class youth.[34] There are several reasons for this which relate to the rite-of-passage concept. Alienation from adult society generally results in strong identification with one's peer group. Though some aspects of adolescent subculture may be regarded as deviant, the pressure for conformity within it makes self-definition difficult. High school does not serve the function of facilitating independence from the family since it is only a day school; moreover, the youth probably experiences less independence at school than at home. The recognition a youth receives in high school is also limited: athletics and school organizations offer peer-group recognition, but the meaningfulness of this with respect to middle-class roles may be dysfunctional for low or underachievers.

From the standpoint of socialization functions, the effectiveness of high school for these groups of young people is likewise tenuous. Pupils are taught citizenship goals and values that are largely removed from social, political, and economic realities. In fact, such programs, inasmuch as they do not reflect reality, are often a source of indignation, frustration, and disillusionment. As far as role models are concerned, the high school has little to offer, except the teachers themselves. Although on rare occasions teachers may offer viable role models, notions of professional distance, objectivity, and impartiality, as well as a generally authoritarian demeanor, more often present formidable barriers to the development of genuine interpersonal relationships between teachers and their pupils, particularly those students who are not interested in the schools.

High schools do not even perform their overriding function—the transmission of culture—very well, at least so far as many young people are concerned. Curriculum is highly selective, and programs are largely geared for the middle-class child who will ultimately go on to college. It is a common conclusion among educational researchers that, given a normal distribution of intelligence and abilities, many young people will not or cannot achieve within the framework of middle-class achievement criteria. Thus, culture in the middle-class sense is transmitted only to those who proceed to college, and even they are increasingly cynical in this regard. High school has no definitive end with respect to formal recognition of adult status: it is, rather, considered by many a transitory step to yet another institution (college), and for others it is merely the end to an alienating process.

## Implications and Conclusions

The systematic process of prolonging the dependency of young people on adult society is a major stumbling block in considering the rights of children. To what extent, in other words, are children necessarily dependent? Certain biological needs must, of course, be met in the course of nurturing the child; similarly, certain emotional demands must be satisfied. Growth is a dynamic, multidirectional phenomenon; we must be careful not to extend dependency where it does not belong and where it retards growth. We have pointed to some areas of psychological, emotional, and social growth where such extensions occur. Maturity is a relative concept; it cannot be conceptualized in the absolute sense that is often the consequence of assumptions drawn from psychological theory. The pervasive notion of an age-grade and age-stage social universe must be repudiated, as it does not afford the kind of determinateness with respect to growth and maturation that was once believed. We must be aware of the confluence of forces which promote or retard dependency and the recognition and adoption of appropriate social roles. We should recognize, in addition, that it is this same confluence of forces—this *Zeitgeist*—that determines the extent to which certain kinds of rights (principally welfare rights) are extended or curtailed.

The child of today, we have implied, is not like the child of other times in this regard: his access to information, his sensitivity to and awareness of global concerns, and his general capabilities are far greater than at earlier ages. This is due mainly to the nature of the environment in which today's children grow—a global village, linked by mass communications. The result is that children know a lot more relative to their elders. Mead, in fact, asserts that the present definition of pupil or student is out of date when we define learner as a child (or at best an immature person) who is entitled to moral protection and subsistence in a dependency position and who is denied the moral autonomy that is accorded an adult.[35] Similarly the traditional lock step concept of school to work is obsolete. Acquisition of knowledge no longer means vertical transmission from wise old teachers to the minds of young pupils. The nature of the transmission of knowledge in our age is lateral, "the sharing of knowledge by the informed with the uninformed, whatever their ages."[36] Age-grade and age-stage distinctions are therefore irrelevant to the notion of maturity and the acquisition of the skills necessary for functional autonomy. In thinking about effective education, Mead cautions, "we should recognize that the adolescent's need and right to work [i.e., function in society] is as great as (perhaps greater than) his immediate need and right to study."[37] This suggests that what it means to be a child today has greatly changed, while what it means to be an adult has remained relatively unchanged.

While adults cling to a traditional notion of conformity and their commitment to an integrated society, the young generation is attuned to the most vital characteristics of the time—diversity and change. It is difficult for adults to accept the notion of culture as "the organization of diversity"; heterogeneity and change, from this standpoint, do not necessarily imply psychological and cultural disorganization or trauma.[38] It does imply a change in the traditional structure of authority in our society, which may be disconcerting if not traumatic to the older generation. In terms of knowledge, skills, and even wisdom, adults must face the fact that they must accept tutelage from those younger than themselves. The major difficulty with this situation is that the problems of sociocultural organization may exceed the capacities of its members to solve them, and this is precisely the problem context with respect to determining the rights of children. As Mead says, "Thus we avoid facing the most vivid truth of the new age: No one will live all his life in the world into which he was born, and no one will die in the world in which he worked in his maturity."[39]

One of the most important concerns for education is clarity of roles. We have seen that certain things involving role definition, role awareness, and role expectation are necessary for the development of adult responsibilities. Yet adults and socializing institutions, rather than clarifying role expectations and responsibilities, tend to present them with ambiguity, if not conflict. While age-stage development constitutes integrative elements for the formation of new physical capacities and new self-awareness, it does not clarify the social context for such awareness. Though a child may sense that new emotional and social behaviors are required by virtue of biological changes within himself, he cannot adequately serve these internal needs unless the specific nature of the new social demands are made clear to him. The problem of role clarity is compounded if normative transitions (such as becoming an adult) involve discontinuous role behavior. For instance, American society encourages openness, idealism, asceticism, and innocence in childhood, but demands ruthlessness, pragmatism, and expediency of adults. Consequently, it seems that the function of education, rather than prolonging dependency, is to promote continuity and to facilitate the transition toward fully functioning adulthood. Role clarity, in this sense, is not achieved by simply defining roles according to traditional political and social ideas, but by providing young people with access to actual duties and responsibilities in a participatory sense. Young people must be given the opportunity to explore and experiment with the diversity of their world in order to be in the position where they can begin to understand the plenitude of roles from which they will gain adult status.

An important consequence of increased role clarity and expanded role participation for young people will be increased pressure for the extension of adult rights and privileges. Maturity, though relevant in the consideration of rights, is a complex and protracted phenomenon. Definitive answers to questions of responsibility and judgment will not be found in developmental concepts and psychological models. Nor can we expect to anticipate all the relevant circumstances and conditions that would be necessary to draft definitive juvenile rights legislation in advance of specific claims. For adult society to deal with increased demands for the extension of rights prudently, but justly, we suggest that a more relative procedure be established that takes into account more of the variously relevant factors. We recommend, specifically, that schools, particularly middle and high schools, adopt a conflict-resolution model similar to the adversary model of our legal system, the function of which would be twofold: first, to adjudicate the legitimacy of any particular claims to welfare rights (as we defined them earlier) and/or rights to due process; and thereby, second, to establish tentative operational limits on children's rights—precedents, but subject to future challenges within the framework. The reasons for our advocating such a procedure should now be clear. Reliance on scientific disclosure models for facile classifications of "maturity" is inappropriate for determination of rights. Arbitrary decisions decreed by adults are, on the other hand, equally unacceptable on ethical grounds. The obvious alternative is to place such deliberations within a democratic process of conflict resolution, in the context of open adversary debate. We advocate this not only because it seems the only reasonable alternative but also because the traditional concept of in loco parentis is losing its grip on the authority structure of the school. An adversary conflict-resolution model, we feel, is a most viable substitute. It is consistent with the democratic notion of due process. It is also supported by the spirit of the *Tinker* decision, in which Fortas suggests that children are to be considered persons in the full constitutional sense, and, thus, rights must be extended to them pursuant to their legal suit.

A few words on the utility of psychological disclosure models are appropriate as a concluding statement. Reliance on psychological-age distinctions in questions of maturity and rights generally ignores the realities of contemporary life. They foster false universals (such as "adolescence"), inflexible norms, and static expectations with regard to age behavior on the part of adults. Since culture-specific tasks are communicated to the child through adult expectations, it is easy to see that expectations based on presumptions of a universal developmental process may have an inverse effect on the growth and development of a child's capacities. Cognitive development should be seen in the context of the particular cultural characteristics of an individual's environment. The mental and social demands culture places on the individual will play a large part in determining the level of maturity he may reach. Cognitive growth, then, depends not so much on naturally unfolding structures as on the unlocking of inherent capacities by exposure to the specialized environment of the individual.[40]

Psychological competency tests have neither necessary connection nor categorical relevance to questions of social maturity and rights; thus they cannot be legitimately used as rationales for the denial of rights. As young people continue to thwart institutional efforts at prolonging their dependency, as they continue to press for increased role clarity (such as reaching majority at the age of eighteen) and more adult responsibilities and privileges, authorities will find little refuge in psychological theory. Neither will they find adequate rationales in traditional age-grade distinctions. Studies tend, in fact, to support the concept that institutionalization is inadvisable for promoting growth, whether in terms of physical, social, emotional, or cognitive development.[41] In the schools and in the courts, the denial of children's claims to rights cannot require prior theoretical and statistical assurances based on psychological age-grade or age-stage competencies. We feel such claims should be viewed and evaluated structurally in terms of the ecological relationships among social and psychological structures,[42] and adjudicated within the context of a democratic conflict-resolution model. Broad psychological and sociological considerations and individual idiosyncracies will be relevant in varying degrees, depending upon the particular circumstances of any given claim. What is important is that children are to be regarded as complete persons, possessing autonomy and integrity, and therefore entitled to the rights and privileges due to adults. Exactly what these rights are or will be remains to be seen. One thing is certain, however: we cannot expect the rights of children to be adequately determined by simple judicial or administrative decree. Though we can legislate the controlling principles, the specific nature of the rights will unfold as children and adults actively pursue them, whether in collaboration or in opposition. The responsibility of adult authorities is to provide the kind of institutional structures that will facilitate rather than frustrate the process.

## Notes

1. See Robert S. Peters, "Concrete Principles and the Rational Passions," in *Moral Education: Five Lectures,* ed. James M. Gustafson *et al.* (Cambridge, Mass.: Harvard University Press, 1970), 29-55.

2. See Claude Levi-Strauss, *The Savage Mind* (Chicago: University of Chicago Press, 1966), and *Structural Anthropology* (New York: Basic Books, 1963).

3. *Tinker* v. *Des Moines Independent Community School District,* 393 U.S. 503, 89, S. Ct. 733 (1969).

4. In Chapter 5 the term "rights of recipience" is used synonymously with "welfare rights."

5. "Human rights" are referred to in Chapter 5 as "option rights," including both rights to "free action" and to "due process."

6. Sometimes the notion of human (option) rights overlaps that of welfare rights, thus presenting difficult cases. Good examples of this are to be found in the area of sexual mores, practices, and behavior, the difficult question being whether sexual freedoms are inviolate regardless of one's age or maturity, or whether, in the case of juveniles, sexual activity is to be considered a welfare right.

7. See J.W.M. Whiting and Irwin L. Child, *Child Training and Personality* (New Haven, Conn.: Yale University Press, 1953).

8. Robert F. Peck and Robert J. Havighurst, *The Psychology of Character Development* (New York: Wiley, 1960).

9. Harold Orlansky, "Infant Care and Personality," *Psychological Bulletin* 46 (January 1949): 1-48; William H. Sewell, "Infant Training and the Personality of the Child," *American Journal of Sociology* 58 (September 1952): 150-59.

10. Margaret Mead, "Comments on Professor Piaget's Paper," in Leo Kanner and Barbel Inhelder, *Discussions on Child Development* (New York: International University Press, 1960), 49; Jerome Kagan, "A Conversation with Jerome Kagan," *Saturday Review of Education* 1 (April 1973): 41-43.

11. Mary Ellen Goodman, *The Culture of Childhood* (New York: Teachers College Press, 1970), 109-10.

12. Kurt Lewin, *Field Theory in Social Science* (New York: Harper and Row, 1964); Solon Kimball and J.E. McClellan, Jr., *Education and the New America* (New York: Vintage, 1962).

13. Carl F. Calkins, Ronald Lukenbill, and William J. Mateer, "Children's Rights: An Introductory Sociological Overview," *Peabody Journal of Education* 50 (January 1973): 103.

14. *Ibid.*, 99; Paul Goodman, "Introduction," in Paul Adams *et al.*, *Children's Rights: Towards the Liberation of the Child* (New York: Praeger, 1971), 1-2.

15. Paul Goodman, quoted in Calkins, Lukenbill, and Mateer, *op. cit.*, 100 (footnote).

16. Kurt Lewin, "The Field Theory Approach to Adolescence," in *The Adolescent: A Book of Readings*, ed. Jerome Seidman (New York: Dryden, 1953), 33-34.

17. Roger V. Burton and John W.M. Whiting, "The Absent Father and Cross-Sex Identity," *Merrill Palmer Quarterly* 7 (April 1961): 85-96.

18. Erik Erikson, *Childhood and Society* (New York: Norton, 1950), 249.

19. Mary Ellen Goodman, *op. cit.*, 146-47.

20. George D. Spindler, "The Education of Adolescents," in *Adolescents*, ed. E.D. Evans (Hinsdale, Ill.: Dryden, 1970), 155.

21. Mary Ellen Goodman, *op. cit.*, 149-50.

22. Margaret Mead, "The Implications of Culture Change for Personality Development," *American Journal of Orthopsychiatry* 17 (October 1947): 633-46.

23. It should be noted that stage theorists themselves do not assume any direct or necessary correlation between age-stages and culturally relative notions of maturity; the criticisms here are directed toward the use of the stage theory concepts by educators, legislators, jurists, and others, and not toward stage theory itself.

24. Ruth Benedict, "Continuities and Discontinuities in Cultural Conditioning," *Psychiatry* 1 (May 1938): 16-67; A.F.C. Wallace, *Culture and Personality*, 2d ed. (New York: Random House, 1970).

25. See Thomas J. Cottle, *Time's Children* (Boston: Little, Brown, 1970), Chapter 9; also Kenneth Keniston, "Growth and Violence: The Context of Moral Crisis," in *Moral Education*, ed. Gustafson *et al.*

26. Paul Goodman, *Growing Up Absurd* (New York: Vintage, 1956), Chapter 11.

27. Edgar A. Friedenberg, *Coming of Age in America* (New York: Random House, 1965).

28. See Wallace, *op. cit.*, 159 ff.; also David Riesman, *The Lonely Crowd: A Study of the Changing American Character* (New Haven, Conn.: Yale University Press, 1950).

29. Friedenberg, *op. cit.*, Chapter 1.

30. *Ibid.*, 13.

31. Charles Goodell, *Political Prisoners in America* (New York: Random House, 1973).

32. Friedenberg, *op. cit.*, 7.

33. *Ibid.*, 5; see also Kimball and McClellan, *op. cit.*, 54 ff.

34. See George Spindler, "Education in a Transforming American Culture," and "The Transmission of American Culture," in *Education and Culture*, ed. George Spindler (New York: Holt, Rinehart, and Winston, 1963).

35. Margaret Mead, "A Redefinition of Education," in *Inquiries into the Social Foundations of Education*, ed. A. Lightfoot (Chicago: Rand McNally, 1972), 70.

36. *Ibid.*, 72.

37. *Ibid.*, 73.

38. Wallace, *op. cit.*, 123 ff.

39. Mead, "Redefinition of Education," 71.

40. See Jerome Bruner, *The Process of Education* (New York: Vintage, 1963).

41. See Erving Goffman, *Asylums* (Garden City, N.Y.: Doubleday, Anchor, 1961); also Wolf Wolfensberger, "The Origin and Nature of Our Institutional Models," in Wolf Wolfensberger and Robert B. Kugel, *Changing Patterns in Residential Services for the Mentally Retarded* (Washington, D.C.: President's Commission on Mental Retardation, 1969).

42. See Jean I. Roberts, *The Scene of the Battle* (Garden City, N.Y.: Doubleday, Anchor, 1971); Elizabeth Eddy, *Walk the White Line* (Garden City, N.Y.: Doubleday, Anchor, 1967).

# 4. Student Rights and the Misuse of Psychological Knowledge and Language

*Paul C. Magnusson*

What are the proper functions of psychological knowledge in student rights controversies? The beginnings of a plausible answer to this question must take into account the prevailing and sometimes latent functions of psychological knowledge and its attendant language in educational contexts and the limitations of those functions when viewed from a perspective of student rights.

## The Question of Function

Within the last decade numerous conflicts have arisen between students in junior and senior high school, who are now considered "persons"[1] under the Constitution, and those school officials and teachers who still cling tenaciously to some of the autocratic in loco parentis practices of days past. Usually the conflicts involve issues of freedom of expression, personal rights (such as hair and dress preferences), procedural due process, marriage and pregnancy, the police in the schools, and corporal punishment.

Psychological knowledge has become an increasingly appealing aid to those school boards, administrators, and teachers seeking to refurbish the traditional in loco parentis claims in these areas of conflict, particularly as the knowledge lends weight to arguments differentiating an "adult" entitled to full legal rights from an "adolescent" or other nonadult whose rights should be selectively restricted. These differentiations among people in terms of attained levels of cognitive and moral development—when based on "scientific" evidence and stated in terms of possessed knowledge and wisdom—support renewed claims of dependency in which the school argues its right and duty to prolong its jurisdiction over certain student behaviors until a desirable adult level of maturity or competency is attained. A prolonged jurisdictional argument resting on such credible evidence also satisfies the public mandate that schools simultaneously protect the best interests of the developing students and those of society which desires productive members.

As they actually occur in schools, these dependency claims appear straightforward and sensible. When asked why a student cannot publish or distribute an underground newspaper on school property, for example, school officials are apt to answer that the student is not sufficiently aware of the complexities of the school environment, that he is not mature enough to understand the broad implications of his acts or to appreciate the sensitive political milieu in which the school operates, that he is not fully capable of perceiving the potentially damaging effects his newspaper may have on students who are less sophisticated and more impressionable than he.

Statements like these rarely represent the complete procensorship "custodial" positions argued by school officials, especially in court.[2] Since the famous Supreme Court case of *Tinker* v. *Des Moines Independent Community School District,* school authorities are forced to show that their attempts to establish or enforce a particular rule were based on evidence that enabled them "to forecast substantial disruption of or material interference with school activities."[3] In the day-to-day school situations where evidential requirements are less stringent, however, the questionable actions of these newly enfranchised "persons" meet with the former sort of arguments more commonly, and here the issues usually stop. For this reason, if for no other, it is important to look carefully at the language used in such arguments.

In the first place the language is deceptively "straightforward and sensible." Rationales such as the above for denying the student his rights to free expression under the First Amendment are couched in everyday, "common-sense" terms—awareness, maturity, capability,

perception, understanding—whose current meanings have been largely appropriated from modern psychology and have become sedi-
mented into the vernacular. The terms are, moreover, typically given
an unquestioned patina of "scientific" legitimacy and credibility
when used by educators because of the close association of psychology and education throughout the twentieth century. But regardless
of this historical and conceptual association of disciplines, the fact
remains that most schoolmen are psychological laymen. Thus, when
school officials use psychologically derived terms to assist in the
adjudication of student rights, most do so as lay people outside the
psychological community. They tend to view the terms as though
they represented "reality," as true descriptors of people, rather than
as the highly contestable theoretical postulates of a constantly evolving scientific discipline, which, of course, is the way psychologists
view them. To make or justify moral and legal decisions on such
speculative scientific constructs is, moreover, outside the realm of
what can logically serve as the source for generating or legitimating
decisions concerning rights.

What makes the hypothetical case of the student's curtailed freedom of expression even more problematic is the fact that his student
status is largely the cause of his predicament. Rights and privileges in
America are generally granted, whether de facto or de jure, on the
basis of age: if you are old enough, you can do it. At age sixteen
most adolescents can quit school or obtain a driver's license; at eighteen they can vote in local, state, and national elections. While it is
not the case that most existing laws that restrict conduct because of
age were founded on modern psychological evidence, it is commonly
the case that they and a host of quasi-legal school dicta and practices
are defended on that basis. The arguments in the hypothetical case
concerning censorship are typical of those presented in many controversies over rights, both in school and out. There is a crucial difference, however: rights and privileges are differentially granted to students and nonstudents.

Schools, courts, and advocates on either side of disputes over student rights must carefully reexamine their uses of psychological
thought and language and even more carefully determine what
psychology can and cannot do in these contexts. They should exhibit
great caution when looking to psychological knowledge, or to any
knowledge, in the behavioral sciences for the bases upon which to

determine or justify what rights should be granted to students. These disciplines cannot yield definitive conceptions of childhood, adolescence, cognitive and moral competence, maturity, and responsibility to serve as templates to stamp out student rights decisions. Such determinations are never simply the mirror image of psychological thought. On the other hand, psychology and all other disciplines that study man can and should illuminate rights disputes by increasing our understanding of the complex of behavioral and contextual factors that shape them.

All rights decisions are ultimately and irrevocably grounded in moral, social, and political positions. Here they are generated, and it is primarily from here that changes in student rights can be made and legitimated. Presently, however, these moral, social, and political substrata are too often obscured in schools and courts by the misuse of psychological ideas and language. In the remainder of this chapter an attempt will be made to show some of the ways in which this misuse occurs and then to suggest the beginnings of a new, more useful role for psychology in student rights controversies.

## A Theory of Moral Development

To demonstrate what psychology cannot do in its current role, we must first examine what a psychological theory, seemingly appropriate in a rights context, seems to be able to do—or at least promise to do. We have selected for that purpose Lawrence Kohlberg's theory of moral development, a stage development theory of moral reasoning arising from the cognitive and moral development tradition of Jean Piaget. These theoretical roots are highly respected and enjoy considerable currency, in both popular and scholarly literature. In addition, Kohlberg's theory draws heavily on the fields of ethical philosophy and social psychology and meets two important criteria for use in rights disputes. First, it addresses itself directly to conceptions of responsibility and maturity that are of interest to those charged with protecting the public weal. Second, for this use, the importance it grants to field or contextual factors makes it less subject than many psychological theories to the objection that its focus is too narrow.

In a strong sense Kohlberg's work can be viewed as archetypal. What enables his theory to stand as a model of moral development theories, for our use here, is the important fact that it shares with the theories of Piaget, Freud, Erickson, and others a conception of "internalized moral standards" that is of paramount interest to those charged with determining and adjudicating student rights. "Rules are said to be internalized if they are conformed to in the absence of situational incentives or sanction, i.e., if conformity is intrinsically motivated."[4] We want to know, fundamentally, when a child will conform to cultural rules freely and responsibly. And each of the theories, with Kohlberg's as representative of the group, attempts to provide that information. By the same token, many of the applications and the limitations of Kohlberg's theory to a rights context hold true for the other theories too.

This is particularly the case for Piaget's theory of moral development, from which many of Kohlberg's ideas derive, and to which many of his conclusions correspond. Piaget's theory states that a child moves from an initial "amoral" stage of development, to "heteronomous" morality, and finally to "autonomous" morality.[5] At the heteronomous stage, extending roughly from ages three to eight, he sees all rules as external absolutes, and he has an unquestioning respect for the authority of his parents and other adults. At the autonomous stage, reached at about age eight to ten, he perceives rules not as external authoritarian commands but as logical external principles of justice. In Piaget's terms, he has acquired a "sense of justice," a concern for reciprocity and equality among individuals, which is largely independent of adult precept.[6]

Kohlberg's research largely supports Piaget's findings,[7] particurlarly his assumption that there exists a "culturally universal age development of a sense of justice, involving progressive concern for the needs and feelings of others and elaborated conceptions of reciprocity and equality"[8] —a finding of considerable importance to those involved in granting rights to young people. In his own cross-cultural research Kohlberg elicited children's responses to a number of hypothetical moral dilemmas. Each response was reliably classified into one of six categories or stages of moral development devised by Kohlberg and his colleagues.[9] The six stages were then divided into three major levels of development as follows:

## I. Preconventional level

At this level the child is responsive to cultural rules and labels of good and bad, right or wrong, but interprets these labels in terms of either the physical or the hedonistic consequences of action (punishment, reward, exchange of favors), or in terms of the physical power of those who enunciate the rules and labels. The level is divided into the following two stages:

Stage 1: *The punishment and obedience orientation.* The physical consequences of action determine its goodness or badness regardless of the human meaning or value of these consequences. Avoidance of punishment and unquestioning deference to power are valued in their own right, not in terms of respect for an underlying moral order supported by punishment and authority (the latter being stage 4).

Stage 2: *The instrumental relativist orientation.* Right action consists of that which instrumentally satisfies one's own needs and occasionally the needs of others. Human relations are viewed in terms like those of the market place. Elements of fairness, of reciprocity, and of equal sharing are present, but they are always interpreted in a physical pragmatic way. Reciprocity is a matter of "you scratch my back and I'll scratch yours," not of loyalty, gratitude, or justice.

## II. Conventional level

At this level, maintaining the expectations of the individual's family, group, or nation is perceived as valuable in its own right, regardless of immediate and obvious consequences. The attitude is not only one of conformity to personal expectations and social order, but of loyalty to it, of actively *maintaining,* supporting, and justifying the order, and of identifying with the persons or group involved in it. At this level, there are the following two stages:

Stage 3: *The interpersonal concordance or "good boy-nice girl"* orientation. Good behavior is that which pleases or helps others and is approved by them. There is much conformity to stereotypical images of what is majority or "natural" behavior. Behavior is frequently judged by intention--"he means well" becomes important for the first time. One earns approval by being "nice."

Stage 4: *The "law and order" orientation.* There is orientation toward authority, fixed rules, and the maintenance of the social order. Right behavior consists of doing one's duty, showing respect for authority, and maintaining the given social order for its own sake.

III. Postconventional, autonomous, or principled level

At this level, there is a clear effort to define moral values and principles which have validity and application apart from the authority of the groups or persons holding these principles, and apart from the individual's own identification with these groups. This level again has two stages:

Stage 5: *The social-contract legalistic orientation,* generally with utilitarian overtones. Right action tends to be defined in terms of general individual rights, and standards which have been critically examined and agreed upon by the whole society. There is a clear awareness of the relativism of personal values and opinions and a corresponding emphasis upon procedural rules for reaching consensus. Aside from what is constitutionally and democratically agreed upon, the right is a matter of personal "values" and "opinion." The result is an emphasis upon the "legal point of view," but with an emphasis upon the possibility of changing law in terms of rational considerations of social utility (rather than freezing it in terms of stage 4 "law and order"). Outside the legal realm, free agreement and contract is the binding element of obligation. This is the "official" morality of the American government and constitution.

Stage 6: *The universal ethical principle orientation.* Right is defined by the decision of conscience in accord with self-chosen *ethical principles* appealing to logical comprehensiveness, universality, and consistency. These principles are abstract and ethical (the Golden Rule, the categorical imperative); they are not concrete moral rules like the Ten Commandments. At heart, these are universal principles of *justice,* of the *reciprocity* and *equality* of human *rights* and of respect for the dignity of human beings as *individual persons.*[10]

Kohlberg concludes from his studies that this progression of stages implies "something more than age trends." First, he suggests that the data suggest an invariate developmental sequence: "Each child must go step by step through each of the kinds of moral judgment outlined."[11] This was consistently supported by a twelve-year longitudinal study of seventy-five American boys and the series of cross-cultural studies. The movement is usually irreversibly forward in direction, although speeds of movement vary and any given child can become "fixated" or stop in the progression at any level. Second, "stages define 'structured wholes,' total ways of thinking, not attitudes toward particular situations."[12] A given individual responding at Stage 3 on a situation involving the morality of the war in Southeast Asia is likely to be Stage 3 on a situation concerning theft, lying, or civil disobedience, even though it is also the case that all children are likely to be "partly in their major stage (about 50% of their ideas), partly in the stage into which they are moving and partly in the stage they have left behind."[13] Third, "a stage concept implies universality of sequence under varying cultural conditions. It implies that moral development is not merely a matter of learning the verbal values or rules of the child's culture, but reflects something more universal in development, something which would occur in any culture."[14] This conclusion is supported by the striking similarity of the pattern of development across religious, social, and economic lines and in urban, suburban, and rural settings in the United States, Mexico, Taiwan, Yucatan, and Turkey. The rate of development differs from culture to culture, but the ascendancy pattern is the same.

This brief discussion does a disservice to Kohlberg's theory and research. An extended description of the theory itself is unnecessary for our purposes, however, since only those implications and research findings pertinent to disputes concerning student rights need to be discussed further. It is sufficient, in summary, to reiterate that the extensive research conducted by Kohlberg and his colleagues to date supports the conclusions that "these stages or 'fundamental principles' on which people differ (a) are culturally universal, (b) occur in an invariate order of development, and (c) are interpretations of categories which are universal."[15]

## Moral Development and Student Rights

The following two sections of the chapter will examine the potential and actual denial of rights to students legitimated by psychological thought. It is not to challenge Kohlberg's theory or its intellectual origins nor to discredit in any way the multifaceted discipline of psychology itself. The ensuing discussion of various applications of psychological thought and language to educational contexts is intended only to demonstrate their serious implications for the rights of students. As has been said, many criticisms of the applicability of Kohlberg's theory apply as well to other theories of moral development.

Kohlberg's theory is potentially attractive to advocates on either side of rights disputes for at least two reasons. First, its use of "disclosure" is valuable and sound. Second, out of Kohlberg's work has come an elaborate coding procedure for validly assessing a person's level of moral development.[16] This time-consuming procedure holds within it the potential for constructing a simpler procedure of perhaps twenty-five to fifty items that will accomplish the same task in a fraction of the time.[17] This test could be administered to young people whenever we wished to assess their moral development, much as we presently do with intelligence and academic achievement tests when we wish to assess intellectual development.

There are two potential uses for our test of moral development, both of which are supported by precedent. It is common knowledge, for example, that the results of intelligence, achievement, and psychological deviance tests are used regularly to influence administrative decisions about the academic program of individual students. That is their stipulated function: to aid administrators, counselors, and teachers in "tracking" students, recommending specific courses, course loads, "special" programs, and so on. One of their tacit functions in these and other "academic" decisions is decidedly moral and political, but is less commonly identified as such. To varying degrees of subtlety, the "bright" student, the "high achiever," and the "good" boy or girl enjoy many more rights and privileges in schools than most of their classmates—in everything from course options and achievement opportunities to "pass privileges" and locker searches. This same evidence, particularly intelligence and deviance test data, has long been used in courtrooms to give information about specific individuals and group norms. The point here is simply that the influence of these psychological test results on rights and privileges in schools (whether openly admitted or not) and in courts is not without pervasive precedent.

Our test of moral development, then, could have the same individualistic and normative usefulness. It could assess the level of moral development of student plaintiffs in school or court cases, and this illuminating personal information could aid each individual rights decision. Or, from a normative point of view, the age-stage correlations might be useful in supporting overarching decisions on a constitutional level; they would, for example, affect all preadults. These decisions would affect adult privileges primarily, whenever the issue in question implied a need for some specifiable level of maturity or responsibility.

What are some of these possible applications? If, as Kohlberg suggests, the definition of Stage 5 is "the 'official' morality of the American government and constitution," we might safely assume that it also reflects the unofficial or popular ideal for the thought and action of American citizens. Actually, constitutional and statutory law together reveal a "national moral rationality" which is a combination of Stages 4 and 5. The Constitution focuses on the preservation of general individual rights and specific rational procedures for making and changing law in order to maximize the welfare of individuals, to the extent that such decisions are agreed upon by the whole society. This corresponds to a Stage 5 orientation. Statutory law, on the other hand, focuses on maintaining law and order, on defending the individual and the social order against its common enemies, that is, those who do not respect law and order—criminals, dissidents, and enemies abroad. This corresponds to a Stage 4 orientation. The relative stage emphasis varies with the fluctuations in national mood: on some days George Wallace is the standard-bearer; on others it is Ralph Nader or a particularly vocal civil libertarian.

If the above assumptions, or some close approximation of them, are at least tacitly correct, we might go on to suggest that, given convincing evidence from our test, the granting of certain legal rights and privileges should depend upon the attainment of at least a Stage 4 level of moral development. Again, this simply parallels the use of aptitude test results and demonstrated academic achievement in the everyday life of elementary, secondary, and college students. These decisions would be justified by the argument that those clearly below the Stage 4 level usually do not seek to maximize the welfare of all citizens; nor are they particularly concerned with the defense and protection of the social order. We would, in effect, have a pragmatic test of competence in public realms of interpersonal and social responsibility.

If we were to extend this method logically, we might argue that it should be consistently applied throughout society: a thirteen-year-old at Stage 5 would be granted voting privileges, and a thirty-five-year-old at Stage 2 would be denied them. We might also envision the scenario of a fourteen-year-old suspended for wearing a black arm band in symbolic protest against the continued bombing of Cambodia, despite the fact that no noticeable disruption resulted from the act. The adolescent subsequently sues the principal for

denying him freedom of expression and the right to an open hearing
before the suspension. It is revealed in court that the student reasons
at Stage 6, a fact persuasive enough in the face of all opposing
evidence to sway the judge to proclaim him an adult in the eyes of
the court and society and to award him his justly deserved adult
rights to free expression.

These hypothetical applications of Kohlberg's moral development
research are admittedly discomforting. The notion of granting or
denying rights and privileges solely on the basis of competence—
moral, cognitive, or even emotional—is objectionable when taken out
of the sheltered school environment and extended to adult society.
But is it any less objectionable to deny certain rights to students
solely on the same basis? In extreme circumstances it is. If we have
convincing psychological evidence, but only that evidence, to show
that the student walking down the hall with a knife in his pocket is
clearly psychotic, we would be well advised to act solely on that
evidence and deny him his right to have the knife. But extreme cases
alone can never refute an argument; nor can they be used to justify
the common case. The de facto bias against students remains a logically untenable position. With Kohlberg's stages of moral competence, for example, even though the progression of development
appears invariate and no stage can be skipped, it simply cannot be
posited without incurring solid opposition that Stages 4 or 5 are
morally "better" than Stages 1, 2, or 3 (regardless of whether or not
they might correspond to an American ideal), and that people on
lower stages should have fewer rights. They are better in the sense
that those stages are applicable to a wider range of moral decision-
making situations, but to claim that Stage 4 reasoning is "more
moral" than Stage 3 is philosophically debatable. And philosophical
claims of "goodness" and "rightness" are not derivable from empirical psychological data, a point of view developed more extensively
later in this chapter and extended to other notions of competence
from other schools of psychology.

Additional objections to any casual application of Kohlberg's
theory to the area of decisions concerning rights have been raised by
Kohlberg himself (but for different reasons than the above). In his
article "From Is to Ought" he discusses several requisite conditions
for the development of moral judgment.[18] First among these antecedents of moral development is a specifiable degree of cognitive

maturity or intellectual judgment. Kohlberg hypothesizes that each new stage of moral development requires new and more sophisticated logical operations than the one before it, and his research supports the conclusion that a person must be cognitively mature to reason morally (although "you can be smart and never reason morally").[19] He adds that intelligence tests also correlate with moral maturity, but not as well as cognitive stage tests.[20] Using a moral development test to parcel out rights and privileges would, therefore, be prejudicial against some people on the basis of intelligence.

Second, in his discussion of affective-volitional antecedents, he suggests that, since a person is able to reason morally at a level below that at which he operates cognitively but not higher, it may be to his advantage in some cases to choose to reason at Stage 2 and not Stage 6: "Stage 6 may be the cognitively most advanced morality, but perhaps those *capable* of reasoning that way do not wish to be martyrs like Socrates, Lincoln, or King, and *prefer* to reason at a lower level."[21] Intimidation, for example, may indirectly affect the rights granted to some, and our hypothetical test might become an unjust standard because the level of moral judgment in some individuals may not be symmetrical with their cognitive potential because of their ability to will it for personal safety.

The third antecedent of moral development of concern here is the degree of social role taking the person has been exposed to, a central factor in Kohlberg's and Piaget's theories. Those children and adolescents deprived of warm face-to-face encounters with groups and institutions have retarded moral development. Among other supporting evidence, Kohlberg cites the findings of Thrower, who discovered that a large majority of sixteen-year-olds in traditional orphanages still reasoned at Stages 1 and 2,[22] levels considerably lower than those occasioned by more typical populations at that age.[23] The implications for injustice here are clear: our test would likely discriminate against those individuals who, by reason of geography, health, home and school environments, and other factors have been deprived of close personal relationships.

Fourth, it appears that social environments or institutions also facilitate moral development if they operate according to the structure of justice based on reciprocity and equality. "Impressionistic observation suggests that many reform schools have an official level of justice which is a stage 1 obedience and punishment orientation, while the inmate peer culture has a stage 2 instrumental exchange orientation. An inmate high in participation in either of these structures is not likely to advance in moral judgment, even though in another sense he may be provided with 'role-taking opportunities.' "[24] Perhaps Kohlberg's present investigation of the perceived level of justice in high schools will yield similar conclusions. In any case, the relevant implications from existing research on social environment[25] are again clear: sole reliance on our moral competence test would handicap those persons considerably affected by home or institutional environments that are severely restrictive, punitive, or self-serving.

Fifth, Kohlberg suggests that another necessary antecedent to development is the experience of cognitive conflicts, verbal clashes in which the child actively participates and through which he senses discrepancies between his own cognitive schemata of moral reasoning and those above his level of reasoning. Without this sociomoral conflict less and slower development will occur,[26] a condition likely to be disadvantageous to the socially withdrawn or culturally and educationally isolated.

Perhaps these hypothetical applications of Kohlberg's moral development theory and the arguments raised against them are not applicable to those everyday instances in which psychological testing, learning theory, or cognitive development theory has actually determined student rights. Granting that possibility raises additional objections to this use of psychology, but at a higher level.

## The Limits of Psychological Knowledge

In order to establish a framework for a broader analysis of the relationship between psychology and student rights, it would be useful first to establish some conceptual framework for the field of psychology itself. As Huebner asserts, "psychology, in-and-of-itself, is an independent discipline, with its own *raison d'etre*. It is its own 'Society of Explorers' . . . who search for truth, warranted assertions or theories to serve as policy guides for further experimentation. Psychological knowledge, as a product of a society of explorers, is self-correcting and has built-in forms of criticism which govern the use of the knowledge in man's future."[27]

A problem arises, however, when psychological knowledge is

removed from the self-correcting community of explorers where it originated and is used by other explorers in other enterprises. The users, whether those who devise curricula or those who advocate student rights, risk the possibility of two deleterious outcomes.[28] First, by taking it out of its self-correcting context, it may reify and "sediment into the habits" of the borrowing group, because of the tendency of the borrowers to view the knowledge as a body of relatively unchanging, agreed upon "truths." There is a second difficulty. Once the reified "tool" has passed its time of value or usefulness, it becomes difficult to dispose of, by virtue of its reification. According to Huebner, psychological knowledge is validated by its value as truth within the community of psychologists, its society of explorers. But for those who would use it outside the field of psychology, in this case to determine or illuminate controversies over rights, it must be valued for its usefulness. To that end, it "must compete in the market place of other useful knowledge tools."[29]

Psychological knowledge is useful for its possibilities of "disclosure," that is, to the extent that it can yield penetrating glimpses or insights that disclose something new in the phenomena under examination. As defined by Ramsey, "disclosure models" are valuable in the natural sciences for "generating deductions which are then open to experimental verification and falsification."[30] But in the area of student rights, which in no way resembles the formal disciplines of physics or chemistry, the disclosure model is perhaps better valued for its "empirical fit," its stability "as an overall characterization of a complex, multi-varied pattern of behavior which is impossible in a particular case to specify deductively beforehand."[31] The potential use of psychological theory for disclosure in controversies over rights, then, is to furnish revealing glimpses into the complexities of person, issue, and context that define them.

It follows from Ramsey's ideas that a sharpened perspective is needed for sifting through the numerous competing theories propounded by each independent discipline. According to Kuhn, no single theory or paradigm can be viewed correctly as the only valid conception of a given body of phenomena.[32] Each has a built-in perspective toward the phenomena of interest, and the perspective of each is limited by the scientific rules of procedure unique to the discipline. In what Kuhn calls "normal science" the working scientist accepts the dominant paradigm of his field and attempts to articulate those phenomena that the paradigm already supplies. No part of the normal scientists' aim is to call forth the perception of novelties of fact, new phenomena, anomalies, or any other of nature's violations of paradigm-induced expectations. In fact, when successful, he finds none. Traditionally, however, anomalies and new phenomena accumulate to a point where a new paradigm must be provided to account for them. This leads to a scientific revolution in which the new paradigm replaces the old—as with the Newtonian and Einsteinian revolutions—and a new perspective dominates the field, holding out new possibilities for unexpected discoveries. In short, theories are neither true nor false, although their implications or derivations may be either; and no theory accounts for all relevant aspects of a given phenomenon.

It is appropriate to view new and old paradigms within the behavioral sciences and psychology in the same light. Each is a potentially useful disclosure model, yet each carries the perceptual and methodological limitations inherent in all explanatory paradigms.

Here is the crux of the matter. Student rights disputes are unique situations existing wholly outside the conceptual and methodological perimeters of psychology's society of explorers. Each dispute is composed of a unique issue, context, and group of individuals. Psychological knowledge is, likewise, unique, arising from a unique scientific tradition in which no single theory is true or false, none is without perceptual and methodological limitations, and none accounts for all the relevant factors of a given body of phenomena. It is not surprising, therefore, given even the greatest of cautions, that, in some situations where psychological theories and research findings have been applied to problems outside psychology itself, they have not produced the anticipated results. Or, what is worse, a deteriorated condition has resulted, or detrimental side effects and misuses have appeared.

Well-documented accounts of these very results in the field of education are easily cited, some with direct effect on the rights of students to equal educational opportunity. Most of these cases are well known in educational and legal circles, and since several have been considered extensively elsewhere, only five will be discussed here. In 1954, in the case of *Brown* v. *Board of Education of Topeka*, the United States Supreme Court rejected the doctrine of "separate but equal" educational facilities on the basis of the psychological findings cited in the now famous "footnote 11" of the decision. The nation's entire educational system was altered by research that has since been discredited and shown to be far too limited in perspective to account for the many factors affecting the lower academic achievement of blacks and other minorities.[33] The next two cases, while quite different from each other in substance, produced some similar popular responses. Among the findings of the Coleman Report of 1966, was the claim that the quality of schooling was not as important as social and economic factors in explaining variance in academic achievement.[34] Jensen's 1969 normative study of intelligence elicited the claim that genetic factors, not schooling, accounted for lower achievement among blacks.[35] Despite the methodological challenges to Coleman's work and the moral charges leveled against Jensen, both of these reports were greeted in some quarters with ready-made proposals to reduce financial support to physically deteriorating schools, usually those with primarily black enrollments, and to eliminate local bases for programs like Head Start. Fourth, in 1968 Rosenthal and Jacobson identified the "Pygmalion effect" in the classroom. This refers to the teacher's foreknowledge of fictitious intelligence scores and phony expectations of academic achievement that were claimed to have a favorable effect on the teacher's treatment of students, actual intelligence scores, and academic performance. The initial findings were criticized strongly for methodological reasons,[36] and yet the hypothesis still stands, showing some support from subsequent research findings[37] and much anecdotal support among teachers. There is one final example: during the last several years, the behaviorism of B.F. Skinner has entered the schools in the form of "behavioral objectives" for student learning and "performance contracting" for students and teachers, and yet there exists no convincing evidence to date that these operant reinforcement techniques are appropriate and valid in school learning situations.[38]

In each of these cases the rights of students to equal educational opportunity have in some way been threatened or denied. In all but the Coleman case the predicament concerning rights has come directly from some form of abuse of psychological findings or methodology. The ultimate effects of these situations are not, unfortunately, on "schools" or "achievement" but on actual children.

On the surface the language we use in schools to describe

"students" appears to be scientifically neutral, that is, based in fact, and appropriately descriptive of actual educational conditions. Upon closer examination, however, we often find this perception false. Instead it appears that the supposedly neutral (scientific) and beneficial act of "educational" labeling by educators and its consequences are distinctly moral and political, reflecting a covert institutional and social bias toward the labeled individuals.[39] The psychiatrist Szasz levels a similar charge at "deviance" labeling by psychotherapists.[40] His analysis is helpful in several ways for understanding the situation in education. Psychotherapy, he claims, is essentially a moral and political enterprise that "de-ethicizes and depoliticizes" human relations and social conduct largely by characterizing verbal and behavioral expressions of nonnormative sociopolitical views in the psychomedical language of deviance.

The dialectical interplay of the opposing tendencies or themes of freedom and slavery, liberation and oppression, competence and incompetence, responsibility and license, order and chaos, so essential to the growth, life, and death of the individual, is transformed in psychiatry and allied fields, into the opposing tendencies or themes of "maturity" and "immaturity," "independence" and "dependence," "mental health" and "mental illness," and "sanity" and "insanity."[41]

What we characterize as "mental diseases," then, are in reality mainly conflicts among values, communications of generally unacceptable ideas, or individual struggles to develop a personally satisfying life style.[42] And, thus, the supposedly neutral acts of diagnosis and treatment are actually partisan acts, allying the therapist with the forces of normative self-interest.

As in education, this is not to say that certain identifiable nonnormative behaviors should not be controlled or treated in some way. It does say, however, that by characterizing all behavioral issues in medical and psychological jargon, the therapist inadvertently supports the interests of those with whom the patient may be in conflict and thereby acts as a partisan agent. In this capacity, his labels of "abnormality" serve to oppress the troubled—students, blacks, women, homosexuals, the poor, the elderly—and effectively subvert their troubled claims.[43] This is the point that was made at the outset about the language typically used by school officials to suppress the publication or distribution of objectionable printed matter on school property. Whatever the objectionable quality of the publication happens to be, the issue is most commonly translated into a question of "maturity" and "responsibility"; thus the possibility of a more difficult sociopolitical confrontation is avoided.

Such educational deviance labels as "poorly motivated student," "reluctant reader," and "linguistically deprived" tend to "objectify" a person and reduce his complexity into technical terms of control.[44] Thus, upon the student's "diagnosis" as any one of these special forms of "learner," he can then be educationally "treated." The financial, material, and personal resources of the school can be mobilized and focused on that otherwise elusive aspect of him which is termed his "learning problem." These labels, as terms of control, imply the power that educators have over students to direct and shape their lives—clearly a moral and political relationship as well as an educational one. No one would deny that these categories are educationally useful to educators. Because of the massive numbers and limitless diversity of children they encounter, educators must utilize such labels in order to identify and deal with those students who actually are "discipline problems" or "underachievers." But this important psychological-educational function masks two more critical functions: the suppression of unpopular sociopolitical claims; and the degradation and humiliation of each individual child who is so labeled.[45]

It must be noted that labels have both essentializing and durable qualities. A child who is labeled a "discipline problem" or "linguistically deprived" in one context is likely to carry the label in other contexts. That is, the label is commonly generalized, and the essence of the child when he is in school is captured and encompassed by that single term. This is clearly dehumanizing, regardless of how subtle it may be. Further, the term is usually tinged with moral significance. The child labeled as "deviant" is likely to be poor and of an ethnic minority group; he is also likely to be perceived by those who labeled him as not simply different but inferior, as somehow morally culpable for the difference that others perceived in him.[46] And, whether a label is favorable ("bright student") or not, it proves to be exceptionally durable. A child identified in the early grades as nonnormative in some way carries the label not only from class to class but from year to year, and rarely is he reclassified.[47]

What we see here is a serious threat to the rights of students—in some instances an outright denial of rights—arising from various actual abuses of psychological test results, learning theory, and normative psychological data. Durable and essentializing deviance labels have arisen repeatedly from incomplete individual histories of learning, from a child's inability or refusal to adapt to the conventions of learning theory as practiced in his school and from intelligence and achievement testing. The misuse of psychological data has had serious moral and ethical repercussions for "slow learners" or "poor readers" who are emotionally damaged by overt and covert sanctions that extend beyond the beneficial intentions of the labels. Where the misuse has camouflaged social and political challenges to the accepted order in schools, the acceptability of psychological data for educationally valid "diagnosis" and "treatment" has been abused since the generalization to this type of political issue is logically and ethically an unwarranted extension of scientific data.

This bodes ill for psychology and education. When the harmful effects of deviance labels *are* perceived by educators, the data themselves are typically faulted instead of the use made of them, and this is where the problem usually lies. In short, the schools hunt for better data rather than question the applicability and extensions of the data they have; consequently, their misuse of the data reflects negatively on the data themselves and the discipline from which they originated.

In the middle of the dispute stands a child who may have suffered an irretrievable loss of prestige and self-esteem at the hands of educators (and his own peers who innocently responded to him as though his designated difference made a difference). Were we to suggest to the average middle-class adult in our society that some of his rights be denied solely on the basis of his ability to read or speak, or his expressed dissatisfaction with governmental policy, he would be outraged, and rightly so. And yet his own child may be suffering a similar fate in school; to the extent he is aware of it, it usually goes unquestioned, let alone being challenged in court.

Up to this point we have attempted to show that it is highly problematic to make determinations concerning rights contingent upon normatively based expectations of mature or responsible behavior for two reasons: the existence of various predictions; and the difficulty of application. In response to the possibility of a more limited role for psychology, we shall now attempt to show that it is equally problematic to maintain this normatively based contingency standard for various philosophical, moral, political, and social reasons, some of which have been alluded to already.

## Psychology and Disclosure

Decisions about what rights should exist and who should possess them are largely moral, social, and political questions, with answers not derivable from empiricism, nor so derived historically. Witness the gradual extension of the franchise to vote, at first granted only to free males who owned a specified amount of property, then to all adult males, then to women, and now down from age twenty-one to eighteen. It must be admitted that for a time the exclusion of women from the franchise was based on a quasi-psychological claim of mental inferiority to men, but only recently have other kinds of denials of rights been derived from or legitimated by modern psychological evidence.

Logically, however, this cannot be done. Psychological findings do not and cannot generate human rights; nor are rights derivable from such findings. To do so is to commit what Moore in the field of ethics called "the naturalistic fallacy," essentially deriving "ought" from "is," in this case deriving conceptions (in the form of prescriptions) of what people "ought" to be and what rights they "ought" to have from descriptions of what they are, cognitively, morally, and behaviorally. For example, Kohlberg's research shows that some people develop "universal principles of *justice,* of the *reciprocity* and *equality* of human *rights*, and of respect for the dignity of human beings as *individual persons*"[48]—his Stage 6 of moral reasoning. This empirical fact alone does not generate or justify the claims that because Stage 6 is the highest (last attained), it is morally "better" than each of the five before it, or that more or all people "ought" to reason at this level, or that the attainment of this level "ought" to be a condition for receiving certain rights and privileges. It simply says that some people reason this way. To justify the claim that higher stages are in any way better than lower stages, Kohlberg appeals to criteria independent of his empirical data. He argues that higher stages of reasoning can solve more moral problems and that the reasoning at each successive stage is applicable to a wider range of situations requiring moral decisions. It is more satisfactory, requires less adjustment, and meets fewer situations it cannot resolve.[49]

The same conditions hold true of cognitive development stages, intelligence test scores, or even reading levels. A "smarter" child is not a "better" child morally, and there is nothing in the data themselves to suggest that those at lower intelligence levels or with lower reading scores are in any way lesser human beings or less deserving of rights or privileges. No respectable social or behavioral scientist would make such claims about his data, and, again, the justification for that sort of claim requires criteria independent of the empirically derived data themselves.[50]

We return to two central questions. How must we evaluate the usefulness of psychological theories for disclosure in controversies over rights? To what extent do they furnish insights into the complexities of person, issue, and context that define them? Attention to psychological justifications for granting or denying rights has served to conceal the essentially moral and political nature of these disputes. The pervasiveness of psychological thinking in schools, legislative chambers, and courtrooms would make it seem that rights must be earned by demonstrating the absence of deviance or the attainment of some nebulous level of moral or cognitive competence. This is a curious reversal since the rights of life, liberty, and the pursuit of happiness were viewed historically, as inalienable, granted to people by virtue of their being human. Such rights as due process, freedom of speech, and freedom from illegal search and seizure, while not inalienable, were guaranteed to people by virture of their being citizens. Today the young, students, and those otherwise disenfranchised find themselves in a position of having to justify receiving many of these rights. And those who misuse psychological thought and language in schools, directly and indirectly, consciously and unconsciously, intentionally and unintentionally, are in the political center acting as collaborators in this subterfuge.

Efforts to control behavior in this context, then, are clearly misdirected, and efforts to predict behavior seem too narrowly focused and highly problematic. At best, the scientific models of behaviorism and learning theory splendidly illuminate that portion of ourselves which is open to observation in controlled environments. But their topic, and that of all of psychology, is a person who logically will never be transparent to any or all models, whose knowing and meanings defy psychological explanation.[51] We are all aware of the logical discrepancy between a theory or model and the insight which gave birth to the model and by which we know ourselves to be distinctly ourselves. The model, in short, does not nor cannot encapsulate us. In Ramsey's words, it "deals in hints rather than identities."[52] It attempts to disclose our common-sense views of ourselves and to open up broader avenues of self-exploration that may enable us to see our complexity rather than define ourselves out of existence.[53]

A model of the individual man as the subject of considerations regarding rights need not stand or fall with the possibility of experimental verification. Ramsey's "empirical fit" may be our best bet: stability over the widest range of phenomena and the consistent ability to incorporate diverse and newly perceived phenomena. While it may well be that humans are too intricate and complex to be treated scientifically at all, it is certainly true that the power of each psychological theory or model to illuminate needs to be constantly "related to and supplemented by other models more characteristic of the social activity which is distinctly human,"[54] models of humans in relation to other humans, institutions, and cultures.

Again, the enemy is not psychology itself but its misuse, its bastardization in educational contexts. Just as psychological testing, for example, can be abused by wrongly relegating a child to an unwarranted remedial track, so can it be used to prevent this from happening. But when psychological research, procedures, or terminology are used merely to confirm present institutional obligations or to maintain existing bureaucratic frameworks in schools, that use is political, not scientifically neutral.[55] It is unlikely that, in this context, there can be an honest disposition of an issue concerning rights.

The models and theories needed for the illumination of disputes over rights should, ideally, come from all of man's disciplines and creative enterprises—psychology, sociology, anthropology, philosophy, political science, economics, poetry, religion, art, drama, and so on. Disputes over student rights require models that do greater justice to our uniqueness as persons and the complexity of our environments and associations: "We are organisms, and we are interacting social units; we are both, because we are peculiar enough to be ourselves and to possess a first-person subjectivity understood in, but never exhausted by, the diversity however diverse of that third-person language in which all models, scientific or social, trade."[56] By seeking help from various disciplines, we raise the issue of rights above the orientation of certainty—prediction and control—and out of the realm of cognitive, moral, or behavioral competence.

## Notes

1. *Tinker* v. *Des Moines Independent Community School District,* 393 U.S. 503 (1969) at 511.

2. Christopher Smith, "The Constitutional Parameters of Student Protest," *Journal of Law and Education* 1 (January 1972): 58-61.

3. *Tinker* v. *Des Moines Independent Community School District,* 514.

4. Lawrence Kohlberg, "Moral Development and Identification," in *Child Psychology,* Sixty-second Yearbook of the National Society for the Study of Education, Part I, ed. Harold Stevenson (Chicago: University of Chicago Press, 1963), 277.

5. Jean Piaget, *The Moral Development of the Child* (Glencoe, Ill.: Free Press, 1948), 5-410.

6. *Ibid.,* 195.

7. Lawrence Kohlberg, "Moral Development," in *International Encyclopedia of the Social Sciences* (New York: Macmillan Company and Free Press, 1968), X, 488-89.

8. *Ibid.,* 488.

9. Lawrence Kohlberg, "From Is to Ought: How to Commit the Naturalistic Fallacy and Get Away with It in the Study of Moral Development," in *Cognitive Development and Epistemology,* ed. T. Mischel (New York: Academic Press, 1971), 167. The categories were derived from Piaget's structural analysis of cognitive development; Piaget derived the categories from Kant's analysis of pure reason.

10. *Ibid.,* 164-65.

11. *Ibid.,* 167.

12. *Ibid.,* 169.

13. *Ibid.,* 171.

14. *Ibid.*

15. *Ibid.,* 177.

16. Lawrence Kohlberg, "Moral Reasoning Scoring Manual," mimeograph (Cambridge, Mass.: Human Development Laboratory, 1972).

17. Such a test is currently being devised by James Rest, Department of Psychological Foundations of Education, Burton Hall, University of Minnesota, Minneapolis.

18. Kohlberg, "From Is to Ought," 180-95.

19. *Ibid.,* 18.

20. *Ibid.*

21. *Ibid.*

22. *Ibid.,* 191.

23. *Ibid.,* 172.

24. *Ibid.,* 192.

25. See Erving Goffman, *Asylums* (Garden City, N.Y.: Anchor Books, 1961). Goffman argues that institutionalization is strongly contraindicated for social, psychological, and cognitive development.

26. Kohlberg, "From Is to Ought," 193-95.

27. Dwayne Huebner, "Implications of Psychological Thought for the Curriculum," in *Influences in Curriculum Change*, ed. Glenys G. Unruh and Robert R. Leeper (Washington, D.C.: Association for Supervision and Curriculum Development, 1968), 29.

28. Michael Polanyi, *The Tacit Dimension* (Garden City, N.Y.: Doubleday, 1966), xi-108.

29. Huebner, *op. cit.*, 30.

30. Ian T. Ramsey, *Models and Mystery* (London: Oxford University Press, 1964), 14.

31. *Ibid.*, 38.

32. Thomas Kuhn, *The Structure of Scientific Revolutions*, 2d ed. (Chicago: University of Chicago Press, 1970), v-210.

33. See Irwin Katz, "Review of Evidence Relating to Effects of Desegration on the Intellectual Performance of Negroes," *American Psychologist* 19 (June 1964): 381-99; and Jean C. Olson, "Research Evidence on the Effects of School Segregation on School Achievement of Negro Students: 1954 and Now," M.A. thesis, University of Wisconsin, 1968.

34. See *On Equality of Educational Opportunity*, ed. Frederick Mosteller and Daniel P. Moynihan (New York: Vintage Books, 1972), for a full discussion of conceptual and methodological criticism; and Gerald Grant, "A Review of *On Equality of Educational Opportunity*," *Harvard Educational Review* 42 (February 1972): 109-25, for an analysis of significant issues in the Coleman Report and all post-Coleman studies through 1972.

35. See the debates between William Schockley and Arthur Jensen and N.L. Gage in *Phi Delta Kappan* 53 (January, March 1972): 297-312, 415-27.

36. See Russell M. Grieger, "Pygmalion Revisited: A Loud Call for Caution," *Interchange* 2 (Spring 1971): 78-91.

37. See D.H. Meichenbaum, K.A. Bowers, and R.R. Ross, "A Behavioral Analysis of Teacher Expectancy Effect," *Journal of Personality and Social Psychology* 13 (December 1969): 306-16; and J.M. Parlady, "What Teachers Believe—What Children Achieve," *The Elementary School Journal* 69 (April 1969): 370-74.

38. See chapters by Michael Apple and Albert H. Yee in *Perspectives on Management Systems Approaches in Education*, ed. Albert H. Yee (Englewood Cliffs, N.J.: Education Technology Publications, 1973); and Michael Apple, "Behaviorism and Conservatism," in *Perspectives for Reform in Teacher Education*, ed. Bruce R. Joyce and Marsha Weil (Englewood Cliffs, N.J.: Prentice-Hall, 1972).

39. See Michael W. Apple, "Common-Sense Categories and Curriculum Thought," paper presented at the conference "Toward the Reconstruction of the Curriculum Field," Philadelphia, May 10-11, 1973; and Robert A. Scott, "A Proposed Framework for Analyzing Deviance as a Property of Social Order," in

*Theoretical Perspectives on Deviance,* ed. Robert A. Scott and Jack Douglas (Garden City, N.Y.: Doubleday, 1966).

40. Thomas Szasz, *Ideology and Insanity* (Garden City, N.Y.: Doubleday, Anchor, 1970).

41. *Ibid.,* 2.

42. *Ibid.,* 6-21

43. Seymour L. Halleck, *The Politics of Therapy* (New York: Science House, 1971).

44. Apple, "Common-Sense Categories"; Dwayne Huebner, "Curriculum Language and Classroom Meanings," in *Language and Meaning,* ed. James B. Macdonald and Robert R. Leeper (Washington, D.C.: Association for Supervision and Curriculum Development, 1966).

45. Szasz, *op. cit.,* 58; Halleck, *op. cit.,* 99-117.

46. Apple, "Common-Sense Categories."

47. Ray C. Rist, "Student Social Crisis and Teacher Expectation: The Self-Fulfilling Prophecy in Ghetto Education," *Harvard Educational Review* 40 (August 1970): 411-51.

48. Kohlberg, "From Is to Ought," 165.

49. *Ibid.,* 222.

50. The analysis of claims of justice as the proper basis for determinations of rights in schools is enormously complex. Here the attempts of investigators such as John Rawls, *A Theory of Justice* (Cambridge, Mass.: Harvard University Press, 1971), to elucidate warranted moral stances is very important.

51. See, for example, the analysis of "discursive" and "presentational" symbolic processes in Susanne K. Langer, *Philosophy in a New Key* (New York: Mentor Books, 1951), especially 75-94; and the discussion of two senses of "knowing" in Gilbert Ryle, *The Concept of Mind* (London: Hutchinson's University Library, 1949), 25-61.

52. Ramsey, *op. cit.,* 9.

53. Apple, in Yee, *op. cit.,* 35.

54. Ramsey, *op. cit.,* 35.

55. Michael W. Apple, "The Process and Ideology of Valuing in Educational Settings," in *Educational Evaluation: Analysis and Responsibility,* ed. Michael W. Apple, Michael J. Subkoviak, and Henry S. Lufler, Jr. (Berkeley, Calif.: McCutchan Publishing Corp., 1974).

56. Ramsey, *op. cit.,* 41.

# 5. The Nature of Claims for Student Rights

*Guy Leekley*

A traditional controversy in Anglo-American political and social life has revolved around the questions of who is to be included in the protection of civil rights and how broad should be the range of that protection. Arguments and conclusions regarding rights have generally been formulated in quite different ways by those who look at the issues from the various viewpoints of law, politics, or philosophy. Whatever the approach or prescription, however, until quite recently the mainstream arguments assumed that the population to be protected by "rights" was composed of adult, white males. The perimeters of the protected group have been gradually expanded during this century, but it was not until the 1960s that claims by students of rights against school authorities began to be recognized and enforced by American courts.

In the last decade the number of court decisions that have supported student claims of rights in relation to their schools has increased considerably. Knowledge of this increase sensitizes students to the possibility of seeking protection against excesses of authority and tends to encourage claims of the right to be so protected. As this new dimension is added to the general ferment of school life, every element involved—courts, teachers, parents, students, and school administrators—must learn to distinguish among various kinds of claims that students might make and must generally develop an understanding of the nature of those claims. In order to increase that understanding, we will need to determine what a student means when he makes such a claim, and we will have to examine some judicial decisions to see what has happened when claims of student rights have been tested in the courts.

This analysis of the nature of such claims should not be confused with studies that have been made by philosophers and political scientists of the concept of "rights." Claims by students of rights, and the response of school officials and courts, are forms of human interaction that have become important enough to deserve close inspection. As was pointed out in a recent study of children's rights, "The term *rights* is commonly used in a quasi-legal or moral sense to identify 'something to which one has a just claim.' Such a definition connotes that rights are a given or pre-existent entity, inherent in nature, embodied in tradition, or incorporate in law, which one can demand or assert. This popular understanding of what constitutes rights does little to explain where rights originate, who may exercise rights, or how rights are secured and maintained."[1] Such an explanation of what it means to seek positive recognition of a right does not depend on the determination of the validity of any particular rights; that determination would be a legal or moral issue. Here we are limiting ourselves to the study of the meaning of a specific form of communication among students, administrators, and other interested parties—a claim on the part of students that they have rights, and the responses to that claim. This inquiry is worthwhile because an improved understanding of the nature of this form of communication will result in more effective communication, which, in the arena of human relations in the schools, is sorely needed.

As we turn to claims on behalf of students that they have rights, we notice that they are actually claims directed toward two different social entities. In one sense, the claim is directed toward school authorities, who generally have the power to control their actions, limit their freedom, or provide desired goods and services. It is an assertion that they have an obligation to act, or to refrain from acting, in certain specified ways. In another sense, the claim is also being directed at judicial authorities who have the power to restrain or coerce school authorities. The student is claiming that the

judiciary has a duty to see to it that obligations of the school officials are fulfilled. The issues that must be considered in support of
this second sense have to do with the court's jurisdiction over the
question and the court's authority to enforce its decisions regarding
actions of the school officials.

This discussion will be limited to an analysis of the first sense of
the claim (directed to school authorities) and will leave a treatment
of the second sense (directed to the judiciary) for a more specifically
legal context.[2]

The analysis of claims as they are directed to school authorities is
presented in two parts. The first part attempts to show how the
assertion of a claim for student rights indicates that an obligation is
being demanded of the school authorities. The remainder of that part
consists of an examination of the various kinds of obligations for
which a school official might be held responsible. The conclusion is
that the nature of a particular student rights claim can be determined
by identifying the nature of the corresponding obligation.

The second part attempts to show that all claims for student rights
are based on an appeal to an existing rule, which, if enforced, would
require the school authorities to perform the claimed obligation. This
is followed by an examination of the range of rules to which appeal
might be made and demonstrates how the nature of the claim depends on the scope of the particular rule on which the claim is
grounded.

Throughout this analysis reference is made to adjudicated legal
cases in which questions regarding student rights were tested, thus
illustrating the variety of claims that can be raised and the responses
with which they have been met.

## The Nature of the Obligation

To see how claims of rights on behalf of students imply the assertion that school authorities have a certain obligation due to the
students, we need only consider the form and manner in which such
claims actually arise in the school setting. It would be typical, in
these times, to find a group of high school students speaking to their
principal or school board to the point that the student body had a
right to the provision of their own area of free speech, or to the
elimination of all dress or appearance codes, or to the assurance of a

fair hearing in the case of a threatened suspension of a student. In each of these examples, if the administration were to agree that such a right existed, it would be admitting to the existence of a duty to perform certain actions, or to refrain from acting in certain ways. It is also clear that, in response to a refusal by the administration, the students might be able to convince a judge to enforce their claim, in which case the administration would be required to meet the obligation implied by the claim. Thus the question "What rights do the students have?" can be rephrased in terms of the presence of obligations that are being demanded of the authorities and the means by which those demands might be enforced. Whether it is termed a "right" or a "duty," the attempt is to articulate a particular kind of relation or interaction between students and the school administration.

A way of determining the kind of right that is being claimed by students is to classify its corresponding obligation or duty. Looking at the first example suggested above, we can see that the claim for a right to an area for free speech really implies two different obligations. The students first wish to require the administration to provide space and facilities and second to make sure that the administration will not interfere with their activities in this area. These obligations are quite different from each other. The one is an obligation to do something and provide something. The other is an obligation not to do something, an obligation to refrain from acting.

In the example of students claiming a right to attend school without the restrictions of a dress or appearance code, we see again that the corresponding obligation would be to restrain from interfering with the appearance of the students.

When students claim the right to a fair hearing, the emphasis in the corresponding obligation is that the administration should proceed in a certain prescribed manner. This category of obligation can, of course, be clearly distinguished from obligations to do something and from obligations to restrain from interfering with student actions or appearance.

These are the three categories into which claims of student rights can be organized by distinguishing among the kinds of obligations entailed by the various claims. Each of these categories will be examined more closely and will be illustrated by actual court cases.

## The Obligation to Refrain from Interfering

When we examine school situations where students are claiming a right to act or speak freely, or a right to be left alone, the corresponding obligation they are asserting is the obligation to refrain from interfering with that speech, action, or appearance. The most important litigation in that category is the *Tinker*[3] case, where high school students in Des Moines had been suspended for refusing to remove arm bands worn in a silent demonstration in opposition to the Vietnam war. The issue was whether the school authorities had a right to interfere with such a demonstration. The students claimed that their silent demonstration was protected by provisions of the First Amendment against state infringement on free speech.

In the *Tinker* case the students were successful in gaining support for their claimed right. The Supreme Court ordered the school officials not to interfere with the peaceful demonstration, essentially finding an obligation to refrain, which corresponded with the student claim of a right to act freely in this endeavor.

In 1969, soon after the *Tinker* decision, the case of *Scoville* v. *Board of Education of Joliet Township High School*[4] was decided by a federal court of appeals. Several high school students had been expelled upon a determination that they were guilty of "gross disobedience and misconduct" after they had published "objectionable" material in their underground newspaper. The students claimed that this interference violated their constitutional rights and that the school authorities should be enjoined from action in the matter. The court of appeals agreed. "We conclude that absent an evidentiary showing, and an appropriate balancing of the evidence by the district court to determine whether the Board was justified in a 'forecast' of the disruption and interference, as required under *Tinker,* plaintiffs are entitled to the declaratory judgment, injunctive and damage relief sought."[5]

What principle seems to underlie the reasoning in these cases involving student claims that a right of free action has been violated? The above cases show that the courts are resting on the classical libertarian position that one can insist on noninterference by the state in personal actions or speech as long as others are not harmed or seriously disrupted. It is important to note that in the face of such a claim, it is up to the officials to prove that their interference was justified by the reasonable forecast of such disruption.

The students in the *Tinker* case argued that they deserved the same constitutional protections that had been enjoyed by some elements of our society since the passage of the Bill of Rights. As indicated in the Constitution, those protections are the right of "persons." We should note that a constitutional amendment was required to include in the category "persons" those people (presumably the adult males) in our society who had been slaves and those races whose skins are not white. It took another amendment to establish that the class of "persons" also included adult women, at least to the extent of allowing one of the prerogatives enjoyed by that class (the right to vote). There has been no such amendment allowing nonadults the protections afforded to "persons," but that appears to be the effect of the *Tinker* decision.[6]

## The Obligation of Performance

In our example of students claiming a right to be provided an area for free speech, they were not only insisting on a right to act freely in that area, but they were also claiming a right to be provided adequate space and facilities. The obligation that students were here attempting to require of the school authorities was, therefore, one to provide something or to give something to the students. They were saying that they have a right to receive something, which corresponds to an obligation to provide something. In other words, the students insisted on a right of recipience which corresponds to an obligation of performance.

A number of other student claims can clearly be classified in this category of right and obligation, for example, a claim to access to certain information or a claim to be provided an education. A case involving the former situation arose in Maine,[7] where in 1968 a student claimed that he had a right to be shown the recommendations that his high school officials were writing about him and sending to college admissions offices. The court agreed with the student and required the high school to make the recommendations available to him.

The case of a student claiming the right to an education has arisen in a variety of forms in courts across the country. A good example is the *Ordway* case (1971)[8] where school officials in Massachusetts informed a high school senior that she could no longer attend regular classes because she was pregnant and unmarried. The administration

was operating under a rule that provided that "whenever an unmarried girl enrolled in North Middlesex Regional High School shall
be known to be pregnant, her membership in the school shall be
immediately terminated." The student claimed that she had a right
to be provided an education and that her pregnancy did not constitute a valid reason for depriving her of that right. After reviewing the
evidence and the arguments, the court concluded its opinion in these
words:

In summary, no danger to petitioner's physical or mental health resultant from
her attending classes during regular school hours has been shown; no likelihood
that her presence will cause any disruption of or interference with school activities or pose a threat of harm to others has been shown; and no valid educational
or other reason to justify her segregation . . . .

*It would seem beyond argument that the right to receive a public school
education is a basic personal right or liberty.* Consequently, the burden of justifying any school rule or regulation limiting or terminating that right is on the
school authorities [italics mine].[9]

The basic authority on which this court relied was the *Tinker* case,
"where the Supreme Court limited school officials' curtailment of
claimed rights of students to situations involving substantial disruption of or material interference with school activities."[10] This is a
very broad interpretation of the *Tinker* case and appears not to notice
that the nature of the right claimed in *Ordway* is quite different from
that claimed in *Tinker*. In *Tinker* the students were not raising the
question of whether they had a right to an education, since they
would have objected to any other form of punishment or curtailment
as well as to expulsion. In the *Ordway* case, the student did not argue
that her right to get pregnant was being curtailed. She argued that
her pregnancy was not an adequate justification for curtailing her
right to be provided an education.

    Rights of recipience have also been referred to as "welfare
rights" and "human rights": "Since the eighteenth century, we have
come to regard the state less as a hostile, if necessary, intruder in
private affairs, and more as an instrument for promoting welfare.
Accordingly, the duties imposed by more recent declarations require
positive action, not merely non-interference. Whereas 'natural rights'
required only that governments as well as private persons should
respect a proper sphere of personal autonomy, 'human rights' also
require positive performance for their realization."[11]

There has not been a clearly formulated policy to justify the enforcement of claims to rights of recipience, and sometimes, as in the *Ordway* case, it is simply assumed that such rights have become "beyond argument." Grave doubt has recently been cast by the Supreme Court (in the *Rodriguez* case) on the notion that a personal right to receive a public school education is "beyond argument."[12] And it is generally felt that reasons have to be given to support claims of rights to be provided such benefits as jobs, social security, and education. The principle that is usually referred to in support of such claims has either to do with need or desert (earned) or a combination of the two.[13] When stated with some care, these principles more specifically refer either to a decision that we as a people do not wish to live in a society that includes the particular stated unfulfilled need (such as illiteracy or poverty), or to a decision that we as a people wish to reward certain efforts or risks by granting to those so identified specified rights or privileges (such as diplomas and income tax deductions).

Before going on to examine our third category of rights and obligations, we should remind ourselves of the difference between the first two. In the *Tinker* case the students wanted to require school officials not to interfere with their demonstration. This would be classified as claiming an obligation to refrain from interfering, which corresponds to the claim of a right to act freely. The *Ordway* case, in comparison, falls into the category of claims for a right to receive something (an education) and an obligation on the part of officials to do something (provide the education).

## The Obligation to Proceed in an Appropriate Manner

All claims for student rights that are not characterized as claims for the right to recipience or the right to free action will fit the category of claims for the right to due process. These claims arise out of situations where the school administration is taking an action that seems to pose some threat to students, and the students claim that they deserve due process. The corresponding obligation on the part of the administrators is that they should proceed in their action in a certain specified manner that is clearly fair to all parties.

A typical example of this form of claim to rights on behalf of students is presented by the case of *Jones* v. *Gillespie* (1970).[14] Here a ninth-grade student was suspended from school for taking a ten-cent box of cookies from a fellow student. The student claimed that he had a right to a hearing prior to suspension and that this right had been denied. Another way of stating the student's claim is that the authorities had an obligation to include a fair hearing as part of their response to his alleged misconduct. The court in *Jones* v. *Gillespie* accepted, and applied to the public school context, the proposition that due process requires a hearing whenever substantial rights of individuals are affected by government action. Once the student could show that substantial rights were threatened (presumably his right to an education), the burden was on the school to show that this was an emergency that did not allow time for a hearing. This the school failed to show. The court decree ordered that

defendant School District shall establish, by written regulations, effective procedures to ensure conformity to the aforesaid provisions of this decree, and defendant *School District shall, in the preparation of such regulations, consider matters including but not limited to: formation of the hearing committee, notice by the principal to the committee, time, place, notice to the student, right to counsel, evidence to be considered, form of hearing and appeals therefrom, and consequences of failure to hold a hearing within five days.* Such regulations shall be effective no later than September 30, 1970 [italics mine].[15]

The burden of justifying the fact that correct procedures were not followed falls on the school as soon as a student can show that the procedure constituted a substantial threat and that due process was not followed. It is important, therefore, to determine what is going to count as a substantial threat. The *Madera*[16] case in New York gives an indication of the kind of school procedure that might not be considered a substantial threat to the student. There a fourteen-year-old boy had been suspended by his principal for behavior problems. According to New York School Board rules a guidance conference is required during the period of suspension to bring together parents, teachers, counselors, and others in an attempt to resolve the conflict. The rule specifically denies student or parent the opportunity to have present at this conference an attorney representing them. Madera claimed that not allowing counsel at this conference violated his right to due process. The U.S. Court of Appeals did not agree. It found that the possible outcomes of the conference did not pose a threat serious enough to the student to warrant his attorney's being present. The student's claim to this right was, therefore, not enforced.[17]

There are a number of both differences and similarities between the third category of claims and the first two. The claim of a right to due process entails a demand that officials are obliged to proceed with an action in a certain way. This demand is similar to a right of recipience, or welfare right, in that it calls for action on the part of officials, while the third form of claim calls for inaction or noninterference. The claim for due process is different, however, in that the student would prefer that no threatening action be taken at all. He certainly is not requesting that action be taken against him. He is saying that if such a threatening action *is* to be taken, it must be done properly and fairly. It is the form, or manner, that is in question.

Note, also, that claims for rights of due process are like claims to the right of free action in that both are assumed to be enforceable by persons threatened by the state, and in both the burden of argument shifts to the state (or school) once that threat has been shown to be substantial. When we examine the obligations entailed by each of these claims, however, we find that the claim of a right to free action requires the officials simply not to interfere with the students' action or speech, while the claim of due process requires that the officials proceed with their interference in an appropriate manner.

## The Scope of the Rule

In the first part of the chapter we have attempted to distinguish among various categories of claims for student rights according to the character of the obligations implied by those claims. We shall now examine the nature of these claims by analyzing the rules to which they appeal. One way of understanding the importance of rules to the claim for every type of right is to remind ourselves of the manner in which enforcement of those claims is sought.

We can assume that a claim of a right is made by students, or on behalf of students, because of a desire to see the corresponding obligation either agreed to by the school officials or enforced by the judicial and executive branches of government. The process, in our society, for gaining enforcement of such a claim in the courts is to argue that the official actions of the school officials are governed by rules, that something in those rules requires the obligation that one is demanding, and that the officials are not abiding by those rules. One identifies the rule, argues that the school is bound by that rule, and then shows that his case falls within that rule.

It is not necessary, however, to look to the enforcement process in order to determine the importance of the nature of rules in claims for student rights. Once it is clear that rights and obligations are two ways of talking about one relationship, we see the importance of understanding the different categories of obligations. We also realize that what we mean by "obligation" is behavior that is prescribed by rules. Whenever we talk about obligations, we always have a rule in mind, and if the rule points to a beneficiary of the obligation, we say that the beneficiary can successfully claim a right. At the time such a right is claimed, appeal is made to what seems to be the appropriate rule. If logical categories can be found by which those rules can be organized, we will have available another framework by which to analyze claims for student rights.

The characteristic of our system of rules that seems likely to produce the most useful set of categories is the fact that some rules are created by a small number of people simply to govern relations among them, other rules are created to govern relations among larger groups of people, while some rules have to be created to regulate rulemakers. When we have identified and characterized the various categories in this range of rules, we will be able to ask of any claim to rights the scope of the rule with which it identifies itself.

Rules of the narrowest scope are those created by individual parties to regulate ways in which they interact with each other. These rules are contract relations, and in our society such privately created rules are generally upheld and enforced by courts if the parties to the contract had the authority to create rights and obligations among themselves. Quite often students will base a claim of right on what they take to be an agreement or contract with school authorities. For example, students in a particular high school may feel that because of an agreement with their principal they can claim the right to be provided a smoking lounge. Even if the students could produce evidence of that agreement, the question would be raised as to whether the principal had legal authority to enter into the agreement.

Next wider in scope to private contracts are those rules at the statutory level. They directly regulate the official actions of school administrators. A common form of claim would be an attempt to show that statutes created a specific obligation on the part of school administrators and a corresponding right on the part of the students and that the administrators were not conforming to the rule.

An example of this form of claim is the case of *Jones* v. *Gillespie,* which resulted from a widespread practice of suspending high school students for indeterminate periods without a prior hearing. The student claimed a right to a hearing when threatened with a suspension of five days or more. In support of this claim, the student appealed to a rule at the statutory level, a section of the school code that dealt in an ambiguous manner with the question of suspension. The court upheld the student's reading of the statute. Thus, we can classify this as a claim of a right to due process that is grounded in a rule at the statute level.

The set of rules that governs the actions of legislatures is next in scope; these constitutional rules authorize and limit the scope of the statutory rules. This level of rules is most often associated with claims for student rights. When a claim is based on a rule at this level, the student is saying that not only do the actions of the administrator violate the rule, but so also does the statute that requires or allows the offending administrative action.

In the *Scoville* case the high school students asked the court to require that school officials not interfere with the students' publication of an "underground paper"; they were claiming a right to free action. To support their claim they relied on a rule from the constitutional level, the protection of free speech granted in the First Amendment. They were successful in this claim because the judge could turn to the *Tinker* decision, which had ruled that the Constitution required school officials reasonably to forecast "substantial disruption or material interference" before they could interfere with student communications.

The rules with the broadest scope in our system are the moral rules of the community. Students will at times feel that a moral rule exists on which they can base a claim, in spite of the fact that neither contracts, statutes, nor Constitution support such a rule. One example of this is the occasionally successful attempt by students to gain community support for their claim to their own smoking lounge.[18]

Another example is the *Ordway* case, where the pregnant, unmarried student was attacking both her expulsion and the school board rule that required her expulsion. One might expect that such a rule would have been attacked on grounds that it discriminates for no good reason and that it violates the Equal Protection clause of the Constitution. But here the student was not simply claiming a right to be left alone, a claim she could have supported by appeal to a rule at the constitutional level. She was claiming a welfare right to be provided an education. It is clear from the language in the court's opinion that the student succeeded in an appeal to the level of rule higher than the Constitution, the moral rules of the community. Recall the language of the judge: "It would seem beyond argument that the right to receive a public school education is a basic personal right or liberty." We have already seen that this is not a constitutional right (see note 12).

## Summary

We have examined the nature of claims for student rights by analyzing the forms of obligation that correspond to the rights claimed and by analyzing the categories of rules on which such claims might be grounded. Students making claims, or those who must respond to those claims, will be able to communicate more effectively if they can share an understanding of the underlying nature of the claim. Are the students asserting that the administration should refrain from acting, that it should act in providing goods and services, or that they should proceed with threatening procedures in a fair and orderly manner? Are the students claiming that the obligations stem from a contract agreement they have with the administration? Or do they look to a broader, statutory rule that they feel proscribes the official actions they find offensive? Do they turn to the Constitution to support their objection to the action, or inaction, of the administrators? Or are they seeking the broadest possible base of support in the attitudes of the community?

At this point it might be helpful to enumerate the advantages gained by organizing claims for student rights according to the categories developed in this chapter.

1. The categories allow the person or institution against whom the claim has been made to determine the nature of the obligation demanded of him, and they provide the student a means of becoming clearer about his own claim. It may even be that claims of rights by students would be accepted more often by school officials if they

recognized the demanded obligation as one already accepted by their school, or by other schools.

2. Each category of claim is based on a somewhat different principle or rule, which an individual claim would have to invoke before it could gain support or enforcement. It is important to recognize the basis in principle of the particular claim with which one is faced.

3. The nature of what a defending school district is going to have to prove varies from category to category, as does the question of who has the burden of defending his position in a disagreement over a claimed right.

The cause of much confusion in responding to the possible claims of student rights is the lack of clarity regarding the distinctions detailed in this chapter. It is to be hoped that the habit of applying the framework developed here will result in speedier and more effective resolution of conflict.

## Notes

1. Carl F. Calkins, Ronald W. Lukenbill, and William J. Mateer, "Children's Rights: An Introductory Sociological Overview," *Peabody Journal of Education* 50 (January 1973): 91.

2. In March 1972 the Supreme Court refused to hear an appeal of the case of *Billie Freeman* v. *Almon Flake et al.* (No. 71-956). Justice Douglas wrote the following dissenting opinion: "Today the Court declines to decide whether a public school may constitutionally refuse to permit a student to attend solely because his hair style meets with the disapproval of the school authorities. The Court also denied certiorari in *Olff* v. *Eastside Union High School*, which presented the same issue. I dissented in *Olff*, and filed an opinion. For the same reasons expressed therein, I dissent today. I add only that now eight circuits have passed on the question. On widely disparate rationales, four have upheld school hair regulations . . . and four have struck them down . . . . I can conceive of no more compelling reason to exercise our discretionary jurisdiction than a conflict of such magnitude on an issue of importance bearing on First Amendment and Ninth Amendment rights." Here we see an example of a claim for a student right remaining unsettled because the Court refused to agree to the implication in the claim that it had an obligation to resolve the issue.

3. *Tinker* v. *Des Moines Independent Community School District*, 393 U.S. 503 (1969).

4. 425 F. 2nd 10 (7th Cir. 1970), cert. denied, 400 U.S. 826 (1970).

5. *Ibid.*, 15.

6. "First Amendment rights, applied in light of the special characteristics of the school environment, are available to teachers and students. It can hardly be

argued that either students or teachers shed their constitutional rights to freedom of speech or expression at the school house gate." *Tinker* v. *Des Moines Independent Community School District.*

7. *Creel* v. *Brennan* (*Bates College Case*), No. 3572, Superior Ct. of Androscoggin City, Maine (1968) (cited in *Student Rights Litigation Packet*, Center for Law and Education, Harvard University, May 1970, 430).

8. *Ordway* v. *Hargraves*, 323 F. Supp. 1155 (D. Mass. 1971).

9. *Ibid.*, 1158.

10. *Ibid.*

11. S.I. Benn and R.S. Peters, *The Principles of Political Thought* (New York: Free Press, 1959), 117, 118.

12. *San Antonio Independent School District* v. *Rodriguez et al.*, 93 S. Ct. 1278 (1973). In this case the Court refused to strike down the Texas system of financing public education. In the majority opinion, written by Justice Powell, the Court said: "We have carefully considered each of the arguments supportive of the District Court's finding that education is a fundamental right or liberty and have found those arguments unpersuasive" (p. 1299). Also, "Education, of course, is not among the rights afforded explicit protection under our Federal Constitution. Nor do we find any basis for saying it is implicitly so protected" (p. 1297).

13. In support of the view that rights can be validly based on both need and desert, see D.D. Raphael, "The Rights of Man and the Rights of the Citizen," in *Political Theory and the Rights of Man*, ed. D.D. Raphael (Bloomington, Ind.: Indiana University Press, 1967), 115.

14. *Jones* v. *Gillespie*, Court of Common Pleas, Philadelphia, April 22, 1970 (reprinted in *Student Rights Litigation Packet*, 183).

15. *Ibid.*, 184.

16. *Madera* v. *Board of Education of the City of New York*, 386 F. 2d 778 (1967).

17. Note that in *Jones* v. *Gillespie* the student was granted rights to counsel, notice, appeal, and so forth, when faced with the threat of a suspension of more than five days, while in the *Madera* case right to counsel was denied for a suspension "conference." This is an area badly in need of judicial clarification, especially considering the potentially damaging experience of those students punished by a series of short suspensions.

18. For example, Homewood-Flossmoor High School, in a suburb of Chicago, has been experimenting with an area for student smoking since 1970. This resulted from the suggestion of a community committee formed to evaluate the student claims for a right to a place where there would not be interference with their smoking.

# 6. Legal Precedents in Student Rights Cases

*Sharon L. Koenings* and *Steven L. Ober*

We were almost into the twentieth century before this society began to see the need for procedures of juvenile justice separate and distinct from those applied to adults. The first American juvenile court, opened in Cook County, Illinois, in 1889, was brought about by Jane Addams and a similarly spirited and concerned group of individuals who recognized the need for procedures designed to deal specifically with the problems of juveniles and juvenile justice.

The court attempted to extend the sheltering arms of a substitute parent, a right previously falling under the sole domain of the public school system within the doctrine of in loco parentis. But, as with the schools, all the good intentions and benevolent ideas soon tended to erode into rules and regulations designed not to benefit the juvenile but rather to serve societal demands for regimentation and expediency. Power fed on power, and soon the doctrine of in loco parentis had evolved into an elaborate system of laws that denied youth even the basic rights guaranteed under our Constitution. As Chief Justice Earl Warren so aptly stated, children and their rights have been "swept under the rug." But a change has taken place. Beginning in the early 1960s with Berkeley's Free Speech Movement, the fight for juvenile and student rights has trickled down into the secondary and even elementary school systems, where the struggle is just beginning.

Secondary school students have now brought their plea for rights into the court systems of the United States, testing the practices of the country's traditional school systems and questioning the legal authority of their school administrators. Students want the courts to settle their disputes with school authorities. Basically these disputes center around two levels of disagreement. First, students question the basic methods used by school officials in forming policies and deciding on forms of discipline, feeling schools often institute unfair rules and apply capricious disciplinary actions without warning or proper hearings. Second, they question the legal right of the school authorities to make rules that curb their freedoms. For example, should administrators and teachers dictate rules that disregard free expression or personal liberty?

These two levels of arguments for student rights can legally be termed procedural issues and substantive issues. The first involve those questions of structure and process used to determine discipline and establish rules; they question "how" the regulation is made and "how" the discipline is administered. Procedural issues are concerned with such things as proper notice of charges and the right to a hearing. Substantive issues are involved with the reasons behind the rule or the details of the discipline. They center around the "why" or "what," concerning themselves with rights to free speech, rights to privacy, or rights to personal liberty.

Two landmark Supreme Court cases set precedents concerning both the procedural and the substantive rights of students. *In re Gault* is a strong case containing a firm opinion handed down by the Supreme Court. The decision lists in detail the obligations of the juvenile court system to the individual juvenile and establishes without a doubt the fact that juveniles have the constitutional rights of due process established under the Fourteenth Amendment. Though *Tinker* v. *Des Moines Independent Community School District* is weaker than the *Gault* case because its opinion is written in very general language, it is important nonetheless. It was the first high court ruling on substantive rights of students.

## In re Gault and Subsequent Cases on Procedural Due Process

*In re Gault* is the most important case to date on juvenile rights. Prior to its appearance before the United States Supreme Court each juvenile court in the country was run at the discretion of its presiding judge. This varied as the individual characteristics of the judges varied, therefore subjecting a juvenile's fate to the ideals, whims, and personal convictions of the judge under whose jurisdiction he might fall. Such infirmities can be seen, certainly, in other court structures besides that of the juvenile system, but not in such preponderance. The juvenile court had a completely informal atmosphere devoid of the due process procedures inherent in the adult courts. Such absence of procedural due process thrust the juvenile into alien courts that did not accord him the constitutional safeguards guaranteed those entering the adult court. As likely as not this subjected the juvenile offender to situations more devastating and severe than those of the adult. *In re Gault* exemplifies such a situation; its appeal to the Supreme Court dictates its position as the turning point in juvenile due process law.

On June 8, 1964, Gerald Gault, a fifteen-year-old boy from Gila County, Arizona, was taken into custody because of a verbal complaint concerning a telephone call in which indecent and lewd remarks were made. Gerald, at the time of this complaint, was under six-month probationary sentence resulting from his presence with another boy who had stolen a wallet.

When Gerald was picked up by the sheriff his parents were not at home, and no notice was left that he had been taken into custody. One of Gerald's friends supplied the information leading to the discovery that Gerald had been taken to the Children's Detention Home. Upon appearing at the detention home, Mrs. Gault was informed that a hearing had been scheduled on the following day.

A probation officer filed a petition on the day of the hearing, but neither Gerald nor his parents were given a copy of the petition. It did not state any charges; it merely recited, "said minor is under the age of 18 years and is in need of the protection of this Honorable court and that said minor is a delinquent minor." It pleaded for a hearing regarding "the care and custody . . . [of the] minor [Gerald]."[1]

On June 9 proceedings began in the court of Judge McGhee,

although the complainant was not present. Judge McGhee decided at this time to "think about"[2] the case and sent Gerald back to the Children's Detention Home. There was no record or memorandum made of these proceedings. At a later hearing, in fact, a problem arose because no one could remember if Gerald admitted making some of the indecent remarks or merely dialing the telephone. When Gerald was finally released, no explanation was given for his detention, but June 15 was set for a further hearing.

At the hearing on June 15 the complainant was still not present; nor had she been spoken to by the judge. She had merely been called by telephone once by the probation officer. Judge McGhee stated that her presence at the hearing was unnecessary. After this hearing the probation officer filed a referral with the judge that finally stated the charge: "Lewd Phone Calls." The Gaults were not informed of this referral nor of the charge. Judge McGhee subsequently committed Gerald to the State Industrial School for the period of his minority or until he was twenty-one. Whereas Gerald was committed to a state institution for six years, an adult in Arizona would have been fined between five and fifty dollars and/or sentenced to serve two months in jail for the same offense. Although an appeal appeared in order, no appeal procedures were permitted for a juvenile in the Arizona court system. Gerald's parents consequently filed a writ of habeas corpus. This hearing was held in the Superior Court of Arizona where Judge McGhee was vigorously cross-examined. He testified that Gerald was "habitually involved in immoral matters."[3] He was convinced of this because of a referral two years earlier in which Gerald had allegedly stolen a baseball mitt from another child. Even though there was no official record of this 1962 offense, however, the Superior Court dismissed the writ.

The appellants sought review in the Arizona Supreme Court. The issue of constitutional rights to due process was raised at this time. This court affirmed dismissal of the writ saying the rights of due process did not apply to this specific case.

The Gaults then took their appeal to the United States Supreme Court where the decision was reversed, and an array of rights was demanded for the child. Justice Fortas, delivering the majority opinion for the Court, recapped a brief history of the juvenile court system stating that due process had initially been taken away from the child for reasons of protection. The juvenile judge was to be a father figure helping the child to find himself within an informal setting. Fortas stated that this system was created with good intentions, but "free discretion of the Judge however benevolently motivated was a poor substitute for the principles of procedure."[4] Justice Frankfurter had stated earlier: "Procedure is to law as scientific method is to science."[5] The Stanford Research Institute, for the President's Commission on Crime in the District of Columbia, stated that 66 percent of the delinquents between the ages of sixteen and seventeen were repeaters in the juvenile court system.[6] Fortas concluded, therefore, "an absence of constitutional protections does not reduce the crime rate . . . . The unique benefits of the Juvenile Court system will not be affected by constitutional domestication."[7]

The Arizona Supreme Court had held that "the policy of the juvenile law is to hide youthful errors from the full gaze of the public . . . ."[8] This juvenile law was instituted in order to protect the child, but in reality enabled courts to bypass legal procedures of record keeping, thus militating against parental petitions and proper notification of charges. The U.S. Supreme Court stated its disagreement with this practice in saying that "a notice to comply with due process requirements must be given sufficiently in advance of scheduled court proceedings so that reasonable opportunity to prepare will be afforded, and . . . must set forth the mis-conduct with particularity."[9]

The U.S. Supreme Court also disagreed with the Arizona Supreme Court on the right of the child to have counsel at juvenile court proceedings. Juvenile procedures, at the time of *Gault*, relied on the parent or probation officer to protect the child's interests. The juvenile judge was also supposed to act as a guiding and interested father figure. The informal atmosphere of the juvenile court was, in general, to be beneficial to the child. Fortas argued that in actuality "the essentials of due process may be a more impressive and more therapeutic attitude so far as the juvenile is concerned."[10] The power of the juvenile court over the child's future is in reality very far reaching. The child can be placed in an institution that restricts his liberty for years. He can be taken from parents and home and placed in the setting of institutional life including guards, custodians, and delinquents. The U.S. Supreme Court concluded: "the Due Process Clause of the Fourteenth Amendment requires that in respect of Proceedings to determine delinquency which may result in commitment to an institution to which the juvenile's freedom is curtailed, the child and his parents must be notified of the child's right to be represented by counsel retained by them, or if they are unable to afford counsel, that counsel will be appointed to represent the child."[11]

In the *Gault* case the complainant, to whom the lewd calls had been made, was never present at the hearings and was only contacted by phone once. The Supreme Court was appalled at this procedure. The opinion stated: "confrontation with sworn testimony by witnesses available for cross-examination is essential . . . ."[12]

Gerald Gault's commitment to the State Industrial School for the period of his minority was made solely on the basis of his confessions. Gerald was neither informed of his right to remain silent nor assured that he would not be punished for so doing. The Supreme Court was thorough and firm in its opinion on this point. "It would indeed be surprising if the privilege against self-incrimination was available to hardened criminals but not to children . . . confessions by juveniles do not aid in individualized treatment . . . we conclude that the Constitutional privilege against self-incrimination is applicable in the case of juveniles as it is with respect to adults."[13]

The Court disposed of the case on the grounds that the juvenile was constitutionally entitled to adequate notice of charges, right to counsel, right to confront and cross-examine his accusers, and privilege against self-incrimination. It did not, however, deal with the issues of a right to the transcript of proceedings or a right to appellate review. The language used in the case seems to indicate the view that these are also significant rights and that a later case raising these arguments would be given favorable consideration. "In view of the fact that we must reverse the Supreme Court of Arizona . . . for other reasons, we need not rule on these questions in the present case . . . [but] the consequences of failure to provide an appeal, to record the proceedings, or to make findings or state the grounds for the Juvenile Court's conclusion may be to throw a burden upon the machinery for habeas corpus . . . and to impose upon the Juvenile Judge the unseemly duty of testifying under cross-examination . . . ."[14]

The Court's decision *In re Gault* set down specific standards and guidelines of due process applicable to juveniles and is a landmark in juvenile law because it is the first such decision handed down with authority and precision. The Court dealt with due process firmly and directly; it answered specific questions and outlined its opinion in blunt and direct terms.

An earlier case, *Kent* v. *United States*, raised similar issues on juvenile rights. The main issue of this case, however, was waiver, which refers to the situation wherein a juvenile is tried in an adult court. Such a situation occurs when it would be against the best interests of society and the child to keep the case in the juvenile sphere. Juvenile drinking, for example, is more severely dealt with than adult drinking, and waiver of such a charge to an adult court would be to the distinct advantage of the youth. To date there has been no universal or absolute criterion used for waiver proceedings. Consequently the Supreme Court on receiving the *Kent* case decided it solely on the issue of waiver, "because we remand the case on account of the procedural error with respect to waiver of jurisdiction, we do not pass upon these questions [right to counsel, right to notice of charges, and privilege against self-incrimination]."[15] The Court did decide in *Kent*, however, that "it is incumbent upon the Juvenile Court to accompany its waiver order with a statement of the reasons or consideration therefore . . . the statement should be sufficient to demonstrate that the requirement of 'full investigation' has been met and that the question has received the careful consideration of the Juvenile Court . . . ."[16] Hence, even though *Kent* dealt only with one issue—waiver—it opened the door to other issues on the constitutional rights of due process. It can be said that *Kent* became a stepping-stone to or foundation of the *Gault* case.

Subsequent cases concerning due process rights of juveniles used aspects of the *Gault* decision in their own decisions. These cases include those concerning procedures of juvenile courts and those concerning procedures of educational institutions. We shall examine both types of cases, emphasizing, however, those concerning educational institutions.

### Procedures of Juvenile Courts

*In re Winship* began in the New York Family Court. A twelve-year-old boy was found guilty of stealing money and was sentenced to confinement in a state training school for as long as six years. The judge found the boy guilty on a preponderance of the evidence, reflecting the contention that due process required proof beyond a reasonable doubt. An appellant division of the New York Supreme Court affirmed the opinion of the family court. The New York Court of Appeals then affirmed the same decision.

On appeal to the U.S. Supreme Court the decision was reversed. The Court confined itself to the question of whether proof beyond a reasonable doubt is a part of due process required during the adjudicatory stage, when a juvenile is being charged, and established the fact that this type of proof has been a part of criminal proceedings since the founding of the nation. "The reasonable doubt standard plays a vital role in the American scheme of criminal procedure. It is a prime instrument for reducing the risk of convictions resting on factual error."[17]

When returning to the issue of whether juveniles also are entitled to the long-established right to proof beyond a reasonable doubt, the Court said, "The same considerations that demand extreme caution in fact-finding to protect the innocent adult apply as well to the innocent child."[18] The *Winship* opinion, then, used *Gault* to back up its decision. It quoted *Gault*, saying "Observance of the standard of proof beyond a reasonable doubt will not compel the States to abandon or displace any of the substantive benefits of the juvenile process."[19]

The juvenile courts are finding it necessary to adhere to the decisions of the Supreme Court regarding due process procedures. The implications are quite clear. Juveniles have the same due process rights as adults have under the Fourteenth Amendment. Courts dealing with children must award them the right to counsel, the right to confront and cross-examine accusers, the right to notice of charges, and the privilege against self-incrimination. These procedures will add to the benefits already acquired in juvenile court. The guiding and understanding juvenile judge and the informal hearings can certainly still exist. The extension of due process rights to juveniles will merely assure that the child receives the rights he or she is entitled to under the Fourteenth Amendment.

*In re Gault* set strong standards for due process procedures in juvenile courts. While its influence on educational institutions was not as thorough and far reaching, it did affect the area of educational administration in that it increased the concern for the rights of students.

## Procedures of Educational Institutions

The legal aspects of student discipline have come to be of paramount importance when that discipline involves long-term suspension or expulsion from public schools. Cases are raising the issue of whether the student's rights to due process have been adhered to by school administrators. The emerging case law gives more flexibility to due process procedures within the school than *Gault* gave to the juvenile court. It seems that schools must have rules that are fair and reasonable that are applied in fair and reasonable terms. It also seems certain that a hearing must be granted (if required by state statute) before disciplinary action is taken. The hearing does not, however, have to be formal in nature.

There is a growing concern to supply procedural due process rights in secondary school disciplinary actions. Such is evident because of the increasing number of state and federal court cases on the constitutional issue of due process in secondary schools. The influence of the *Gault* decision and the struggle for rights by college students have certainly led to the movement for securing rights of students in secondary schools.

*Dixon* v. *Alabama State Board of Education* is a college case that influenced subsequent secondary school cases. *Dixon* concerns several college students who were expelled after participating in a series of civil rights demonstrations. The notice of expulsion was sent to each involved student; it did not, however, state the charges, but merely used the general term "the problem"[20] as reason for expulsion. It was then taken to a United States Court of Appeals where the previous decision was reversed. During the court proceedings questions concerning due process rights of notice of charges and of opportunity for a hearing were raised. The court handed down an affirmative decision. "The notice should contain a statement of the specific charges and grounds which, if proven, would justify expulsion under the regulations of the Board of Education. The nature of the hearing should vary depending upon the circumstances of the particular case . . . . This is not to imply that a fulldress judicial hearing, with the right to cross-examine witnesses, is required . . . the student should be given the names of the witnesses against him and an oral or written report on the facts to which each witness testifies . . . ."[21] From this decision secondary school administrators and students could decide the direction upon which they wished to embark in the area of student rights. Several similar cases are evidence of an active approach to student rights.

*Vought* v. *Van Buren Public Schools* was a case concerning expulsion from a secondary school. The court followed the guidelines of *Dixon* in deciding the case. In summary, a high school student was suspended for possessing a copy of a newspaper that contained obscene material and that was not allowed on school property. The student was informed he could appeal the suspension before the local school board and that he would be notified of the board's date of meeting. The student was not notified of the meeting and was therefore not present when the board decided to expel him for the remainder of the year. With counsel present, the student was allowed to address the board at its next meeting. The board would not, however, reconsider its previous decision on expulsion. The student then sought relief in the U.S. District Court of Michigan. That court's opinion stated: "plaintiff here was not treated fairly. The lack of fair treatment is such as to, in our opinion, constitute denial of due process to this plaintiff in these circumstances. He was entitled to the observance of procedural safeguards commensurate with the severity of the discipline of expulsion."[22] The court then ordered the school board to hold a hearing, saying, "such [a] hearing [is] to be conducted in accordance with the guidelines laid down in *Dixon* v. *Alabama State Board of Education.*"[23]

In another secondary school case involving expulsion, *Sullivan* v. *Houston Independent School District*, the court agreed that procedural due process is a right of high school students. Two students were expelled for writing and distributing a newspaper that was critical of school administrators and school policies. They were expelled by the high school principal for the remainder of the school year. Both students had good academic and behavioral becords; the expulsion was based solely on their connection with the newspaper. An assistant superintendent of schools affirmed the expulsion. The only avenue open to the boys, within the Houston School District, was to try and find another school that would admit them; this proved unsuccessful. During all this time they had never been granted a hearing or given a written notice of charges. In fact, the school's rules and regulations were not even written down for the students to read and follow.

The students took their case to the U.S. District Court of Texas.

(Though many issues were raised during the court proceedings, at this time only those concerned with due process will be discussed.) The court answered the charge of violation of due process of law under the Fourteenth Amendment in the affirmative. "When severe discipline is contemplated—either expulsion or suspension for a substantial time—the student and his parents should be given ample time before the hearing to examine the charges, prepare a defense and gather evidence and witnesses. And, it goes without saying that the disciplining official should endeavor to maintain a neutral position until he has heard all of the facts."[24] The court then ordered that the Houston School District could not suspend or expel students for a substantial period of time "without compliance with minimal standards of due process: (1) formal written notice of the charges and of the evidence . . . [students] must be provided . . . (2) formal hearing affording both sides ample opportunity to present their cases by way of witnesses or other evidence, and (3) imposition of sanctions only on the basis of substantial evidence."[25]

In *Hobson* v. *Bailey* the U.S. District Court of Tennessee ordered the Memphis City Schools to reinstate a student in the exact school from which she was suspended. In this case a student was suspended because of participation in several racial protests. She was an above average student and had never been a discipline problem. Her first notice of suspension came the day after she stayed home from school in observance of a city-wide protest. The principal informed her that she was given a "home suspension," and she must return to school within three days with a parent. The mother accompanied her to school within the terms of the "home suspension." They were both informed that the girl was now on "board suspension" because of picketing she had done during her "home suspension." After reviewing the suspension, the assistant superintendent of public services informed the student she could not return to school. Later the attendance division of the school system reviewed the suspension and told the student she could go back to school, but not to the one from which she was expelled. A suit in the district court was then filed. The court reinstated the student in her original school because of the absence of due process procedures used by the school district, stating "the court is of the opinion that the procedure followed in the disposition of the board suspension did not meet the minimum standards of due process as guaranteed . . . under the Fourteenth Amendment of the United States Constitution."[26]

The issue of procedural due process has been expanded to legal representation in any situation involving serious educational discipline, although the outcomes have not always benefited the student. In the case of *Madera* v. *Board of Education of the City of New York*, the Second Circuit Court of Appeals upheld the New York Board of Education's plea that a student be withheld the right of counsel at a guidance conference. In this situation a junior high school student was expelled for disciplinary reasons. He and his parents were informed of the suspension and notified of a conference to be held. After receiving notice of the conference the parents retained legal counsel. The attorney wrote to the district superintendent asking to be allowed to appear at the conference on behalf of the boy and his parents. This request was refused. The case was taken to a New York district court which issued a permanent injunction upon the school district, forbidding its suspension of the student without a hearing where counsel was allowed to be present. The school board appealed the issuance of the injunction.

The issue the court preferred to address was whether a guidance conference is similar enough to a criminal hearing to render necessary the right to counsel by the student. The court consequently found the guidance conference a unique situation that only helps the child in his education: "the Guidance Conference . . . is not intended to be punitive, but it is, rather, an effort to solve his school problems . . . to place the child in a more productive educational situation."[27] (In spite of the court decision, the reader should be aware that no preponderance of evidence exists supporting the contention that guidance counselors serve the interests of the child alone. Social pressures and societal preconceptions often cloud juvenile guidance, and, no matter how ingeniously it is conceived, it may serve social norms rather than individual needs.)

It is obvious from the above due process cases that the court systems of our country are set up to dispose of cases as efficiently as possible and as thoroughly as necessary. This often happens when a court rules on a case on procedural grounds. Procedure is a unique set of steps in the legal process; if only one of these steps is overlooked or misused the entire case can be disposed of on that single point. When case after case is ruled on procedural issues, a definite pattern of due process develops. This due process becomes law for all cases; it gives lawyers and judges a set of steps to follow when determining the fairness of the particular legal actions taken in each individual case. Procedural law guarantees a consistent approach to all cases, regardless of variations in their actual facts.

Hence, from the above cases a pattern of procedural guarantees seems to be emerging that sustains the Fourteenth Amendment rights of students. *Gault* provided an immense step toward this goal by recognizing juveniles as persons under the Fourteenth Amendment, whereas *Dixon* made the initial step that brought due process within the confines of educational institutions. Subsequent state and federal cases have strengthened the case law on procedural rights of students by ruling against unjust procedures in secondary schools. It seems evident, therefore, that secondary schools must form policies regulating student behavior that are fair and reasonable. It would not be surprising if the next area of contention would be that of students in middle and elementary schools.

There are no absolute guidelines controlling student procedural rights as there are controlling juvenile court proceedings. There has been no Supreme Court ruling that dictates rules of conformity to every school district in the country, but there do exist strong state and federal court decisions following the guidelines set down in *Dixon*. The strictness of adherence to these guidelines varies with each state; it seems generally accepted, however, that secondary students should be afforded the rights of fair and just procedures, although these procedures may be informal.

## Tinker v. Des Moines Independent Community School District and Succeeding Cases on Substantive Rights

As the first case to deal directly with the substantive rights of students, *Tinker* v. *Des Moines Independent Community School District* has come to be considered the landmark case on student rights. Never before had the Supreme Court rendered an opinion on such an issue, and to date it remains the sole high court case pointedly involving the rights of secondary school students under the First Amendment.

Although *Tinker* is referred to as a landmark case on student rights, its significance is not equal to that of *Gault*. The latter delineated specific procedural rights whereas *Tinker* merely raised the issue of substantive student rights without dictating decisive action to be taken. As a result *Tinker* has not had a consistent influence on subsequent cases. *Gault,* on the other hand, because of its precise delineation of procedural rights, has had an immense influence on subsequent cases involving procedural issues and juvenile court proceedings. The *Tinker* opinion is so broadly written that it allows for a vast freedom of interpretation. Its nonspecificity in outlining student rights or administrative responsibilities left those cases decided in favor of the students open to exceptions and a variety of explanations. The same was true for all reprimands made of school administrators. Although the *Tinker* opinion was not specific and therefore did not clearly identify student rights or their bounds, it did take the monumental step of raising the issue of the substantive rights of students to a high court level. Never before had the Supreme Court handed down a favorable decision on First Amendment rights of secondary school students. Though its opinion was not precise in legal wording, its affirmative implications gave the struggle for substantive student rights its first encouragement from the high court.

Before we take a detailed look at *Tinker,* it is necessary to recognize a previous case that influenced an important section of the *Tinker* opinion. *Burnside* v. *Byars* emphasized that school officials could not make rules or regulations that infringed on a student's right to free expression unless there was absolute certainty that such expression would be disruptive to the school atmosphere. In *Burnside* a group of black students were suspended from a Mississippi high school for wearing "freedom buttons" that said "one man one vote."[28] The students wore the buttons in order to participate in a city-wide effort to encourage members of the black community to register to vote. The case was heard in the U.S. Court of Appeals, Fifth Circuit. The principal of the high school testified that "the children were not suspended for causing a commotion or disrupting classes but for violating a school regulation."[29] (The regulation forbade the wearing of said buttons.) The court granted an injunction forbidding the school to enforce the rule. It said, "the school is always bound by the requirement that the rules and regulations must be reasonable . . . . [School officials] cannot infringe on their students' rights to free and unrestricted expression . . . where the exercise of such rights . . . does not materially and substantially interfere with the requirements of appropriate discipline in the operation of the school."[30]

*Tinker* involved issues similar to those of *Burnside*. In December 1965 a group of adults and students in Des Moines, Iowa, held a meeting and decided to protest the Vietnam war. This was to be done by wearing black arm bands and by fasting on December 16 and New Year's Eve. Upon becoming aware of the plan to wear arm bands, the principals of the Des Moines schools established a policy that those wearing an arm band to school would be asked to remove it. If they refused, they would be suspended until they returned to school without the arm band. Students involved in this case were fully aware of the policy.

On December 16 two high school students and one junior high school student wore black arm bands to school. They were suspended by their principals and told they could not return to school unless they came back without their arm bands. The students did not return to school until after New Year's Day, which was after the planned period for the wearing of arm bands.

The parents of the students filed a complaint with the district court, requesting an injunction to restrain school officials from disciplining the students for their actions. The court dismissed the complaint and upheld the constitutional right of the officials to exercise their authority forbidding the wearing of arm bands. The court used the measure of the *Burnside* case on disturbance and said the Des Moines principals made a reasonable policy in order to prevent trouble. An appeal was made to the Eighth Circuit Court, which affirmed the district court's opinion. Because the circuit court was evenly divided on this case, it affirmed without a written opinion.

The Supreme Court granted a hearing and reversed the rulings of the lower courts. Justice Fortas, delivering the opinion, took great care in pointing out the issues to which the Court was limiting itself in this case. It is important to realize that in the *Tinker* case the Court addressed itself solely to the topic of freedom of expression for students and not to an array of other First Amendment rights. Fortas wrote: "The problem posed by the present case does not relate to regulation of the length of skirts or the type of clothing, to hair style, or deportment. It does not concern aggressive, disruptive action or even group demonstrations. Our problem involves direct, primary First Amendment rights akin to pure speech."[31]

The Supreme Court's interpretation of the *Burnside* case disagreed with the interpretation used by the district court, which based its decision on the point that school authorities anticipated a disruption should arm bands be worn. The Supreme Court stressed that fear of disruption is not enough to curb the freedom of expression: "undifferentiated fear or apprehension of disturbance is not enough to overcome the right to freedom of expression."[32] The Supreme Court did not find the Des Moines principals justified in their anticipation of disruption. It found, in fact, that the students "neither interrupted school activities nor sought to intrude in the school affairs or the lives of others."[33] Fortas pointed out the necessity to avoid allowing the fear of disruption from limiting free speech: "our Constitution says we must take this risk [of disturbance] . . . our history says that it is a sort of hazardous freedom . . . that is the basis of our national strength . . . ."[34]

The Supreme Court felt that the Des Moines principals established the policy forbidding the wearing of arm bands because it involved the controversial issue of the Vietnam war. The policy also was found to be inconsistent with policies concerning the wearing of other symbols (political campaign buttons were allowed, as was the Iron Cross, a traditional symbol of Nazism). The Court was outraged in its disagreement on this point: "In order for . . . school officials to justify prohibition of a particular expression of opinion, it must be able to show that its action was caused by something more that a mere desire to avoid the discomfort and unpleasantness that always accompany an unpopular viewpoint."[35] The court ruled, "In the absence of a specific showing of constitutionally valid reasons to regulate their speech, students are entitled to freedom of expression of their views."[36]

The main concern of the Supreme Court was the First Amendment right of students involving free expression. This stems most likely from its overall concern for freedom of speech in our country. "Under our Constitution, free speech is not a right that is given only to be so circumscribed that it exists in principle but not in fact."[37] The Court saw the *Tinker* situation "closely akin to pure speech" and saw students as persons under the Constitution: "students in school as well as out of school are persons under our Constitution . . . . It cannot be said that students shed their Constitutional rights to freedom of speech or expression at the schoolhouse gate . . . ."[38]

### *Limitations to* Tinker

From the above it is easy to see the favorable encouragement the *Tinker* opinion gave the movement for student rights. The vagueness of the language of the opinion is, however, just as obvious, which gives rise to definite questions concerning what the Court was actually saying.

The *Tinker* opinion was careful to limit its discussion to rights of free expression, stressing that it was not concerned with dress, hair styles, or group demonstrations. In fact, the opinion limited itself solely to freedom of expression to those peacefully wearing black arm bands. "Their deviation consisted only in wearing on their sleeve a band of black cloth . . . they caused . . . no interference with work and no disorder. In the circumstances [those particular to *Tinker*], our Constitution does not permit officials . . . to deny their form of expression."[39]

The vagueness of the "disruptive" measure used in *Tinker* leaves considerable room for an array of interpretations (for example, the term "disruption" is never defined). This leaves it open to a variety of uses depending upon the contextual situation in which it is to be applied. The particular situation, the unique understanding of the term by school authorities, and the wide discretion of the courts constitute only a few of the situations in which it can differentially be interpreted. "Disruption" has evolved into a catchall term with no specified, but only contextual, meanings, allowing almost any behavior by students to be termed "disruptive."

When the *Tinker* decision discusses students as persons under the Constitution, its language becomes vague and thereby broadly interpreted. It talks of students as persons when it says, "they are possessed of fundamental rights which the State must respect, just as they themselves must respect their obligations to the State."[40] But, what is meant by "fundamental rights" or by "obligations"? The opinion goes on: "The Constitution says that Congress [and the states] may not abridge the right to free speech . . . we properly read . . . [this] to permit reasonable regulation of speech-connected activities in carefully restricted circumstances."[41] Here the phrase "reasonable regulation of speech-connected activities" is not explained. The entire issue of whether students possess the same First Amendment rights as adults is never positively answered in the *Tinker* decision. In fact, Justice Stewart, in a concurring opinion, disagrees entirely with the assumption that children have such rights under the Constitution.[42] He insists the *Tinker* opinion contradicts an earlier Supreme Court ruling, *Ginsberg* v. *New York*, which said: "A State may permissibly determine that, at least in some precisely delineated areas, a child—like someone in a captive audience—is not possessed of that full capacity for individual choice which is the presupposition of the First Amendment."[43]

A great number of cases concerning the substantive rights of students flowed into the lower court systems. Though this wave of cases may have been influenced by the affirmative opinion of *Tinker*, the decisions of the lower courts show no consistency with the *Tinker* decision. Some cases ignored the rulings of *Tinker*; others disputed parts of the decision; still others agreed with the Supreme Court. All in all there were a large number of interpretations of the *Tinker* opinion.

A discussion of cases supporting rights for students follows. It includes cases that address themselves to a variety of issues on substantive rights. There is a similar discussion dealing with the same substantive rights, but citing cases that support school authorities and their policies.

## Substantive Cases Upholding Rights of Students

The case of *Aguirre* v. *Tahoka Independent School District* was ruled exactly as was the *Tinker* case. The circumstances surrounding both cases are also very much the same. In *Aguirre* a group of students had been suspended from a Tahoka, Texas, high school for wearing brown arm bands which symbolized their dissatisfaction with certain educational policies. The court ruled in favor of the students' First Amendment rights to free expression. It was determined that the school officials adopted the policy of suspension for wearing arm bands only after these bands appeared at school; this was unreasonable because it was inconsistent with the established dress code. The court also stressed that no substantial disruptions of the school atmosphere could be found, and so there was no justification for prohibiting the wearing of arm bands.[44]

*Scoville* v. *Board of Education of Joliet Township High School District 204* was heard by the U.S. Court of Appeals, Seventh Circuit, thus making its decision of significance to the student rights movement. It is interesting that the court heard this case twice. At the first hearing the lower court's decision to dismiss the complaint was upheld. The second hearing, en banc, was held after *Tinker*, and the court chose to reverse its previous decision.

Two students were expelled from Joliet High School in Illinois for writing and selling a newspaper that contained material critical of school officials and their policies. The students wrote the material off campus and sold it in the school.

The circuit court, in its second hearing, used the *Tinker* language of disruption to find the actions of the school administration unreasonable. Because the conduct of the students did not cause disruption of classes, the students were protected under the guarantees of the First Amendment. The facts also showed that the school administration could not have reasonably forecasted any substantial disruption because of the publication or its distribution as required under *Tinker*. For these reasons the court reversed its former opinion of agreement with school officials and recognized the injustice of the students' expulsion on grounds that the students had been denied First Amendment rights.[45]

### Dress Codes and Hair Length

One of the few cases dealing with the issue of dress as a freedom of expression under the First Amendment is *Bannister* v. *Paradis*. It is also one of the only cases decided in favor of the student.

A sixth-grade boy was sent home from school because he was wearing blue jeans. The case was taken to the U.S. District Court of New Hampshire. The court found no evidence indicating that the wearing of blue jeans caused disturbance or constituted any discomfort or interference to other students. The court felt that the school dress code intruded upon the personal liberty of the student, even though it was a small intrusion. Deciding that the rule against the wearing of blue jeans was invalid and unconstitutional, the court ordered the school to stop enforcing that section of its dress code.[46]

*Richards* v. *Thurston* is a leading case on the issue of whether length or style of hair is a valid right guaranteed under the Constitution. This decision chose to address itself to the concept of personal liberty and only casually referred to parts of the *Tinker* ruling.

The student in this case was suspended from a Massachusetts high school because his hair was "falling loosely about his shoulders,"[47] and he refused to have it cut. This case was heard on appeal by the

U.S. Court of Appeals, First Circuit. The court rejected the notion
that the choice of hair length was sufficiently a communicative expression protected under the First Amendment. Rather it established
the core of this case to be a part of the Fourteenth Amendment
where it protects the personal liberty of every individual from unreasonable intrusions. The *Richards* decision reasoned that liberty
encompasses small personal aspects of life (such as hair length) as
well as the more momentous ones of free speech. The court concluded that, "Within the commodious concept of liberty, . . . em-
bracing freedoms great and small, is the right to wear one's hair as he
wishes."[48]

The *Richards* court used reasoning similar to that used in *Tinker*.
It acknowledged that at times, for reasons of public interest, a person's personal liberties must be curbed. Long hair at school should
not be objectionable to the public; mere unattractiveness in the eyes
of others cannot justify proscription of personal liberty. Conformity
is not a necessary part of the educational process.

*Sims* v. *Colfax Community School District* is a unique "hair case"
because it involves the hair length of a female student. The court
relied heavily on the *Tinker* decision to write its opinion.

The student was suspended from an Iowa high school because she
refused to change her hair style which was longer than the forbidden
"one finger width above her eyebrows."[49] This case was heard in the
Southern District Court of Iowa. The decision sustained the student's
right to wear her hair as she wished.

Ground rules from *Tinker* were stressed in the *Sims* decision. "Only those school rules and regulations that are reasonable are
permissible."[50] Such rules become reasonable when they are justi-
fiably made in apprehension of substantial interference with the educational atmosphere. "In other words, school hair rules are reasonable and thus Constitutional only if the school can objectively
show that such a rule does in fact prevent some disruption or interference of the school system."[51]

*Parker* v. *Fry* was heard in the Eastern District Court of Arkansas.
It also concerned suspension because of a student's length and style
of hair. The court was solicitous to school authorities, ruling in favor
of the student only after an energetic but fruitless search of all the
evidence. The court succumbed to its decision because of the belief
that the burden of proof rests on school officials to show that a rule

is reasonable and has an effective relationship to the educational process. The decision concluded halfheartedly: "After hearing all of the evidence at the trial on the merits, the Court may conclude otherwise, but at this point, the defendants have failed to sustain the burden of justification."[52]

### Substantive Cases Upholding the Authority of the Schools

While the above cases sustain the constitutional rights of students, there were many decisions, made during this same period, that uphold the school's rules and regulations.

In Cleveland, Ohio, a high school student was suspended for wearing a button that advertised a student demonstration. School policy prohibited all types of buttons and other insignia. This rule was challenged in the court case of *Guzick* v. *Drebus*.

A district court in Ohio heard the case and ruled in favor of the school administration. A significant portion of this decision was founded upon the litigation of the *Tinker* case. Two points are of main concern. This particular high school had an informal rule, of some forty years standing, that forbade the wearing of buttons, emblems, or other insignia on school property during school hours. The school was also beset with a potentially explosive racial situation, and the court found the school administrators justified in their "undifferentiated fear or apprehension of disturbances likely to result from the wearing of buttons."[53]

*Butts* v. *Dallas Independent School District* strongly distinguishes itself by its use of the *Tinker* decision. The school authorities, applauded for their actions, were found to be completely justified in their anticipation of disruption.

The Northern U.S. District Court of Texas explicitly stated that it would rule only on the facts of the case before it and that it would not be influenced into forming a decision similar to *Tinker*. This court saw *Tinker* as having quite the opposite facts as the *Butts* case.

The suspension in *Butts* involved the wearing of black arm bands to demonstrate against the Vietnam war. Because there had been group demonstrations and a variety of other circumstances causing interference with school work, the principals of the Dallas School System felt the arm bands might trigger further disruptions. The court agreed with them and added, "It occurs to this court that one obligation students have to the state is to obey school regulations designed to promote the orderly educational process."[54]

In the case of *Hernandez* v. *School District Number One, Denver, Colorado*, it is clear that the element of disruption caused the court to decide the case in favor of the school system. The school principal suspended several high school students of Mexican descent for wearing black berets. The berets symbolized the Mexican culture and the dissatisfaction the students felt toward the treatment of their people. The principal, also of Mexican descent, sympathized with the students' feelings and in the beginning allowed them to hold various demonstrations to celebrate the Independence Day of the Republic of Mexico. The group of students wearing the berets later became a discipline problem, however, disturbing several classes and numerous students. The principal consequently asked them to stop wearing their berets at school; he also talked with their parents. The students continued wearing the berets and continued such behavior as shouting "Chicano Power" in the hallways and blocking the passage of other students. As a result, they were suspended. The U.S. District Court of Colorado supported their suspension.[55]

In *Schwartz* v. *Schuker* a New York City high school student was suspended for defiance of school rules and officials. His defiance concerned the distribution of a student newspaper. The newspaper criticized the school principal and contained "four letter words, filthy references, abusive and disgusting language, and nihilistic propaganda."[56] The Eastern District Court of New York upheld the school in its suspension of this student.

The students in the case of *Baker* v. *Downey City Board of Education* complained to the court that they had been refused freedom of expression and due process in their suspension. The Central District Court of California disagreed with them.

The students had printed and distributed (off campus) a newspaper containing "profanity or vulgarity." Evidence was presented that showed that the newspaper had caused confusion and chaos in some classes. The suspension was upheld, therefore, on the point that substantial disruption did occur. The court also felt the students had been awarded all necessary steps of due process.[57]

The "hair case" of *Jackson* v. *Dorrier* was heard by the U.S. Court of Appeals, Sixth Circuit. Two boys were suspended after the school held several hearings and conferences because their hair was so long that school officials considered it "distracting attire." A district court in Tennessee granted approval to the school board's suspension of the two boys. On appeal the circuit court affirmed the lower court's decision. The opinion stated that, because the students did not define their hair styles as a symbol of any verbal expression, their constitutional protections under the First Amendment were not violated. The court also felt they were awarded proper due process procedures.[58]

A Texas district court found the school board's action of suspension because of long and unkept hair clearly necessary to protect the school atmosphere. In *Pritchard* v. *Spring Branch Independent School District* the court used the explanation of disruption when it confirmed the school officials' reasons for insisting that all male students are responsible for suitably groomed hair.[59]

In *Brownlee* v. *Bradley County, Tennessee Board of Education* a Tennessee district court concluded that the school had carried the substantial burden of justifying the regulation of male students' hair. The school had argued that students with long hair are discipline problems and often do poorly academically.[60]

The above cases on substantive rights for students show little consistency in their reasoning and logic. The breadth of interpretation has been limited solely by the discretion of the presiding judge in every court, with substantial influence being exerted by state and community atmosphere. This, coupled with the realization that each case constitutes a somewhat factually different situation and consequently can be dealt with somewhat differently, makes one aware of the tremendous difficulties arising from the application of substantive rights for students and the emergence of case law.

It should be noted that the terms "disturbance" and "disruption" play a significant role in the cases concerning substantive rights. As stated previously, the application and influence of this term on a case will depend on the particular atmosphere of the court and the particular facts of the case. The burden of proof concerning the fairness and reasonableness of rules and regulations, however, belongs to the school, with the thoroughness of the proof again depending on the requirements of the individual court.

Until and unless the Supreme Court hands down some clear decisions regarding student rights, the lower courts will continue to handle the cases in the same apparently capricious manner as in the past. It seems inevitable, however, that within a few years the Supreme Court will grant certiorari to a student rights case, the outcome of which will be in direct correlation to the atmosphere and tenor of the Court at the time of the hearing.

## Summary

The movement for student rights has entered the arena of the legal system, where it is seeking court sanction for procedural and substantive rights in schooling. Court systems across the country are not taking any consistent approach to this new student litigation; some decisions reflect optimism for the student movement while others give firm support to school authority. As of now, there appear to be no definitive legal answers to the issues concerning rights of students.

Substantive rights of students are those which are the least clearly defined by the legal system. Freedom of expression through symbols such as buttons and arm bands, student newspapers, and control over one's personal appearance has been recognized in some courts and in some cases, but still awaits total legal sanction. The problem lies in the definition of the term "disruption." Although the term is loosely used in courts by lawyers and judges, the final determination of its meaning has not been legally defined. As a result of its vague interpretations, answers on issues of substantive rights still remain unclear to students and school administrators and confusing for lawyers and judges.

Procedural rights have survived the legal system with a higher degree of success than have substantive rights; they tend, that is, to be more explicitly defined. This is especially true in the juvenile court system. Under the Constitution the child is now entitled to adequate notice of charges, the right to counsel, the right to cross-examine witnesses, and the privilege against self-incrimination. The juvenile courts have definite guidelines to follow; strictness of procedural rules is not, however, as well defined for the schools. Educational institutions are responsible for only a small portion of the procedures required of the juvenile court systems, and this portion is mostly confined to disciplinary actions concerning suspension or expulsion. When school authorities resort to such action, case law seems to indicate that adequate notice of charges and an informal hearing are sufficient requirements of due process. Case law also requires that school officials have justified reasons for making rules and regulations. This last requirement is often too broadly used by schools, courts, students, lawyers, and judges. Therefore procedural guidelines for school authorities remain incomplete.

Not only are the substantive and procedural issues of student rights inadequately handled by the courts; there also remain a considerable number of untouched issues that need to be answered legally before the movement for student rights ends. There are, for example, procedural issues concerning school authority over the student. The right against unlawful search and seizure is presently a disputed area; to date there is little case law on this subject, and all existing decisions uphold the right of the school official to open a student's locker. (The Supreme Court has refused to grant certiorari to any case concerning search of lockers. The legal reasoning used in upholding the right of schools to search lockers argues that the lockers are not assigned for the students' exclusive possession and use.) Along with the need for litigation regarding search of lockers is the need for case law clarifying the meanings of reasonable rules and regulations and describing definite guidelines and requirements for notice of charges and school disciplinary hearings.

The area of substantive rights of students has been barely touched by sound and decisive case law. The whole issue of whether school officials can regulate the appearance of students is inadequately answered, especially on the question of proper dress codes, not to mention policies about hair styles. The right to privacy has not come before the courts yet; nor have cases concerning the right of a student to have access to his records.

Some demands by students are far from being raised successfully in the court systems, including the constitutional right to an education, the right to an education appropriate for the individual, or the right to be taught in school one's constitutional rights. The issue of whether compulsory state education is constitutional has not been challenged; the same is true for a number of other such laws on curriculum and attendance.

It is evident that children do not leave their rights at the schoolhouse gate, but it is unclear what those rights actually are.

## Notes

1. *In re Gault*, 387 U.S. 1, 5 (1967).
2. *Ibid.*, 6.
3. *Ibid.*
4. *Ibid.*, 18.
5. *Ibid.*, 21.
6. *Ibid.*, 22.
7. *Ibid.*

8. *Ibid.*, 24.

9. *Ibid.*, 33.

10. *Ibid.*, 26.

11. *Ibid.*, 41.

12. *Ibid.*, 56.

13. *Ibid.*, 47, 51, 55.

14. *Ibid.*, 58.

15. *Kent* v. *United States*, 383 U.S. 541, 552 (1966).

16. *Ibid.*, 561.

17. *In re Winship*, 397 U.S. 358, 363 (1970).

18. *Ibid.*, 365.

19. *Ibid.*, 367.

20. *Dixon* v. *Alabama State Board of Education*, 294 F. 2d 150, 152 (5th Cir. 1961).

21. *Ibid.*, 158, 159.

22. *Vought* v. *Van Buren Public Schools*, 306 F. Supp. 1388, 1393 (E.D. Mich. 1969).

23. *Ibid.*

24. *Sullivan* v. *Houston Independent School District*, 307 F. Supp. 1328, 1343 (S.D. Texas 1969).

25. *Ibid.*, 1346.

26. *Hobson* v. *Bailey*, 309 F. Supp. 1393, 1401 (W.D. Tenn. 1970).

27. *Madera* v. *Board of Education of the City of New York*, 386 F. 2d 788, 782 (2nd Cir. 1967).

28. *Burnside* v. *Byars*, 363 F. 2d 744, 746 (5th Cir. 1966).

29. *Ibid.*, 748.

30. *Ibid.*, 748, 749.

31. *Tinker* v. *Des Moines Independent Community School District*, 393 U.S. 503, 507-508 (1969).

32. *Ibid.*, 508.

33. *Ibid.*, 514.

34. *Ibid.*, 508-509.

35. *Ibid.*

36. *Ibid.*, 511.

37. *Ibid.*, 513.

38. *Ibid.*, 511.

39. *Ibid.*, 514.

40. *Ibid.*, 511.

41. *Ibid.*, 513.

42. *Ibid.*, 515.

43. *Ginsberg* v. *New York*, 390 U.S. 629 (1963).

44. *Aguirre* v. *Tahoka Independent School District*, 311 F. Supp. 644 (N.D. Texas 1970).

45. *Scoville* v. *Board of Education of Joliet Township High School District 204*, III, 425 F. 2d 10 (7th Cir. 1970).

46. *Bannister* v. *Paradis*, 316 F. Supp. 185 (D.N. Hamp. 1970).

47. *Richards* v. *Thurston* 424 F. 2d 1281, 1282 (1st Cir. 1970).

48. *Ibid.*, 1285.

49. *Sims* v. *Colfax Community School District*, 307 F. Supp. 485, 486 (S.D. Iowa 1970).

50. *Ibid.*, 487.

51. *Ibid.*, 488.

52. *Parker* v. *Fry*, 323 F. Supp. 728, 739 (E.D. Ark. 1971).

53. *Guzick* v. *Drebus*, 305 F. Supp. 472, 479 (N.D. Ohio 1969).

54. *Butts* v. *Dallas Independent School District*, 306 F. Supp. 488, 491 (N.D. Texas 1969).

55. *Hernandez* v. *School District Number One, Denver, Colorado*, 315 F. Supp. 289 (D. Colorado 1970).

56. *Schwartz* v. *Schuker*, 298 F. Supp. 238, 240 (E.D. New York 1969).

57. *Baker* v. *Downey City Board of Education*, 307 F. Supp. 517 (C.D. Calif. 1969).

58. *Jackson* v. *Dorrier*, 424 F. 2d 213 (6th Cir. 1970).

59. *Pritchard* v. *Spring Branch Independent School District*, 308 F. Supp. 570 (S.D. Texas 1970).

60. *Brownlee* v. *Bradley County, Tennessee Board of Education*, 311 F. Supp. 1360 (E.D. Tenn. 1970).

# 7. Trends, Conflicts, and Implications in Student Rights

*Bonnie Cook Freeman*

This chapter is divided into three parts. The first summarizes and synthesizes recent significant case law in a number of important areas of student-teacher conduct and life. The second part identifies and illuminates several broader trends and implications that seem to follow from both the cases discussed in the first part and the larger legal, social, and historical processes that have been treated in the earlier chapters of this book. Part three examines briefly the nature of policymaking concerning student rights and the basic question of who makes that policy.

We do not consider this essay to be a convenient guide to how much the schools can get away with without really trying. We hope, rather, that a greater awareness of the legal and constitutional issues that are involved in the school-pupil relationship will encourage educators to be more circumspect in their actions and more diligent in their protection of the liberties of their students. Furthermore, our emphasis on the courts does not reflect a belief that they are the best or most appropriate forum for the resolution of educational issues. We trust that this essay will help both teachers and students to exercise the informed restraint and reasonableness in their interactions that will lead to nonjudicial solutions to their problems.

## Recent Developments in School Law

In recent years there have been two major developments that have led the courts slowly to abandon the norm of judicial noninterference in educational matters and to begin to create a body of case law in the area. While this process is more fully described in Chapter 6, we can briefly summarize it here. The first development was the rise of dissidence and protest in the universities (on such matters as free speech, the war, and university governance) that led to an atmosphere of general questioning of authority and to the emergence of numerous court cases. At first there was no commensurate growth of protest or case law at the secondary school level, but, as the courts began to review school conflicts, the whole issue of the rights of children was inevitably raised.

The second important development that has led to the intervention of the judiciary into school affairs was the application of the requirements of due process to juveniles. The authors of Chapter 6 have already discussed the *Gault* decision in great detail. All we need do here is point out that once the precedent of *Gault* was established in juvenile court proceedings it was only a matter of time before the claim for constitutional protection would be made by students being disciplined by school administrators.

In this chapter we want to discuss some of the major developments in the law as it bears on particular aspects of school life. Descending from the general and broad-ranging observations of the last chapter, we wish to explore the legal context within which such routine and everyday matters as discipline and evaluation take place.

We should stress the fact that the law in many of these areas is quite undeveloped and sketchy. Those cases which do exist tend to be ambiguous and unclear. The courts have preferred when possible to dispense with cases on the basis of legal technicalities or questions of fact. There are few clear trends to be found in the field of school law. Cases have been decided both for and against students, depending on the particular facts of the case and the idiosyncratic characteristics of the particular court that had jurisdiction in the matter. Because of this, administrators should be very cautious in relying on any conclusions drawn in this section as legal justification for their own behavior.

There are a number of good, detailed summaries of cases relevant to the issue of student rights.[1] They have given more attention to the facts involved in particular cases and the legal technicalities at issue. In this chapter we have thought it wise neither to try to duplicate nor improve upon their efforts. Instead of summarizing every relevant case and describing each particular behavior that has been prescribed or prohibited to either students or teachers, we have chosen only those cases which seem to raise important substantive and process issues of lasting consequence.

## Freedom of Expression

Three basic types of issues may be considered under the rubric "Freedom of Expression": verbal, symbolic, and written.

### Verbal Expression

It appears that the traditional forms of speech that have been protected by the First Amendment for adults will also be guaranteed to children.[2] Because the language of the pertinent opinions is vague and because the legal reasoning employed in them has varied considerably from jurisdiction to jurisdiction, there are still considerable grounds for disagreement on the issue.

In one instance a court took the stance that if the state abridges student expression, the interest of the state must be "compelling" or "fundamental and substantial," and that the regulation must be "reasonable."[3] It is the exact definitions of these terms that is in debate. In other instances there has been only minimal demonstration on the part of the school that a clear regulation existed, that it was required for the proper operation of the school, and that the speech was disruptive and in violation of the regulation, and yet the court has found in favor of the school.[4]

Although the *Tinker* case did not deal explicitly with verbal communication, it did refer to the issue and it is considered an important precedent on the matter. As the Court saw it the key was whether a particular expression of opinion is a right if conveyed "without materially and substantially interfering with the appropriate discipline in the operation of the school and without colliding with the rights of others."[5] The schools traditionally have had the authority to take such measures as were necessary to ensure the orderly operation of the educational process. In this instance the Court concluded that the school had not demonstrated that the wearing of black arm bands in protest against the war in Southeast Asia had actually

interfered with the learning process or that such a danger could be
rightfully anticipated. The Court felt, therefore, that school authorities cannot prohibit the speech or expression of students for reasons
of "undifferentiated fear or apprehension of disturbance . . . ."[6]

## Symbolic Expression

Certain symbolic actions such as the wearing of arm bands to
protest the Vietnam war and the wearing of political buttons have
been found at times to be constitutionally protected forms of free
speech.[7] But not all forms of such behavior are considered "speech"
and therefore within the ambit of the First Amendment and the
"preferred position"[8] of First Amendment guarantees. As one court
noted, "as the non-verbal message becomes less distinct the justification for the substantial protections of the First Amendment becomes more remote."[9] Accordingly some hair styles and beards may
go unprotected, at least as forms of free expression. As is often the
case, one can see that once constitutional protection is admitted in
principle, the terms of the debate then become the "finer distinctions" of what discrete sets of acts, behaviors, and symbols will fall
within the "protected" category. One court contended, for example,
that a "symbol must symbolize a specific idea or viewpoint
. . . [and] unless it represents a particular idea it becomes meaningless."[10] Thus the possibilities for legal hairsplitting are almost end-
less, and for this reason alone one should be careful in drawing any
firm generalizations about this issue at this stage of the process.
Although all symbolic acts may not be interpreted as within the
protection of the First Amendment, these same issues (such as hair
style) may be considered and appealed as violations of the Fourth
Amendment or the Fourteenth Amendment.[11]

Whether speech-related activities such as stand-ins, sit-ins, and
walkouts may be regulated by the school, and to what extent, is not
yet clear.[12] The issue of disruption would, in general, form the basis
for a decision. One expert notes that "students may not deny ingress
and egress to public buildings, conduct sit-in demonstrations in
school buildings, or otherwise obstruct the normal operations or
functions of the school by use of violence, force, coercion, or
threat."[13]

## Written Expression

One of the most significant developments in recent years in the
schools has been the phenomenal growth of underground or

unauthorized student publications. Their appearance has occasioned most of the litigation involving freedom of written communication and of the press. Exact information is rather difficult to assemble, but Gaddy writes that "Estimates of the number of high school underground newspapers in the United States during the 1969-70 school year range from approximately 200 to 1000."[14] School officials have almost uniformly perceived these papers to be direct threats to their own authority and to the operation of the educational process and have therefore attempted to suppress or censor them. The most common instrument of suppression has been the application of sanctions on the students involved in the publication.

The courts have decided for students at times and for the schools at others; thus it is difficult to draw unambiguous conclusions in this area of school law. One court held that a student has the right to publish and distribute a newspaper on the school premises "so long as it does not unreasonably interfere with normal school activities."[15] The court argued that disagreement with the contents of a paper may not be considered as grounds on which to limit expression or otherwise interfere with its publication. The opinion noted, however, that while students may be permitted to publish such newspapers, the school administrators may regulate and enforce the time, place, and manner of distribution of the papers.

In another case recognizing the need of students to express their political views against the war in Vietnam and their difficulties with school officials who attempted to suppress them, the court granted relief to the students with this commentary: "The lawsuit arises at a time when many in the educational community oppose the actions of the young in securing a political voice. It would be both incongruous and dangerous for this court to hold that students who wish to express their views on matters intimately related to them, through traditionally accepted nondisruptive modes of communication, may be precluded from doing so by that same adult community."[16]

## Freedom of Personal Appearance

Although the Supreme Court has indicated its reluctance to grant certiorari in cases involving appearance codes because it is not considered pure speech,[17] this is the area of student rights in which the greatest number of suits have been brought.[18]

As Gaddy describes it: "Twentieth-century school officials, no less than seventeenth-century magistrates, consider personal appearance a matter of great importance. School officials generally regard dress and appearance regulations as essential for maintaining an educational atmosphere free of distraction or hazard to students."[19] Thus, in seeking to enforce conformity in dress and appearance school authorities have assumed that unconventional dress or "unusual" hair styles so upset normal routine and so distract other students that the only alternative is outright banning of such idiosyncratic expression.[20]

Contrary to the views of school officials, students have regarded these regulations about personal appearance and the sanctions for violations of these codes as an extreme restriction of their personal rights.[21] In the many cases that have been tried, two primary constitutional arguments have been employed on behalf of student rights. Both dress and hair styles have, for example, been found at times to be entitled to First Amendment protection as the symbolic communication of an idea.[22] The difficulty with this argument is that it does not "fit into the categories that have traditionally been accorded first amendment protection."[23] Thus, individual courts will have significant discretion in determining the boundaries of the principle. The second argument has been that one's appearance is a right of personal privacy. Choice of appearance is thought to be "something so intensely personal, so inherent in the fact of being an individual, that the state should not be able to deprive people of the power to make such decisions."[24]

Court cases have been decided for both the school board and the students on the issue of appearance. One court that affirmed the right of each person to determine his own hair style and personal appearance said that school regulations in this area were a violation of the equal protection clause of the Fourteenth Amendment: "the freedom here protected is the right to some breathing space for the individual into which the government may not intrude without carrying a substantial burden of justification."[25]

The question of who must carry the burden of proof—the school or the pupil—is fundamental in the determination of the boundaries of student rights. If the burden of proof passes from the student to the school, the categories of rights extended to children will probably expand. School officials could be required to argue the reasonableness of their regulations and demonstrate the relationship between the sanctioned behavior and the alleged deleterious consequences to the school. The court may, for example, request proof that a particular style caused disruption or distraction. School officials seem to believe that there is some relationship between distraction and low academic achievement. While this assumption may be accurate, it is difficult to demonstrate which specific things distract students because of the variability of other factors, including teacher ability and student intelligence.[26]

As the task of proof becomes more difficult, the school will be likely to retreat from restricting appearance. To the average pupil the question of dress codes appears to be the most salient of all issues concerning student rights.[27] For this reason alone, it might be wise for the higher echelons of the school hierarchy to take direct action to avoid the conflict inherent in costly litigation and disturbed students and parents. The New Jersey State Board of Education has taken the initiative by prohibiting local boards of education from interfering with the styles of dress and hair chosen by students for themselves. The board argued that the issues involved in keeping hair styles within the boundaries of current community standards were simply not of importance and relevance to the operation of the schools.[28]

## Privacy

Adults have rarely considered the child's need for privacy, simply assuming that minors require supervision. The concept of a right to privacy when related to children is, therefore, relatively novel, and the Fourth Amendment has had little application to the protection of children or against the invasion of their privacy.

The question of the child's right to privacy is greatly complicated by compulsory schooling laws. According to Bronars, the school requires enforced intimacy: "a body of students is compelled to come together in a designated place for a designated time for the purposes established by the adult members of a society."[29] It is usually assumed, furthermore, that children do or should enjoy group activities even if the established groups are not voluntary. Children who express a desire to be alone may be seen as maladjusted and antisocial.

Although children of all ages need privacy, the greatest number of cases so far have concerned children in their later school years.

There are an increasing number of requests being made for areas of privacy such as student lounges (comparable to those available for teachers) where a student may either sit quietly by himself or escape the scrutiny of his teachers at least temporarily. Beyond this, however, there is growing resentment over the more invidious techniques employed by the schools to gather information about their pupils.[30] While not all of the following practices have been the focus of court actions yet, all have been challenged as invasions of privacy: searches of lockers, desks, and persons; the use of personality tests; the misuse of student files; the violation of student-teacher confidences; the use of public-address systems for the purposes of listening in on classes; and the use of cameras, two-way mirrors, student informants, and police in the schools. There seem to be no limits to what some school officials will do to detect wrongdoing.

There are few clear judicial guidelines in this area; in the following discussion all conclusions and generalizations must be considered tentative. One commentator has summed up the situation in the following manner: "The rights of students pursuant to the Fourth Amendment are dormant as they have remained in a judicial[ly] abstract form and have not been converted into student rights . . . ."[31]

*Cases of Locker Search*

Cases of locker search have been appealed under the Fourth as well as the Fourteenth Amendment. Cases brought by students are normally based on the argument that lockers should be considered as "personal effects" and that the searches are often conducted without official warrants. School officials have contended that they are not governmental agents and that school lockers are not the exclusive possessions of the students. The disposition of such cases has been ambiguous, and procedures that are acceptable to the courts are yet to be clearly drawn. While many student appeals have been lost, because the courts made special considerations for educational institutions,[32] this is by no means a rule.

Because educational authorities who are found to have conducted illegal or unreasonable searches are subject to personal lawsuits, school administrators should take the precaution of informing themselves of the minimum standards of procedural safeguards prescribed by law rather than seeking reassurance from the cases that have supported teachers. Phay has suggested that the school can protect itself by conducting a search of a locker only when there is either a warrant, probable cause and circumstances that would frustrate the purpose of the search if a warrant were obtained, or a valid arrest.[33]

*Search of Students Themselves*

In the area of personal searches of students, officials should be even more cautious. Swift cites two cases in which teachers were successfully sued in civil courts for trespass.[34] A minimal precaution would be to request that a student empty his pockets rather than the school official doing it for him. A court has held, however, that when a student is believed to possess a concealed weapon a school official has the right to confiscate it.[35]

In the future, other questions under the rubric of privacy will have to be considered by both the courts and professional educators. The following include some of the questions in need of attention and clarification.

First, "Do scholars and scientists have the right to find out anything and everything about children's behavior?"[36] Scholars of child development have raised questions concerning the limitations necessary in their research so that their activities do not result in psychological or physiological harm or invade the child's private life.

Second, does the student ever have a right not to answer questions addressed to him or her? " . . . the expectation that children will reply when called upon is often transformed into the prescription that it is the child's duty to answer all questions put to him by adults."[37] Do the questions that teachers ask constitute invasions of privacy?

Third, "What is the meaning of confidential data in the school setting?"[38] How are children's disclosures of personal information to teachers in confidence to be regarded? The status of confidence in the professional relationship between teacher and child is not clear.

Fourth, do teachers have the right to administer drugs to children in order to control their behavior? It may be argued that such activities interfere with the civil liberties of children in that drugs deprive them of their own reasoning powers.[39]

*Off-Campus Rights*

The law is not clear as to whether school officials can discipline a student for activities carried on away from school and after regular school hours. This appears to be the area where school officials are on their weakest ground in attempting to regulate and punish the behavior of students. The two most traditional and most common justifications for school authority are seriously in question in off-campus cases. The judicial doctrine of in loco parentis is quite obviously of limited applicability since one would assume that when students are away from school the parents, rather than the schools, would take responsibility for the behavior of their children. The courts upheld an appeal against school officials who attempted to require pupils to remain at home and study between the hours of seven and nine in the evening because the rule interfered with parental authority.[40]

The second most powerful argument that school officials may employ is that their actions are necessary to ensure the efficient and uninterrupted operation of the educational process, but it is difficult to charge students with interference with the educational process when their activities take place away from the school.

A Westchester County court in striking down the suspension of two students who had been arrested on drug charges argued that the schools cannot suspend or expel students on the grounds "that they are insubordinate or disorderly; nor that their physical or mental condition endangers the health, safety or morals of themselves or other minors."[41] Exactly what grounds, if any, would be sufficient to justify the disciplining of students for off-campus activities is not clear. The dangers of double jeopardy suggest that the schools should exercise great restraint in such cases. The American Civil Liberties Union holds the position that the school is never justified in punishing a student for something for which he receives or which is subject to civil sanctions: "A student who violates any law risks the legal penalties prescribed by civil authorities. He should not be placed in jeopardy at school for an offense which is not concerned with the educational institution." [42]

### Discipline and Punishment of Students: Authority to Punish

While the principal or teacher in charge of a public school is subordinate to the school board or board of education of his district or city, and must enforce rules and regulations adopted by the board for the government of the school, and execute all its lawful orders in that behalf, he does not derive all his power and authority in the school and over his pupils from the affirmative action of the board. He stands for the time being in loco parentis to his pupils, and because of the relation he must necessarily exercise authority over them in many things concerning which the board may have remained silent. In the school, as in the family, there exist on the part of the pupils the obligations of obedience to lawful commands, subordination, civil deportment, respect for the rights of other pupils and fidelity to duty. These obligations are inherent in any proper school system, and constitute, so to speak, the common law of the school. Every pupil is presumed to know the law, and is subject to it, whether it has or has not been reenacted by the district board in the form of written rules and regulations. Indeed it would seem impossible to frame rules which would cover all cases of insubordination and all acts of vicious tendencies which the teacher is liable to encounter daily and hourly.[43]

For years the sentiments expressed in the above opinion have been thought to be the law on school matters. Operating under the principles of quasi-judicial discretion and in loco parentis,[44] most school officials have believed themselves to have a wide field of discretion in disciplining disobedient students for their own welfare. The legal test has been, in general, whether a reasonably knowledgeable and careful parent might act in the same way. That conventional wisdom is being increasingly challenged today. Most of the cases involving discipline may be considered under the headings of corporal punishment and suspension and expulsion.

The several states differ in legal rights they expressly give teachers to inflict "reasonable" corporal punishment on students.[45] Although nearly all states have some statutes relating to this, it is interesting that "between 1958 and 1963, Virginia, California, North Carolina, South Dakota, and Nevada enacted laws expressly permitting the use of corporal punishments in public schools. Newcomers are Georgia and Michigan in 1964, and Ohio in 1965. New Jersey is the only state which by statute forbids corporal punishment in all schools or educational institutions, public or private."[46] But even the New Jersey law allows exceptions in certain situations.

Whether the relation of in loco parentis exists depends on the facts of each individual situation.[47] Although differing views continue in this area, the majority view that courts seem to be following is that for a person to be found within the bounds of in loco parentis when inflicting punishment he "must not exceed the bounds of moderation and reasonableness and that any act found to be cruel, merciless, unreasonable or immoderate, exceeds the privilege and will subject the actor to liability."[48]

Case law in this area indicates that school officials have been supported generally, with the child receiving the worst of the two worlds as noted by the Supreme Court in the *Kent* opinion: he gets neither the protection accorded to adults nor the solicitous care and regenerative treatment postulated for children.[49]

Although the law on corporal punishment is still largely undeveloped, it no doubt will receive greater scrutiny in the future. Either as in loco parentis is diminished in its thrust, or as the right of parents to corporal punishment is challenged (particularly in relation to child battery cases), corporal punishment in the schools is likely to be far less acceptable.

Among the penalties available to school officials in disciplining students, the one most frequently challenged in lawsuits is exclusion from school by either suspension or expulsion.[50] The supposed educational philosophy behind this practice has been that the school knows best what to do with a wayward student. Although school officials have viewed suspensions and expulsion as both treatment and punishment, in court they tend to stress the former aspect.[51] Critics have argued that these methods are used vindictively and arbitrarily to punish and harass students, intimidate parents, and to rid the school of people labeled "undesirable."

The matter of expulsion is one area of school law in which the courts have not been reluctant to intervene—a reflection of the potentially grave consequences flowing from expulsion. Since termination could lead to limiting one's opportunities for occupational success, "the courts closely examine the grounds on which this particular penalty may be based."[52] The courts have insisted that in this instance the burden of proof is on the school to show that such an extreme action was appropriate. While few states legally set out the procedure to be followed by a school administrator or school board before it expels a student, the attention of the courts has tended to focus on the question of the process by which sanctions for the infraction of rules and regulations are brought to bear on the student.[53] The courts have held in general that a student cannot be expelled or suspended for a long duration without due process of law, but we are far from an understanding of exactly what steps might constitute due process.

The Supreme Court in *Hannah* v. *Larche* (363 US 420, 442 [1960]) said of due process: "Its exact boundaries are undefinable and its content varies according to specific factual contexts.... Whether the Constitution requires that a particular right obtain in a specific proceeding depends upon a complexity of factors. The nature of the alleged right involved, the nature of the proceeding, and the possible burden on that proceeding are all considerations."[54] The nature of due process when applied to students is even more in question.[55] Phay has concluded that the barest minimum of procedures that can be expected to be mentioned by the courts include: there must be an adequate notice of the charges against the student and the nature of the evidence to support those charges; a hearing must be held unless the right is waived by the student; and any action taken by a school official should occur only when it is supported by the evidence.[56]

The following is a concise summary, drawn mostly from the work of Phay, of the procedural requirements in disciplinary proceedings that have been found by the courts to constitute due process in school matters. It is important to note the tentative and artificial nature of these requirements in that they are taken from many cases, and a particular court might not choose to apply all of them in a specific case.

A. Specific rules on student conduct.
   1. Rules must be explicit, clear, detailed, and publicized so that it is understood what conduct is prohibited.
B. Notice.
   1. A statement detailing the conduct subjecting one to expulsion must be given. (See A, above.)
   2. A written statement to the student and his or her parents explaining the violation of a specific rule and giving evidence that the violation was committed is necessary.
   3. Some time must elapse before the hearing.
   4. A student must be informed of his procedural rights before a hearing.
   5. To waive a formal hearing, a form must be available and signed by the student.
C. Hearing.
   1. It must be conducted in accord with the basic principles of due process of law.
   2. The student must have the names of witnesses against him and an oral or written report on the facts to which each witness testifies.
   3. The student should be given the opportunity to present his own defense and offer his own witnesses or affadavits.

4. The student has the right to an impartial tribunal.
D. Right to counsel.
   1. The law is too unsettled to permit a guideline as yet. In *Madera* the process for expelling a student was defined as a guidance conference to help the student and therefore did not require counsel. (See Chapter 6 of this book for details of *Madera*.) Future cases will be contesting this legal point.
E. Inspection of evidence.
   1. Phay notes that he knows of no case where a student's right to inspect evidence was an issue, but he believes that the right to do so should be affirmed.
F. Trier of fact.
   1. The student has the right to an impartial trier under the Sixth Amendment.
   2. "Since a disciplinary hearing is a civil proceeding, reviewable in a court of law, the constitutional requirement of a jury trial has no application."
   3. Although a jury is not required, Phay recommends a hearing panel consisting of a teacher, a parent, and a student to serve as a trier of fact. In the past the principal has played the prosecutional and decision-making roles. In playing both of these roles, plus likely direct involvement with the case, the principal may be biased, and a student should be entitled to a different trier of fact. The student would, however, first have to demonstrate bias.
G. Witnesses.
   1. "In criminal prosecution and in most administrative proceedings, the defendant may confront and cross-examine witnesses, and compel witnesses to attend the trial or hearing."
   2. The student has the right to his own witnesses, and witnesses should be compelled to attend the hearing.
   3. There is some question whether confrontation and cross-examination are within the rights of the student. Courts in college cases have found that it is not a right of due process. Many colleges and secondary schools do, however, permit this right.
H. Self-incrimination.
   1. In juvenile court proceedings a minor is given the protection against self-incrimination. (See the elaborate discussion of the *Gault* case in Chapter 6 of this book.)

2. Disciplinary proceedings at the college and school levels are perceived as administrative proceedings that are thought not to be sufficiently criminal in nature to require protection under the Fifth Amendment. (This issue of self-incrimination particularly will be raised where a student is accused of violating a criminal law, which is also a school offense. Phay claims that protection against self-incrimination is not a basis for postponing an expulsion hearing until the criminal trial is completed.)

3. A *Miranda*-type warning (a reminder to suspects of crime that they may refuse to make self-incriminatory answers to questions and may have the assistance of a lawyer in answering questions) is not applicable to a school investigation of alleged misconduct.[57]

4. Further court challenges will probably occur over the legality of self-incrimination in school proceedings.

Until now the courts have required the rights of due process only in "serious" discipline cases involving long-term suspensions and expulsions[58] and have followed a self-imposed rule of noninterference in cases involving "less extreme" sanctioning of students, such as the prohibition of extracurricular activity and academic failing.[59] While it is likely that the expulsion of a student for getting married might be overturned, for example, it is unlikely that the court would consider prohibition of participation in extracurricular activities as unreasonable.

It is clear that in many cases minor disciplinary measures are the first in a chain of events that eventually leads to more extreme measures. If a student is suspended for a short period of time without the benefit of due process, the chain of events is set into motion. During suspension a student is not fulfilling curriculum requirements. Because there is usually prohibition against the student making up work during this time, he receives failures for not having done the work. The consequence is not only suspension but lower grades and the difficulty of picking up the material covered in class, which leads to low grades on the next round of tests. Because sanctions are not always "severe," this does not mean that they cannot be abused (harassment of students), arbitrarily determined, and incur cumulative and interlocking deleterious consequences for a student. One commentator has noted that "a sanction no matter how slight it may seem is, by its very nature, subject to abuse in particular applications."[60] It would seem, therefore, that the courts should review their concept of less extreme sanctions and extend due process at each stage, particularly where the initial acts set off these processes.

*Compulsory Attendance*

A law requiring that children attend school until a particular age is a restriction on the rights of the child and of the parents since it is one of the few instances in which the government intervenes between the parent and the child.[61] On a number of occasions suits have been brought challenging the right of the state to require attendance in school, but none has been successful (with the exception of the qualified decision concerning the Amish).[62]

One of the few minor exceptions to this general requirement is that which allows children to attend private rather than public schools. State statutes that have attempted to require attendance at public schools only have been overturned repeatedly. Edwards concludes that "it is the policy of the state that children be educated, not that they be educated in any particular way or in any particular place."[63] The courts have held, however, that the state has the authority to regulate those private educational institutions and to set minimum standards they must satisfy.[64]

It seems likely that future challenges to the principle of the state's right to require attendance at either public schools or state-regulated institutions will come in three areas. The first challenge may focus on the state's use of age as the determinant of one's susceptibility to control rather than educational attainment. Individuals may challenge this law on the basis of its deprivation of their liberty.

A more serious line of attack is likely to come from sectarian groups such as the Amish who recently won the right to terminate their children's education before the compulsory age was reached.[65] In deciding such cases, the courts are asked to make the difficult choice between the parents' right to guide the religious and secular education of their children and to pass on and protect a precious heritage and the child's right to have an education equal to that of everyone else. In the Amish case the Supreme Court held that the state's right to compel education was not absolute. Although the case was decided in favor of the Amish, the challenge was not an effective blow to compulsory education because the particular group in question was explicitly made an exception to the rule on the basis of interference with freedom of religion.

A third but less visible challenge to compulsory education is the trend to abandon the public school system and the established private schools and create alternatives such as "free schools." A number of radical reformers have argued that the bureaucratic interests of the educational establishment come into conflict with the education and personal needs of the individual students.

Plasco has identified the school's interests as the "efficient, effective, and orderly conduct of the public school system. Conformity, discipline, and the enforcement of moral and political values are said to be of primary concern."[66] It is questionable whether the movement toward innovative schools will continue, but the efforts in this direction have certainly been noticeable.

Other attempts at innovation have occurred within the public school system. One school within the system may, for example, be identified as experimental. The incorporation of such a school within the public school system provides an outlet for the pressures on school officials as well as for parents and students unhappy with the conventional system. Furthermore, "troublemakers" are removed from the regular schools and placed in an "educational system" supposedly more suited to their individual needs; this is done without effecting the routines of the regular educational establishment. Because such a school does skim off those who would pressure the entire school bureaucracy to change, this same institution becomes the very mechanism that allows the educational structure to continue largely untouched. Thus the private free school and the public experimental school remain at worst an ambiguous challenge to compulsory public education and at best a slightly effective but questionable attempt to change the existing educational structure.

### Testing and Tracking

In our society the use of intelligence and scholastic achievement testing has developed as an ostensibly unbiased means of measuring school outputs and of classifying students. The so-called objective instruments of testing achievement encourage "the illusion that promotion and rewards are distributed fairly."[67] Because the educational bureaucracy accepts the results of intelligence tests with few reservations, those results determine to a great extent which track students will be placed in, the methods by which students will be "educated," and the likelihood that a student will go to college.

In addition, the intelligence test can become a clinical instrument that serves to stigmatize individuals, some of whom may be quite well adapted to their environment.[68] Scores on intelligence tests often determine whether a child will be diagnosed as retarded (a label empirically associated with low-income groups and blacks), and retardation is believed to be primarily a physiological condition often resulting from brain damage. Once labeled retarded, a child is shunted off into separate classes and put into special educational programs. All his subsequent treatment serves to confirm for the child that he is in fact retarded and suffering from "special problems."

Some evidence suggests that the "public school is a mechanism which actually destroys whatever ability the child had when he entered the school."[69] One such example has been noted by Roberts:

As pressures for conformity in school increased, the children's ability to think creatively decreased . . . . Research conducted . . . in Harlem schools showed "non-achieving" Negro children obtained higher scores on tests of creativity than those scores of children who were "achieving"—by the school's standard . . . . Potential to learn is affected not only by the culture in which the child is raised . . . it is also affected by the school and teacher who may, through inhibiting procedures, decrease the child's capacity to use his learning potential. [70]

As the normative as well as scientific questions of testing and tracking have become a public issue, a small number of parents have begun to seek legal remedies. But few courts have ventured into these muddy waters. It is, however, necessary to discuss one landmark case. In *Hobson* v. *Hanson* Judge Skelly Wright found that the ability tests used by the schools were unfair because they resulted in a large proportion of black children being placed in the lower tracks, which prepared them for the less desirable positions in life. He accordingly ordered the abolition of the track system.[71] Wright wrote that the tracking system lacked a rationale and subsequently led to unequal protection under the law. The case is important not only because of its finding, but because of the nature of the considerations: "*Hobson* was the first time a court considered the testing question on its merits, looked at the theory, looked at the data, and found discrimination."[72] While one can only speculate about the long-term ramifications of the decision, its implications are clear. Other courts may request school boards to come up with a "satisfactory" justification other than the intelligence test for the separation of students into tracks[73] or they may demand that educators prove that they can accurately assess each student's ability to learn. According to one opinion in the *Connecticut Law Review*, "If, however, the school officials were unable to effectuate this assessment with a high degree of accuracy, then according to the court, the type of discrimination being exercised by the schools in track assignments was repugnant to the student's constitutional right to equal educational opportunities."[74]

Where serious consequences may follow from labeling a child as "special" or as "retarded," the labeling process itself is going to be subject to the requirements of due process. In one Pennsylvania case, the court ordered "that notice and the opportunity must be extended before the educational assignment of any retarded child or any child thought to be retarded may be changed: And notice and the same opportunity to be heard must be extended automatically every two years thereafter, and upon the request of the parent every year."[75]

This new requirement may also become applicable to the tracking route as well. Tracking has occurred sometimes in the past without the teacher consulting with the student, and shifts have been made subtly by switching a student from one track to another without parental or pupil knowledge.[76] It is possible that, under the constitutional principles of the right to an education and due process of law, educational administrators either may take the initiative to open up their decision-making processes and allow greater input from pupils and their parents in decisions affecting them or they may face the possibility of going to court and subsequently being denied the authority to process students through the tracking slots.

The question of external testing should also be raised here. Recently there has been much criticism directed at the Scholastic Aptitude Test (SAT) of the Educational Testing Service because the tests are relied on heavily as a basis for college admissions—the next step up the educational hierarchy—and because they may be invalid tests of aptitude. It has been charged, furthermore, that the tests have a built-in racial bias. So far there appear to be few, if any, legal remedies against SAT. One source, however, has suggested that state institutions of higher education have a constitutional duty not to impose racial barriers to admission and that "any entrance requirement that discriminates according to race rather than ability is invalid as a violation of the equal protection clause of the Fourteenth Amendment."[77]

*Records*

"Perhaps no workers exchange more information about people than those employed in education."[78] Using a number of criteria, educators place their students in a wide variety of categories. These categories, which are supposed to be of a general and administrative nature, are designed to describe the student's relationship to the school's functioning. Categories such as "slow learner," "exceptional student," "underachiever," and "overachiever" are derived (in theory at least) from such objective sources as achievement and ability tests and are supposed to aid the school in bringing the most appropriate form of educational response to the students within each category. But such labels have invidious and unintended consequences. Because of the permanence of the school record, they become lasting stigmata. Subsequent behavior can alter them only marginally or not at all since teachers act on such labels to a great extent, children tend to internalize the labels and incorporate them into their own self-images, and the labels influence the child's perception of reality and even that reality itself.[79]

In the past students have had little control over the items entered into their records. School officials have assumed that student records, maintained and compiled by a particular school district at public expense, are the property of the school district.[80] The problem, as in all areas of school law, is that there are few administrative guidelines concerning student records. Only twenty states have issued uniform rules; thirty-one states have no rules at all at the state level. Because policy regarding records is delegated to local boards, which seldom put their administrative guidelines into writing, ad hoc decision making results.[81]

The use and compilation of student records have conventionally been considered a positive contribution to a pupil's attempts to achieve his future goals, such as college or a job.[82] More recently much attention has been given to the possibilities of harmful use of records.[83] Cicourel and Kituse consider some of the possible negative consequences of the use of school records.

Should he seek part time employment after school hours or apply for a job or military service upon leaving the school, the student's record may be used as the basis for unfavorable or qualified letters of recommendation to prospective employers. The student's record may be reviewed when police direct inquiries to the school about some "delinquent" actions or his family or peer group may learn about his record when school personnel contact them in the course of investigating cases of stealing, fighting, smoking, vandalism etc.[84]

Depending on the variety of professionals employed in a school (psychiatrists, pscyhologists, counselors, teachers)'and the number of the various professionals, the nature and type of information added to a record could be very harmful. Records include such things as progress reports, grades, intelligence test results, achievement test scores, medical records, psychological and psychiatric reports, guidance notes, evaluations, and "delinquent" reports. The essential questions on this issue are whether some of this "information" may not develop into an invidious label and whether the distinction between "fact and opinion" can be made. A student who complains about school policies may find himself described as immature, psychologically maladjusted, or disruptive with delinquent tendencies. Those who have been particularly active in student rights causes within their school will possibly be intentional targets for such descriptions. School authorities will, at the very least, enter a report of the student's part in an event such as a demonstration. In one case where parents attempted to prevent the communication of such facts to schools, colleges, and employers by initiating a legal suit, the court held that "school officials have the right and . . . a duty to record and to communicate true factual information about their students."[85]

Another controversy over records involves who has the right to see them. School board members apparently have automatic access to them on request.[86] Cicourel and Kituse suggest that information about pupils considered "delinquent" is routinely exchanged between the police and the school;[87] these exchanges have serious consequences for the adolescents involved. But, for parents and the pupils themselves, gaining access has been difficult. At this time no clear legal principle has emerged on the question. According to Butler, recent cases have sustained the right of parents and students to examine their personal files.[88] The crucial criteria in the judicial determination of these cases have been whether a person can demonstrate a need to see the records. Butler notes that "in the absence of constitutional, legislative, or administrative rules, a parent has the right under common law to inspect public school records of his child because of his parental interest maintained in the parent-child relationship." But he also notes that "third parties may establish an interest in student records by statute, board policy, or under common law practices."[89] Cases in the future could involve some serious questions over the exchanges of information between school officials and the police. The courts must define principles to balance the right of inspection against the claim of confidentiality.

While the courts have indicated that information may be placed in a student's file as long as it is truthful, they have not established criteria for deciding what is a fact. Is, for example, a psychological evaluation discussing an Oedipus complex a matter of fact? Without access to their records, how are students to know that false or misleading data have been compiled? Once the student is satisfied that his file contains untruthful information he must request that the courts expunge the offending data, unless the school voluntarily withdraws them, or request the right to insert a response to information in his file.

Because, as Butler notes, student records are both private (in that the information about an individual is highly personal) and public (in that they are compiled and maintained by public officials), the issue of their availability for inspection will continue to be controversial.[90] If the cases should weigh in favor of access by parents and pupils (which, incidentally, could lead to parents seeking scores en masse to see how well their children are educated and then attempting to make boards of education accountable for low scores), school officials will undoubtedly try to protect themselves. One likely adaptive response is the creation of a new system of recording, one that will avoid the issue but not settle the conflict. This new system of record keeping "would separate the information collected about a student into categories depending on the extent of confidentiality."[91] The less confidential information would be available for general use. Those files with more confidential information, including disciplinary measures, intelligence test scores, and so forth, would not be made available.[92]

## Freedom to Learn

The question of student rights is not normally thought to encompass matters of curriculum and instruction. This is reflected both by the neglect of scholars interested in the rights of children and by the paucity of case law that has arisen from challenges to curriculum offerings.[93]

No doubt the most widely publicized and controversial issue dealing with what is taught in the school concerns the doctrine of evolution. In *Epperson* v. *Arkansas* the Supreme Court concluded that "The State's undoubted right to prescribe the curriculum for its public schools does not carry with it the right to prohibit, on pain of criminal penalty, the teaching of scientific theory or doctrine . . . ."[94] Darwin's theory has been the source of continued bitter controversy for many years; it seems probable that the variety and intensity of conflict over curriculum and instruction will increase in the future. And it is likely that the debate will be carried on in terms of the rights of children to learn.

Litigation will probably arise in several areas. First, there may be challenges to the curriculum that charge that it is outdated and has failed to keep up with the growth of knowledge. Complaints may be made that courses are not "relevant" to the world as children know it, and, therefore that they do not properly prepare the child for adulthood. Second, there will surely be conflicts over the degree to which it is proper to allow controversial public issues into the school, either through classroom discussion led by the teacher or outside speakers. Schools have traditionally thrown open their doors to religious leaders and ultrapatriotic organizations while strictly excluding persons who represent anti-war organizations, civil rights groups, or gay liberation. The legal basis for this kind of discrimination is not clear, and it could be argued that such a practice denies the student the opportunity to be exposed to a variety of viewpoints. Third, teachers may be accused of giving biased interpretations in their classrooms. It has been common in the past for instructors to be dismissed for being politically suspect (usually to the left). In the future students may complain about sexist or racist classes. One can only wait to see what legal remedies the courts will afford in these matters. Finally, it seems possible that the practice of restricting certain courses to members of one sex only (home economics or auto mechanics, for example) may come under increasing attack.

## Trends and Implications

In this section we will discuss in broad and analytical terms some of the more significant conclusions that we have drawn about the question of student rights, both from the cases outlined and the long-range historical and social developments identified in earlier chapters.

## The Phenomenology of Public Issues

The emergence of particular social problems as issues of public concern is a sociopolitical phenomenon. No necessary relationship exists between the intrinsic value of an idea and its ability to find a place for itself on the public agenda. Issues or "problems" arise as the result of the convergence of a number of social processes at a particular time. They are partly a reflection of semiautonomous changes in the societal context and partly a reflection of the power distribution within the society. Those social groups which have the resources to make their needs or interests known will do so. Those groups which lack the necessary resources, whose problems are so serious that they cannot be safely ignored by those in power, will see their problems become topics of public debate.

Becoming an issue is, however, only the first step in the process. A problem may be perceived differently by various groups in the society, each seeking to define the problem in the manner most congenial to its own interests. Since the definition of the issue largely determines the type of alternative solutions that may legitimately or reasonably be brought to bear on the problem and the arena in which decisions will be made, this is a crucial stage in the development of social policy. The group that succeeds in having its definition of the problem accepted has already won half the battle.

Those aspects of life that are deemed matters of public concern change overtime. Most public issues exhibit a life cycle, developing as important and salient concerns for usually short periods and then dying away. Whether an issue will be of lasting consequence depends on several factors, including the ability of opponents to suppress it, but the primary determinant seems to be whether it is firmly rooted in a significant social cleavage. Fundamental issues derive their potency from the intensity of the conflict between the social groups involved.

## Student Rights as a Public Issue

The controversy over student rights developed at the end of the wave of activism in the 1960s, as was pointed out in Chapter 2. It can be seen, in part at least, as an outgrowth of the civil rights movement, the tide of antiwar protest, and, in general, the rise of the New Left. A number of special characteristics of the issue of student rights could have significant implications for its future direction and success.

To the extent that student rights is a derivative issue that rode into the political arena on the back of more salient matters such as civil rights and the war, its potential may be closely tied to the success of those other questions. If this is so, proponents of the movement may be in for hard times. The activist phase of the civil rights movement has been dormant for some time, and certainly the spark has gone out of the antiwar cadres. As Vietnam and civil rights recede, it may be more and more difficult to engender enthusiasm for student causes. It is possible that the current spate of litigation is purely a generational phenomenon that will pass as this crop of high school students graduates and is replaced by less vociferous pupils.

Exactly what the social basis of the student rights movement is (if it is not premature even to speak of a movement) is not obvious. One possibility is that it stems from the conflict between generations. A small library of popular and scholarly literature has developed on this subject.[95] If the generation gap is not only real but permanent and if it is the result of social developments that can be expected to continue in the same general direction, then one is justified in predicting that the prospects for a prolonged battle over student privileges are good.

The evidence one would want in order to draw a firm conclusion on this is not available, but it seems likely that the divisions of class, race, and family are more telling than those of generation. The most serious conflicts on the issue of student rights are not, after all, just between the young and the old. They are between students and their parents and educators. They represent in some ways a dispute between the public and the educational establishment. Furthermore, parents and children, as well as educators, of the same social class and race may have more in common in this political conflict than do the young and old of different classes and races. All these factors lead to the conclusion that the division between the young and the old is not the primary basis of the movement. The class and racial origins of the dispute, however, are not clear cut or simple. It appears, on the contrary, that the movement may be divided somewhat against itself in both its major source of support and its goals.

An analysis of the class basis of the issue reveals a number of internal contradictions in the movement for student rights that may have a telling effect on the final outcome of the controversy. One way to begin is to consider the distinction drawn in Chapter 5 by Leekley between option rights and welfare rights. We would argue that these two different categories of rights are the primary concern of different strata in the population and that in a number of important ways they are contradictory.

Option rights include the freedom to express oneself in speech, behavior, and dress as one sees fit. To a degree the issues of free speech and expression are symbolic or style issues.[96] They involve not so much substantive outputs as the acquisition of a certain status by the student (he becomes, for example, a person who is "responsible" or "mature" enough to edit a newspaper without faculty censorship). Wearing beads and beards will not materially alter the education that the child gets, but it may transform the style of that education. It is reasonable to assume that civil liberties are more salient to middle-class children and parents than to lower-class persons.[97] We do not mean to suggest that the latter do not care about such issues. (The struggle for the right to wear Afro hairdos and other cultural artifacts such as the dashiki belies that notion.) The point is simply that the issues of free speech, of the right to have long hair or to print four-letter words in underground newspapers, may be considered slightly superfluous to people who are denied an opportunity to learn basic English and mathematics.

The guarantee that everyone will have such an opportunity is the purpose of the welfare rights orientation in the movement for student rights. Welfare rights may be symbolic (just as option rights may be the means to very real changes in the substantive outcomes of the educational process), but they involve primarily material matters: more teachers, more books, more expenditures per pupil, higher reading achievement scores. Everyone wants such things for his child, but the parents who occupy the lower social and economic echelons of the society may rightly feel that these are of more critical concern to them than civil liberties per se. They are likely to show more concern for the basic issues of school finance and academic achievement as a "right" than are middle-class parents who can afford to buy an adequate education for their children.

There are, then, two aspects of the student rights movement—the demand for option rights and the demand for welfare rights. Theoretically there is no reason why these sets of objectives could not be complementary. Practically, however, they may be at cross-purposes because they arise from different social classes and because they reflect different assumptions about the role of the school.

The two orientations embrace highly divergent conceptions of the proper role of the principle of in loco parentis. Those who favor the option rights orientation are pressing for an enlargement of the sphere of freedoms (freedoms from) that the child and the parent enjoy vis à vis the school. Persons supporting this line of argument are trying to diminish the principle of in loco parentis. The implication of this trend is to circumscribe the authority of the school in its dealing with the child in certain areas. Those who favor the welfare rights orientation are, on the other hand, generally have-nots. They seek to increase the "accountability" of the school in meeting its educational obligations to their children.

To the extent that the first group succeeds in destroying the concept of in loco parentis, they will decrease the possibilities that those primarily concerned with welfare rights can succeed. For to hold the schools accountable for failing to educate their children, parents must argue that the school has the duty to act in behalf of the parent to give the child an education equal to the rest of the members of the community. In loco parentis is not just a justification for spankings; it can also be interpreted to mean that the school is responsible for nurturing and caring for the child as if it were the parent.

But it is not only on the issue of in loco parentis that the two orientations differ. There is a practical contradiction between the two because of the costs involved in their realization and their political bases. Welfare rights are more costly both politically and materially than are option rights. They involve substantive issues; for their realization it is necessary to raise taxes, spend money, and build schools. Option rights may damage the morale of teachers and cause embarrassment or inconvenience in the schools, but on the whole administrators will find them easier to deal with than with the economic costs of welfare claims. When given the opportunity, then, administrators are likely to grant concessions in the form of option rights rather than welfare rights. The Machiavellian decisionmaker will see that he can buy off those persons making both claims of welfare rights and option rights by granting only the latter.

. Even when the educator sincerely wishes to ensure the right of each child to an equal education it is not clear how he or she can do so. The movement for the recognition of educational welfare rights may be asking the schools to do the impossible. In a country where the myth of education as the remedy for all social ills is widely disseminated, it is not surprising that this should be the case. We expect education and the educational establishment to be the vehicle for the social mobility of whole social groups. We expect educational institutions to resolve our social conflicts of class, sex, and race. But it seems overly optimistic to expect the schools to be able to guarantee black children a chance in life equal to whites. To achieve such a goal it is necessary to go beyond the confines of the school system and bring about substantial alterations in the social, economic, and political structures.

Because the implementation of welfare rights entails higher political and social costs than option rights and because the proponents of welfare rights tend to be the least powerful and influential segments of the population, it is likely that this aspect will be the least successful component of the struggle for student rights. Such an outcome would be unfortunate not only for the children of the poor, but for all students. It is to be hoped that the two types of rights will be seen as mutually necessary. Without welfare rights, option rights can be rendered meaningless. For students to be "free" involves not only freedom from intrusion (negative or option freedoms) but the ability to take advantage of freedom (positive or welfare freedoms).[98]

We believe it is vital that those persons who are a part of the growing movement for student liberties (lawyers, parents, students, and teachers) should embrace the goal of an inalienable right to an equal education as indispensable to the meaningful exercise of constitutional freedoms.

In the twentieth century in loco parentis is perhaps an improper principle on which to base the authority or responsibility of the school. But to diminish in loco parentis is a mixed blessing. The push for student freedoms from educational supervision and punishment comes at a time when there is a crisis of authority in the classrooms of urban schools. Educators will view the movement to enlarge the rights of students as detrimental to their ability to maintain any semblance of the educational process. A reaffirmation of in loco parentis is, however, not what is required; what is necessary is the reexamination of the nature of the proper authority that school officials ought to have a different basis to support that authority.[99] Institutional controls are unlike parental controls. If the story of the traditional school situation, whereby the school and the family were in pursuit of common goals, ever existed, it is no longer the case today. Both institutions have changed, as have their relationships to young people,[100] and both must adapt.

The rest of this essay concerns future educational policy on student rights and those who will make it.

## Who Makes Educational Policy?

One general conclusion that can be drawn from both this and the preceding chapter is that the courts are now in effect making educational policy regarding the rights of students. This is the case, first of all, because parents and students see fit to challenge educators' decisions by bringing suits against them. Second, the courts have recently shrugged off at least part of their self-imposed restraint and are directly intervening in the educators' bailiwick. What is most important, however, is that the courts are making policy because the schools have defaulted on their responsibilities in that area. It is not necessary for judges to decide all or even the major questions about student rights. The schools could take the initiative in drawing up guidelines regarding the behavior of students and teachers. One should recognize that who makes policy will significantly affect the shape of that policy. What are the implications for student rights of a judicially determined policy?

### The Courts as Policymakers

The first proposition to be stated is that courts and judges do make policy. The ideology of legalism is entrenched in this country;[101] it holds that judges decide cases on the basis of a recognizable set of abstract legal principles. But increasingly scholars who are willing to examine the courts honestly realize that they do not operate in isolation from the society and its political system. Judges come from particular social strata, and they too, have political values. It is inevitable that these factors influence their decisions; whether this is unfortunate is a question that is beyond the scope of this chapter.

Litigation, then, involves questions of value and choice. The ideological belief in the purity of law, however, has at least two important effects on judicial decisions. The first is that in most instances judges will attempt to ground their decisions on questions of fact or on the narrowest legal or technical considerations available to them. This means that they will normally try to ignore broader, substantive questions. But even though questions of value do influence decisions, they tend to do so only when translated into the technical, professional language of the law.[102] A judicial policy, therefore, will normally focus on questions of process rather than substance. As Dolbeare and Edelman have put it,

The effects of the generally accepted assumptions about the sanctity and importance of the law are many. For one thing, they operate to shift considerations of the merits of issues to specialized arenas and persons . . . . Issues are issues insofar as they can be phrased as such as a result of the understanding and conceptualization of those who deal in the law, and only such decisions as can be articulated by the traditional language of the land can be made by the polity. Instead of a public consideration of preferences and goals for present or future, there can be only a technical and professional dialogue on the question of the precise manner in which things are to be done. To an extent, a politics of means gains precedence over a potential politics of ends.[103]

A policy of student rights formulated by the courts will be piecemeal and ad hoc. It will be created on a case-by-case basis. Although legal principles develop through the reliance on precedent, this occurs only in the long run, so that the influence of particular events and facts on an individual case tends to limit the continuity of such a policy. The courts, besides, must wait for someone to bring a suit, and there is no reason to expect that sufficient cases will be brought to enable the courts to enunciate guidelines in all important areas of concern.

Probably the most impressive argument against policy made by the courts is that such a policy is often more symbolic than real. The power of the courts is primarily hortative and persuasive. They possess no machinery of enforcement. They rely, to a great extent, on voluntary compliance and, if that fails, on executive enforcement. It is quite clear that the executive in this case, the educational institution, will often be the party against which the decision is rendered; thus the temptation to evade the consequences of the case will be strong.

Recent scholarship on the degree to which court decisions are complied with gives us no reason to be optimistic that sweeping changes in the lives of ordinary students will be effected through the judiciary. It is convenient for our purposes that most of the research on the impact of the courts is focused on educational matters, primarily desegregation and school prayers. The most thoroughly studied case is *Brown* v. *the Board of Education of Topeka, Kansas.* Blaustein and Ferguson found that both state and local officials (as well as federal judges) successfully utilized a wide variety of strategies to avoid the implications of *Brown*.[104] They included disqualifying potential litigants (such as the NAACP), setting up separate education on bases other than race (such as intelligence and achievement) but with the same result, and abolishing public educational institutions altogether. Becker has isolated the following factors which seem to predict whether lower court judges will follow higher court directions: "the ambiguity of the command, the proximity of a subordinate to strong community pressures, and his preferences (personal attitudes) will influence execution."[105] Murphy argues that judicial hierarchies, like any other large institution, evidence a kind of bureaucratic drag. He notes that the Supreme Court's adherence to the "vague remand principle" in overturning state decisions gives the state courts considerable latitude for evasion. State courts resisted *Brown*, for example, by "(1) refusing to expand the school decision to other areas, (2) upholding the constitutionality of state efforts to evade compliance, and (3) . . . balking at Supreme Court decisions in related areas of race and federal-state relations."[106]

The case concerning school prayers (*School District of Abington Township* v. *Schempp*) is probably even more relevant to the present discussion. The widespread and open defiance of the Court by local school boards[107] suggests that if abiding by a decision requires a local school board to defy the intense desires of the local community, the board is unlikely to do so.

None of these considerations delves into the broader question of how the law can be used to change attitudes or effect more basic changes within the society. First of all, one must see that the law is obeyed, that judicial principle is put into practice. Given the highly decentralized nature of educational decision making, the lack of direct judicial or police supervision of administrative action, and the idiosyncratic and fragmented structure of the courts, it seems unlikely that much direct compliance will be secured from court decisions. Since that is the case, one can be only skeptical of the judiciary's ability to secure such long-range impacts as a better education through a more open and reciprocal educational process.

It is not entirely clear who benefits from court-made policy. McNeil (Chapter 2) notes that educational administrators have tried to define student conflict in legal, procedural, and nonsubstantive terms. To the extent that, through a court strategy, educators are able to avoid public consideration of broader questions about the role of schools in a democratic society, then those educators benefit. Not all administrators, obviously, want to avoid open discussion. Since the controversy over welfare rights entails questions of public policy of the most fundamental and extensive sort, it would, on its face, seem that a court policy would be detrimental to its proponents. This is not necessarily the case, however; and that it is not only demonstrates how cautious one should be in generalizing about this complicated question. On the basis of present evidence, it appears that the courts may be one of the only available means by which relatively powerless groups may have their claims presented. It seems that the courts in these cases (as with the desegration cases previous to this time) are perhaps the only branch of government sufficiently isolated from community pressure to be able to intervene on behalf of the minority.

Thus, while one is tempted to argue that allowing the courts predominant influence in educational matters (besides all the problems already noted) is undemocratic, it is possible that the judiciary represents the only practicable means of giving poor people, in this case poor children, a fair hearing.

### The Implications of a School-Made Policy on Student Rights

Before directly considering the implications that follow from the possibility that educational officials might themselves develop policy on these issues, we might find it useful to consider what a policy is. There are several alternative definitions of policy: what the school actually does with regard to student rights; the official rules—what the school says it is doing; a coherent argument stating goals, means, and procedures for attaining those goals.

We feel that the third definition is the most useful. It is not necessary to assume that a policy can be rationally implemented without problems. We can assume that many nonrational forces and contingencies will intervene between the policy and the actual decisions made in discrete cases. But this is not a telling criticism against the argument for comprehensive and planned decision making. All one needs to assume is that it is better to have at least some stated program and goal (granted that one cannot always adhere to it) than to make all decisions in a purely ad hoc manner.

A comprehensive policy should have a number of beneficial results. First, it will allow discrete decisions to be made in the context of the long-range goals and purposes of the institution. Second, the performance of the institution can be evaluated. Administrators as well as interested outsiders are provided a means by which they can determine if their purposes are being achieved; policy goals thereby become a standard of evaluation. Third, because the decision maker need not make each determination anew, a certain degree of "efficiency" results.

There is no guarantee that the development of an official policy on student rights would be an unmitigated good. To the extent that it becomes embodied in a set of rules, regulations, and strictures, such a policy may become rigid and self-protecting.[108] Unless the need for periodic reevaluation is taken seriously, an official policy can be much less open to change than purely ad hoc decisions. Furthermore, because school boards are highly subject to local pressures, it is possible that school-made policy will be more conservative than that made by the courts.[109] These potential costs may, on the other hand, be outweighed by the opportunity for a democratic and open discussion of the questions of student rights on its merits, which the development of policies by the schools should entail.

## The Changing Concept of Childhood

In Chapter 1 Naherny and Rosario pointed out that the concept of childhood in the West has evolved over an extensive period of time. They noted that the idea of childhood as a separate and distinct status was a relatively modern concept and that children on the whole possessed fewer rights after the development of the distinction between childhood and adulthood than before. They also concluded that the prevalent concept of childhood played an important role in the development of public policy for children because it could be used as a justification for programs designed for other social and political purposes.

We seem now to be at the beginning of a period in which the clear distinction between a child and an adult will be blurred. The unmistakable but not undiluted message of a number of recent judicial and legislative actions is that children have rights as do adults and that they too are citizens, at least to some extent. Though a number of fascinating questions suggest themselves at this point, all we can do is raise them for discussion.

If historically the development of the idea of childhood as a separate status led to a reduction in the rights of children, then is it likely that an attack on that distinction will lead to an increase in rights for young people? The answer is not clear, since we are not postulating that childhood will disappear. It seems, on the contrary, more likely that the vague and indeterminant period between dependence and adulthood will become longer and more ambiguous. We see no reason to suspect that the social structural processes outlined by McNeil in Chapter 2 will lead to the disappearance of a long adolescence before the young person becomes self-sustaining. What does seem likely is that those social phenomena she stresses—alienation and politicization, for example—will lead to the granting of at least some provisional rights of adulthood to persons who are not yet adults in the current understanding of that term.

## Notes

1. Besides the review found in this volume, others include *Academic Freedom in the Secondary Schools* (New York: American Civil Liberties Union, 1971); Robert L. Ackerly, *The Reasonable Exercise of Authority* (Washington, D.C.: National Association of Secondary School Principals, 1969); William G. Buss, *Legal Aspects of Crime Investigation in the Schools* (Topeka, Kansas: National Organization on Legal Problems of Education, 1971); Henry E. Butler *et al., Legal Aspects of Student Records* (Topeka, Kansas: National Organization on Legal Problems of Education, 1971); Robert E. Phay, "The Courts and Student Rights—Procedural Matters," in *Emerging Problems in School Law* (Topeka, Kansas: National Organization on Legal Problems of Education, 1972); Robert E. Phay, *Suspension and Expulsion of Public School Students* (Topeka, Kansas: National Organization on Legal Problems of Education, 1971); Edmund Reutter, *Legal Aspects of Control of Student Activities by Public School Authorities* (Topeka, Kansas: National Organization on Legal Problems of Education, 1970); Ronald Sealey, "The Courts and Student Rights—Substantive Matters," in *Emerging Problems in School Law; Student Rights and Responsibilities: A Manual for the Development of School District Rules and Policies Governing the Conduct of Students,* ed. Larry Swift (Bellingham, Wash.:

Northwest District Administrators' Association, 1972); and *Training Manual on Public School Life* (New York: School Defense Network, 1969).

2. "Public Secondary Education: Judicial Protection of Student Individuality," *Southern California Law Review* 40 (Fall 1968): 140.

3. *Burnside* v. *Byars*, 363 F. 2d 745 (5th Cir. 1966), cited *ibid.*, 141.

4. For example: *Byrd* v. *Gary*, 184 F. Supp. 388 (S.C. 1960); *Guzick* v. *Drebus*, 305 F. Supp. 472 (Ohio 1969); *Ferrel* v. *Dallas Independent School District*, 261 F. Supp. 545 (Texas 1966); aff'd. 392 F. 2d 697 (1968); cert. denied, 393 U.S. 856 (1968).

5. *Tinker* v. *Des Moines Independent Community School District*, 258 F. Supp. 971, 973 (S.D. Iowa 1966); aff'd. per curiam, 383 F. 2d 988 (8th Cir. 1967); cert. granted, 390 U.S. 942 (1968).

6. *Ibid.*

7. *Ibid.*

8. This is the doctrine that holds that the rights guaranteed in the First Amendment are so basic that any action, statutory or otherwise, that in some way abridges those rights shall come under special scrutiny by the courts. See "Public Secondary Education," 140-41.

9. Cited in Sealey, *op. cit.*, 47.

10. *Davis* v. *Firment*, 269 F. Supp. 524 at 527 (E.D. La. 1967); aff'd. 408 F. 2d 1085 (5th Cir. 1969), cited *ibid.*, 25.

11. *Breen* v. *Kahl*, 296 F. Supp. 702 (Wis. 1969), 38 L.W. 2332; aff'd. 419 F. 2d 1034 (1969); cert. denied, 90 Sup. Ct. 1836, — U.S. — (1970), 38 L.W. 3474, cited in Phay, *Suspension and Expulsion of Public School Students*, 52.

12. Sealey, *op. cit.*, 27.

13. Phay, *Suspension and Expulsion of Public School Students*, 6.

14. Dale Gaddy, *Rights and Freedoms of Public School Students: Directions from the Sixties* (Topeka, Kansas: National Organization on Legal Problems of Education, 1971).

15. *Sullivan* v. *Houston Independent School District*, 307 F. Supp. 1328 (Texas 1969), cited *ibid.*, 20.

16. *Zucker* v. *Banitz*, 299 F. Supp. 102 (S.D. N.Y. 1969), cited *ibid.*, 22.

17. *Akin* v. *Board of Education of Riverside Unified School District*, 68 Cal. Rptr. 557 (1968); hearing denied mem. (Cal. Sup. Ct., July 10, 1968); cert. denied, 393 U.S. 1041 (1969).

18. Gaddy, *op. cit.*, 25.

19. *Ibid.*

20. "Public Secondary Education," 131.

21. Gaddy, *op. cit.*, 4.

22. Reutter, *op. cit.*, 19.

23. "Public Secondary Education," 142.

24. *Ibid.*, 143.

25. *Griffin* v. *Tatum*, cited in Gaddy, *op. cit.*, 31.

26. "Public Secondary Education," 131.

27. Gaddy, *op. cit.*, 8.

28. Warren Gauerke, "Legal Rights of Students in the School Setting," in

*Conference Proceedings* (Topeka, Kansas: National Organization on Legal Problems of Education, 1967), unnumbered.

29. Jane R. Bronars, "Children's Privacy and Compulsory Schooling," in *The Experience of Schooling*, ed. Melvin L. Silberman (New York: Holt, Rinehart and Winston, 1971), 233.

30. *Ibid.*

31. Sealey, *op. cit.*, 29.

32. Buss, *op. cit.*

33. Phay, *Suspension and Expulsion of Public School Students*, 36.

34. Swift, *op. cit.*, 56.

35. *Ibid.*

36. Bronars, *op. cit.*, 228. One set of guidelines produced by scholars can be found in the document *Guidelines for the Collection, Maintenance, and Dissemination of Pupil Records* (New York: Russell Sage Foundation, n.d.).

37. Bronars, *op. cit.*, 228-29.

38. *Ibid.*, 232.

39. Edward T. Ladd, "Pills for Classroom Peace?" *Saturday Review* 53 (November 21, 1970: 68. Issues concerning school records are dealt with in a later section of this essay.

40. Newton Edwards, *The Courts and the Public Schools* (Chicago: University of Chicago Press, 1971).

41. *Howard* v. *Clark*, 299 NYS 2d 65 (1969), cited in Gaddy, *op. cit.*, 46.

42. *Academic Freedom in the Secondary Schools*, 15.

43. *State* v. *Burton*, 45 Wis. 150, 30 Am. Rep. 706, cited in Edwards, *op. cit.*, 605.

44. In loco parentis, we should point out, encompasses much broader considerations than just those of corporal punishment, suspension, and expulsion.

45. Joan G. Brown, "Law and Punishment: Status of State Statutes," *Clearing House* 46 (October 1971): 106.

46. *Ibid.*

47. James L. Edwards, "In Loco Parentis: Definition, Application, and Implications," *South Carolina Law Review* 23 (No. 1, 1971): 114.

48. *Ibid.*

49. *Kent* v. *U.S.*, 383 U.S. 541 (1966).

50. Reutter, *op. cit.*, 50.

51. John Katz, "The Opportunity to Be Heard in Public School Disciplinary Hearings," *Urban Education* 4 (January 1970): 295.

52. Reutter, *op. cit.*, 50.

53. *Ibid.*

54. Charles A. Wright, "The Constitution on the Campus," *Vanderbilt Law Review* 22 (October 1969): 1027-88.

55. Reutter, *op. cit.*, 59.

56. Phay, "The Courts and Student Rights," 19; Robert Phay and Jasper Cummings, *Student Suspensions and Expulsions: Proposed School Board Codes* (Chapel Hill, N.C.: Institute of Government, 1970), 10.

57. Phay, *Suspension and Expulsion of Public School Students*, 21-33.

58. *Ibid.*, 20.

59. In one case, *Goldwyn* v. *Allen*, concerning an accusation of cheating on the New York Regents' Examination, the student was sanctioned by a principal without the benefit of a hearing. The sanction involved waiting a year before she could retake the examination. The court ruled in favor of the student because she was denied the rights of due process.

60. "Public Secondary Education," 137.

61. Reutter, *op. cit.*, 5.

62. Newton Edwards, *op. cit.*, 519.

63. *Ibid.*, 521.

64. *Ibid.*, 46.

65. *Wisconsin* v. *Yoder*, 92 S. Ct. 1526 (1972).

66. Marvin R. Plasco, "School, Student, and Appearance Regulations," *Cleveland-Marshall Law Review* 18 (January 1969): 143.

67. Samuel Bowles, "Getting Nowhere: Programmed Class Stagnation," *Transaction* 9 (June 1972): 49.

68. Jane R. Mercer, "The Lethal Label," *Psychology Today* 6 (September 1972): 44.

69. Kenneth D. Phelps and William J. Perez, "Ability Grouping in Public Schools: A Threat to Equal Protection," *Connecticut Law Review* 1 (June 1968): 165.

70. *School Children in the Urban Slum*, ed. Joan I. Roberts (New York: Free Press, 1969), 22.

71. "Legal Implications of the Use of Standardized Ability Tests in Employment and Education," *Columbia Law Review* 68 (April 1968): 691.

72. *Ibid.*

73. Phelps and Perez, *op. cit.*, 165.

74. *Ibid.*

75. Thomas K. Gilhool, "The Uses of Litigation: The Right of Retarded Children to a Free Public Education," *Peabody Journal of Education* 50 (January 1973): 126.

76. See Aaron Cicourel and John Kitsuse, *The Educational Decision-Makers* (Indianapolis: Bobbs-Merrill, 1963); Aaron Cicourel and John Kitsuse, "The High School's Role in Adolescent Status Transition," in *The Sociology of Education*, ed. Robert R. Bell and Holger R. Stub (Homewood, Ill.: Dorsey Press, 1968), 44-53; and Aaron Cicourel and John Kitsuse, "The Social Organization of the High School and Deviant Adolescent Careers," in *Deviance: The Interactionist Perspective*, ed. Earl Rubington and Martin Weinberg (New York: Macmillan, 1968), 124-37.

77. "Legal Implications of the Use of Standardized Ability Tests," 741.

78. Gauerke, *op. cit.*

79. Robert Rosenthal and Lenore Jacobsen, *Pygmalion in the Classroom* (New York: Holt, Rinehart and Winston, 1968); Cicourel and Kitsuse, "The High School's Role in Adolescent Status Transition," 44-53; Ray Rist, "Student Social Class and Teacher Expectations: The Self-Fulfilling Prophecy in Ghetto Education," *Harvard Educational Review* 40 (August 1970): 411-51.

80. Butler *et al.*, *op. cit.*, 25.

81. *Ibid.*, 43.

82. *Ibid.*, 28.

83. "Parental Rights to Inspect School Records," *Buffalo Law Review* 20 (Fall 1970): 255; Cicourel and Kitsuse, "The High School's Role in Adolescent Status Transition," 44-53.

84. Cicourel and Kitsuse, "The Social Organization of the High School and Deviant Adolescent Careers," 133.

85. *Einhorn* v. *Maus*, 300 F. Supp. 1169 (Pa. 1969).

86. Butler *et al.*, *op. cit.*

87. Cicourel and Kitsuse, "The Social Organization of the High School and Deviant Adolescent Careers," 133.

88. Butler *et al.*, *op. cit.*, 29.

89. *Ibid.*, 31.

90. *Ibid.*

91. *Ibid.*

92. *Ibid.* After this volume was written, the United States Congress passed the Family Educational Rights and Privacy Act of 1974. The purpose of the act is to improve access for students (or for the parents of elementary and secondary school students) to information contained in school files and to restrict the release of such information to others without the students' explicit consent.

93. For exceptions, see Gaddy, *op. cit.*; Newton Edwards, *op. cit.*; *Our Time Is Now*, ed. John Birmingham (New York: Bantam, 1970).

94. *Epperson* v. *Arkansas*, 393 U.S. 107 (1968).

95. See, for example, Lewis S. Feuer, *The Conflict of Generations* (New York: Basic Books, 1969); Richard Flacks, "The Revolt of the Advantaged: Explorations of the Roots of Student Protest," *Learning About Politics*, ed. Roberta Sigel (New York: Random House, 1970).

96. See Murray Edelman, *The Symbolic Uses of Politics* (Urbana: University of Illinois Press, 1964).

97. Lloyd A. Free and Hadley Cantril, *The Political Beliefs of Americans: A Study of Political Opinion* (New York: Clarion Books, 1968).

98. Isaiah Berlin, *Four Essays on Liberty* (London: Oxford University Press, 1969).

99. Arthur Pearl, "There Is Nothing More Loco Than In Loco Parentis," *Phi Delta Kappan* 52 (June 1972): 629-31.

100. Roy C. Howarth, "On the Decline of In Loco Parentis," *ibid.*, 626-28.

101. Judith N. Sklar, *Legalism* (Cambridge, Mass.: Harvard University Press, 1964).

102. See Kenneth Dolbeare and Murray Edelman, *American Politics: Policies, Power, and Change* (Lexington, Mass.: D.C. Heath, 1971), 331.

103. *Ibid.* 331-32.

104. Albert P. Blaustein and Clarence C. Ferguson, *Desegregation and the Law* (New Brunswick, N.J.: Rutgers University Press, 1957).

105. *The Impact of Supreme Court Decisions*, ed. Theodore L. Becker (New York: Oxford University Press, 1969), 63.

106. *Ibid.*, 68.

107. Robert H. Birkly, "The Supreme Court and the Bible Belt: Tennessee Reaction to the 'Schempp' Decision," *ibid.*, 106-14; William K. Muir, *Prayer in the Public Schools: Law and Attitude Change* (Chicago: University of Chicago Press, 1967).

108. Michael W. Apple, "The Adequacy of Systems Management Procedures in Education," *Journal of Educational Research* 66 (September 1972): 10-18; Michael Katz, *Class, Bureaucracy, and Schooling* (New York: Praeger, 1971).

109. See Harmon Ziegler, *The Political Life of American Teachers* (Englewood Cliffs, N.J.: Prentice-Hall, 1967).

# 8. Toward Increasing the Potency of Student Rights Claims: Advocacy-Oriented Policy Recommendations

*Michael W. Apple* and *Thomas Brady*

The essays in this volume have pointed to the complexity of the problems surrounding student rights. They include historical, analytic, sociopsychological, political, and, especially, legal issues. It should be clear that the courts have opened a signal area of contention. Just as clear, however, is the fact pointed to in both Chapters 6 and 7, that there are no easy generalizations to be drawn from the judicial controversy. There are trends, though, and an evolving judicial climate that may be important in the argumentation over claims for student rights. Keeping in mind trends and implications noted in Freeman's discussion and the realization that educators cannot rely totally on the courts, we shall make recommendations here that will be clearly within an advocacy framework.

While we cannot hope to be exhaustive in any list of concrete proposals concerning student rights, we shall advance a number of propositions that are of particular import. Questions dealing with specific rights, such as due process in expulsion, will not be treated. We shall, rather, focus on recommendations that may have just as potent an impact on other expected activity in schools and in university research. We urge the reader to turn to the appendix for an excellent example of a high school bill of rights that provides specific recommendations. It could serve as a model for the development of similar bills of rights in other areas. Included in this model bill of rights are specific policy recommendations covering the following five major areas of possible conflict between school personnel and students: freedom of speech and the press; use of school facilities; freedom of political activity; due process, including the question of record keeping; personal counseling and the right to a quality education. The bill itself will serve as our recommendations for these areas. It should be noted that the bill is not merely a model, but is being used with only minor revisions in Madison, Wisconsin, and elsewhere. Similar codifications of student rights have been accepted as official school policy in many other municipalities throughout the country.

This discussion of the specifics that are found in the high school bill of rights does not in any way cover all necessary policy proposals. Even if such a codification were administratively approved universally, much more would have to be accomplished in order for it to be effective. We shall, therefore, enumerate a range of activities which, if carried out, can serve to make the student rights issue an even more forceful aspect of educational argumentation. This list will concern itself basically with two levels of activity: first, suggestions besides those codified in the student bill of rights that will increase the probability of success of the student rights movement on a local level; and, second, recommendations for an advocacy style of research and action on the part of professional educators. There will be, finally, a number of critical comments concerning the placement of the student rights movement in a broader context.

## Toward Local Responsiveness

1. A student bill of rights should be adopted and disseminated in each district. All too often, student "handbooks" specify rules to follow, yet never clearly articulate the concrete rights students possess within educational institutions.

2. These student rights should be taught; statements regarding student rights have little potency if they are not communicated to the youth within the school setting. Here we include not only high school students, but all students within schools. While the area concerned with the specific rights of elementary school students is still cloudy, even these individuals, in principle, do not lose their

constitutional protections upon entering the school. There are, furthermore, educational as well as legal reasons for advocating and teaching student rights at all levels of schooling, reasons that will be noted later in the discussion.

3. If there is to be weight behind the last recommendation, individuals and professional groups should bring concerted pressure to bear upon publishers of educational materials to develop and distribute curricular materials appropriate for students of different ages that honestly deal with the rights of students. Given the past history of the rather slow and cautious response of the publishing field to racism and sexism in their publications, such organized advocacy may be especially important.

4. Student rights also relate to other people within the school setting. The policy manual of school boards should enumerate the restrictions placed upon educational employees in dealing with students. It could be argued, for example, that "no school official has any more legal right to question students without first apprizing them of their constitutional rights, than has a police officer when the questioning has the purpose for possible prosecution in a juvenile court."[1] It should be clear, therefore, to school people as well as students what specific obligations they incur to act (or not to act).

5. We urge that there be created and actively recruited a student ombudsman who will not serve as an advocate of school policy, but will instead act in a student advocacy position. There are significant precedents for the creation of such a position. For example, juvenile lawyers paid by the administrative apparatus are continually appointed to argue against the court in legal proceedings. And federally and locally funded poverty lawyers have also served to make public institutions more responsive to their clientele. Since it is becoming increasingly evident that the school is to be seen as just such a public institution because of the decline of in loco parentis, the position of student ombudsman with specified powers could act to mitigate the lack of responsiveness in many schools.

6. While realistically it may be too much to ask, school personnel should actively begin the process of sharing power with students; these people should be leading the courts rather than following them in support of student rights. There are ethical and educational as well as legal reasons for this argument. At the foundation of any serious attempt to define an educational environment must be one person's

ethical responsibility to treat another justly.[2] It must, that is, embody reciprocal forms of influence. Also, we have known for a number of years that the actual power to control and make significant decisions about aspects of one's environment is essential to the quality of the educational interaction in schools. One final reason for educators to respond favorably to the rights claimed by students should be recognized. As we have seen, the reasoning employed in the *Tinker* decision rests upon the thesis that the rights guaranteed by the First Amendment are actually "essential to an effective educational environment."[3] Controversy, diversity, and open argumentation—all of which may be generated by specific rights of free speech in schools—are, in essence, to be looked upon not as problems to be eliminated at whatever cost, but as signs of a just and educative milieu. Because of community pressure, bureaucratic exigencies, and the like, local educators may be taking risks in advocating significant changes; the "facts" of these situations can just as often serve as excuses for a lack of genuine commitment and an abrogation of educational responsibility.

7. In order to establish student rights, committed educators, child advocates, community members, and others must act as catalysts within or near schools by questioning students on the types of relationships that dominate their interaction in schools. This is a critical point. It may well be that the educational experience of students engaging in the dispute with others over rights and obligations is equally as or even more important than the granting of the specific rights themselves.[4] These people can assist students by clarifying and helping them focus on the sources of their discontent.

8. As is happening in a number of urban areas throughout the country where community participation has become a critical factor in education, community members should be trained as student advocates. This is especially important in dealing with the problems of younger children. Here the role of the university may become crucial. One function of schools of education could be to establish and support such training within an advocacy framework, thereby in addition exerting leadership within the field itself.

9. Colleges and universities also perform the function of training teachers. Institutions that train teachers should, therefore, focus on the question and implications of student rights and make it an integral part of their program. This should be done in such a way that

teachers are shown that student rights are, in fact, beneficial for them in establishing a responsible educational setting. While in training these future teachers should have an expanded role in decision making within their own programs. It is difficult to establish dispositions favorable to or unthreatened by student rights when one's own personal experience has been centered on a rationale of control.[5]

## Advocacy Models of Research

The activities of universities and, especially, schools of education are not limited to educating teachers. They also act to generate research that is applicable to policy decisions in schools. All too often, however, the forms of research carried out by educators perform the latent function of supporting the bureaucratic regularities that serve as a foundation for the day-to-day life of students in schools rather than leading toward better and fuller understanding. As with other forms of social research, it is difficult for educational research to be neutral. The very questions asked and the modes by which data are collected imply tacit commitments. While we cannot go into detail here, it should be noted that the constitutive logic of much educational research embodies the interests of strict control and certainty in dealing with human interaction.[6] In this way the research, although not necessarily aimed at this end, is ideally suited to support an institution whose own interests unfortunately have historically centered around running the school on the model of an "efficient factory."[7] A number of recommendations germane to the issue of student rights should, therefore, be made to educational researchers.

1. There is a distinct need for research into how and where, both overtly and covertly, rights are abridged in schools. This will require the refinement of techniques such as those used by Goffman[8] and others. We need, for instance, to be able to trace the "moral career" of students, to see the effects the process of labeling has over a long period of time on the distribution of educational "goods and services" within the institution of schooling.

2. Further legal research is also essential on a number of levels. For example, since schools are increasingly being compared to other public and "total institutions," what available precedents exist in involuntary mental commitment cases and the like for arguments concerning compulsory school attendance? This concept needs to be

questioned quite thoroughly. Further, what is the relationship between teachers' rights and students' rights or between parents' rights and students' rights? These are, admittedly, difficult questions, but advocacy necessitates a rather extensive commitment to concrete investigation if legal and educational progress is to be effected.

3. Additional conceptual work is essential to clarify the problem of the rights of young children. While this volume has focused primarily on issues that may seem more appropriate for middle or high schools, educators should not assume that the points made here have little applicability to the elementary school. As one example, it might be wise to think about the constitutional implications of the use of behavior modification drugs or techniques on elementary school children. According to congressional testimony, such use is rapidly expanding and may signify an attempt by some school people to continue to fit the child to the school by rather drastic means rather than taking seriously the task of making school more meaningful to the student.[9] There is a very real possibility that educators may succumb to the temptation to diagnose as hyperactive the bored but bright child or the child for whom schools are oppressive institutions; they may thus prescribe drugs[10] and thereby deny him or her what may be established as certain rights to an educational environment that is responsive to the students' orientation. While it should not need to be said, one further recommendation specifically aimed at young children is required: there is little ethical or educational justification for corporal punishment in schools. It should be abolished. Other examples abound. The general point to be made, however, is the necessity of much scrutiny on, and intense effort to understand, the rights of young children.

4. Other critical questions must also be examined, among which are such difficult issues as a thoroughgoing analysis of the relationship of schools as institutions to other institutions in American society. This should include further historical work similar to that of Katz and Karier[11] and in-depth economic and ideological analyses as well.[12]

5. In addition, fresh insights are essential into the relations between the forms of rationality that dominate educational discourse (for example, vulgar forms of behaviorism and systems management) and the ideology of control in schools.[13]

6. Finally, most educators and researchers hold membership in a

variety of professional associations. Here is another area where progress can be made. One would want research associations to support
the forms of questioning articulated here, and yet there are other
points to be argued. Many professional educational organizations
have exhibited a positive commitment toward making schools responsive to the very real sentiments of students. Much of this commitment has been limited, however, to such safe assertions as supporting a bit less "teacher dominance" or "humanizing the curriculum." As long as this remains on the level of rhetoric it has little
effect. Any serious attempt to grapple with the issue of "humanizing
the schools" cannot afford to neglect the concept of student rights
that is entailed; nor can it continue to remain on a rhetorical level.
Professional organizations can show their earnest involvement with
this issue by commiting funds to support test cases in the courts.
(The concept of a dues check-off system may be appropriate here.)
They can also go on record in support of concrete and specific recommendations concerning the rights of students within the schools.
For this to be accomplished, individual educators within these organizations must organize politically around issues. The various "cau-
cuses" within the Association for Supervision and Curriculum Development provide partial models of such action-oriented groups.

## On Placing Student Rights in an Expanded Context

The discussion throughout this chapter, and throughout the book
as a whole, has focused on student rights as primarily an issue involving
schooling and on analyses of the ways in which educational institutions might be more accountable to the youth who inhabit their
halls. The rights of students need not, however, be considered as only
ends in themselves. They count, rather, as one step toward providing
what Mann has called a "humanizing experience." That is, the advocacy of student rights in educational institutions can be interpreted
as a transitional step, as well as a worthwhile goal in itself, in the
process of engaging students and others in examining many of the
problematic conditions of a number of institutions in our society.[14]
This is not, then, a problem that can be effectively solved by
human relations training and other similar approaches. It is, instead,
a systemic issue concerning bureaucratic institutions and the relationship of the school to the institutional structure of an advanced

industrial society. While concrete steps can and must be taken now to ameliorate certain conditions within school settings, ultimately the real issues may be of a broader political and economic nature.

It is difficult to divorce the lack of responsiveness to student rights in schools from the lack of responsiveness to human sentiment of a number of institutions in our advanced economic and political structure. Schools seem to reflect modes of interaction that predominate in the larger collectivity. When women, blacks, Chicanos, native Americans, and other groups are denied fundamental liberties in varying degrees throughout each region of the country, then one should not be too surprised that students are denied rights and the opportunity to make significant decisions concerning their lives in schools.

The fact that the rights of students are interrelated with the problem of rights in general should not make us lose sight of the fact that changes can be effected in the present. As was noted in Chapter 5, there is no clear direction in the court cases adjudicated so far. Strikingly similar cases have been decided in one instance for the student and in another instance for school authorities. It is obvious that the rights of students are situationally dependent; rulings often reflect dominant community and local sentiment. Such a lack of uniformity should not dishearten advocates of student rights, for it shows that the issues surrounding these rights are exceptionally complex and much less clear than administrators and other educators have supposed. Thus, there may be little justification for the blanket denial of claims for rights based on "mere" authority. By the very fact that the issues are more difficult than has previously been thought, it is harder to dismiss demands by students for constitutional rights on the basis of such traditional arguments as maintaining school discipline.

This is certainly a positive sign, for it was argued at the very beginning of this volume that schools as institutions require a new basis of authority besides in loco parentis. Perhaps that authority can be found in a new conception of the relationship among all individuals within a just educational community.

# Notes

1. Warren D. Gauerke, "Legal Rights of Students in the School Setting," *Thirteenth Annual Conference Proceedings of the National Organization on Legal Problems in Education*, mimeographed (1968).

2. See John Rawls, *A Theory of Justice* (Cambridge, Mass.: Harvard University Press, 1971).

3. Richard L. Berkman, "Students in Court: Free Speech and the Function of Schooling in America," *Education and the Legal Structure*, reprint series number 6, *Harvard Educational Review* (1971): 49.

4. John S. Mann, "The Student Rights Strategy," *Theory into Practice* 10 (December 1971): 361. This is perhaps one of the most articulate statements on some of the very real issues any committed individual must grapple with if he or she is indeed serious about student rights.

5. On the dominance of an ideology of control and certainty in education, see Michael W. Apple, "The Adequacy of Systems Management Procedures in Education," in *Perspectives on Management Systems Approaches in Education*, ed. Albert H. Yee (Englewood Cliffs, N.J.: Educational Technology Publications, 1973), 3-31.

6. Jürgen Habermas, *Knowledge and Human Interests* (Boston: Beacon Press, 1967), 309.

7. Herbert M. Kliebard, "Bureaucracy and Curriculum Theory," in *Freedom, Bureaucracy, and Schooling*, ed. Vernon Haubrich (Washington, D.C.: Association for Supervision and Curriculum Development, 1971), 74-93. For further discussion of advocacy models of research, see Michael W. Apple, "The Process and Ideology of Valuing in Educational Settings," in *Educational Evaluation: Analysis and Responsibility*, ed. Michael W. Apple, Michael J. Subkoviak, and Henry S. Lufler, Jr. (Berkeley, Calif.: McCutchan Publishing Corp., 1974).

8. Erving Goffman, *Asylums* (Garden City, N.Y.: Doubleday, 1961); Roy C. Rist, "Student Social Class and Teacher Expectations: The Self-Fulfilling Prophecy in Ghetto Education," *Harvard Educational Review* 40 (August 1970): 411-51.

9. See *Federal Involvement in the Use of Behavior Modification Drugs on Grammar School Children of the Right to Privacy Inquiry* (Washington, D.C.: Government Printing Office, 1970); see also Edward L. Ladd, "Pills for Class Room Peace," *Saturday Review* 53 (November 21, 1970): 66-68, 81-83.

10. *Federal Involvement in the Use of Behavior Modification Drugs*, 3.

11. Michael Katz, *Class, Bureaucracy, and Schooling* (New York: Praeger, 1971); Clarence Karier, Paul Violas, and Joel Spring, *Roots of Crisis* (Chicago: Rand McNally, 1973).

12. See Herbert Gintis, "Toward a Political Economy of Education: A Radical Critique of Ivan Illich's *Deschooling Society*," in *After Deschooling What?* ed. Alan Gartner, Colin Greer, and Frank Riessman (New York: Harper and Row, 1973), 29-76.

13. Apple, "The Adequacy of Systems Management Procedures in Education"; *id.*, "The Process and Ideology of Valuing in Educational Settings"; *id.*,

"Common-Sense Categories and Curriculum Thought," a paper presented at the conference "Toward the Reconstruction of the Curriculum Field," Philadelphia, May 10-11, 1973.

14. Mann, *op. cit.*

# Appendix

Madison Public Schools
Madison, Wisconsin

## Guidelines to Board of Education Policy in the Area of Student Rights and Responsibilities

*Adopted by Board of Education June 18, 1973*

PREAMBLE

This document pertains to high school students enrolled in the Madison Public Schools.

Conflict, confrontation, and controversy will be channeled constructively and positively if the rights and responsibilities of students are recognized and respected. Students have the responsibility to respect rights of all persons involved in the educational process and exercise the highest degree of self-discipline in observing and adhering to legitimate rules and regulations. Responsibility is inherent in the exercise of every right. It is impossible to list all student responsibility but it must be emphasized that the lack of responsibility means a weakening of rights. Correspondingly, it is impossible to list all the rights of students. Therefore, the following list of rights shall not be construed to deny or limit others retained by students on their own campus in their capacity as members of the student body or as citizens.

# I. FREEDOM OF SPEECH AND PRESS

A. The school shall make no rules respecting an establishment of religion, or prohibiting the free exercise thereof, or abridging the freedom of speech, or of the press, or the right of people to peaceably assemble, and to petition the government for a redress of grievances.

  1. Students shall have the right to post any literature of a non-commercial nature without prior censorship or approval by the Administration or School Board in any designated posting area, provided, however, the principal or his designated representative shall be accorded the right to remove posted material he considers obscene, libelous, or will cause material disruption of the educational environment. The name and address of the person distributing the literature must be listed on the literature itself. The removal of material by the principal or his designate may be appealed to the Area Director. The decision of the Area Director may be appealed to the Superintendent. The decision of the Superintendent may be appealed to the Board of Education at its next regular meeting after the decision of the principal or his designate if the next regular meeting is scheduled to occur more than five days after the removal of the posted material by the principal or his designate. If the removal is made within five days of the next regular meeting of the Board, the decision may be subject to appeal at the Board's following meeting.

  2. Students shall have the right to distribute newspapers or other printed material of a non-commercial nature both inside and outside the school building on school grounds without prior authorization of the school administration or School Board provided, however, the time, place, and manner of distribution may be limited to prevent substantial interference with educational activities. The name and address of the person distributing or posting the literature must be listed on the literature itself. The principal or his designate may curtail distribution of material he considers obscene, libelous, or will cause material disruption of the educational environment. The decision of the principal or his designate may be appealed to the Area Director. The decision of the Area Director may be appealed to the Superintendent. The decision of the Superintendent may be appealed to the Board of Education at its next regular meeting after the decision of the principal or his designate if the next regular meeting is scheduled to occur more than five days after the original decision of the principal or his designate. If the original suspension decision is made within five days of the next regular meeting of the Board, the decision may be subject to appeal at the Board's following meeting.

  3. All student publications shall be produced by students. Editing shall be done by student editors, chosen by the publications staff. The principal

or designated representative shall be accorded the opportunity to review material to be printed prior to publication and may suspend publication of material he considers obscene, libelous, or will cause material disruption of educational environment. The decision of the principal or his designate may be appealed to the Area Director. The decision of the Area Director may be appealed to the Superintendent. The decision of the Superintendent may be appealed to the Board of Education at its next regular meeting after the decision of the principal or his designate if the next regular meeting is scheduled to occur more than five days after the original decision of the principal or his designate. If the original suspension decision is made within five days of the next regular meeting of the Board, the decision may be subject to appeal at the Board's following meeting. The copy of the procedures should be submitted to all editors and staff members of school publications.

4. Students shall have the right to wear buttons, armbands, and other badges of symbolic expression provided these expressions are not obscene, libelous, or cause material disruption of the educational environment.

5. Students shall have the right to choose their own dress, conduct, and personal appearance, insofar as they do not substantially disrupt, pose a clear and present danger to school operations, present an obscene appearance, or endanger health.

## II. USE OF SCHOOL FACILITIES

A. Any student, or group of students, may use any school facility (e.g., meeting rooms, mimeographing, etc.) at cost, provided that it is not needed for a scheduled educational purpose and pursuant to Board of Education policy.

B. Schools shall be open daily to parental observation.

## III. FREEDOM OF POLITICAL ACTIVITY

A. Students may not in any way be penalized for any political or moral beliefs which they have though they may be held responsible for their actions taken in line with those beliefs.

B. Students may form political organizations in the school so long as they do not have discriminatory membership restrictions.

C. Students shall have the privilege to plan and carry out voluntary forums, assemblies, seminars, and school programs of a political nature so long as they do not substantially disrupt or pose a clear and present danger to school operations.

D. Attendance at all assemblies shall be optional for students except those assemblies explicitly called for the efficient operation of the school.

E. Students shall have the right to demonstrate dissent in any lawful manner as long as they do not substantially disrupt or pose a clear and present danger to school operations. Individual students who violate specific school rules or city ordinances are individually responsible for these acts and shall be dealt with according to established procedures.

F. Students have the right to present petitions, complaints, or grievances to school authorities and the right to receive prompt authoritative replies from school authorities regarding the disposition of their petitions, complaints, or grievances.

G. Students have the right to respect from teachers and administrators, which would exclude their being subjected to cruel and unusual punishments, especially those which are demeaning or derogatory, or which diminish their self-esteem or exclude them from their peers.

## IV. DUE PROCESS

A. All students shall have the right to due process of law.

1. Students shall receive annually, upon the opening of school, a publication including, with reasonable specificity, a list of school rules, procedural rights, and the penalties which may be imposed for the violation thereof.

2. In all cases where major punishment may be the end result but not limited to, i.e., forced transfer to another school; refusal to grant a diploma, etc., students shall have the following procedural rights:

   a. The student shall have the right to at least a three (3) day notice in writing, of any charges against him/her which might result in major punishment and before such major punishment is commenced, with enough specificity if he or she so demands, to allow him or her to respond to said charges.

   b. The student or designated counsel shall be allowed to inspect at least 24 hours prior to any hearing exhibits which will be submitted in evidence.

   c. If the student so desires, he/she shall be entitled to a hearing before a Board of Inquiry to be conducted under rules set forth by the City Attorney's office for the City of Madison. This Board shall be composed of one person appointed by the student's School Principal; one person appointed by the parent or guardian of the student; and one person appointed by the President of the Board of Education. Any decision of a majority of this Board shall be final.

This hearing may be public or private at the option of the student and a written request for such hearing must be submitted to the building principal within seven days after the letter has been mailed. Any heretofore decreed punishment under this section shall be stayed pending this hearing which shall be held at the earliest moment practicable.

d. The student shall have the right of representation by a lawyer or some other person of his/her own choice at his/her own expense.

e. The student (and/or counsel) shall have the right to confront and cross examine any witness against him/her; the right to present a defense to charges and to produce oral testimony in his/her behalf.

f. Determination of guilt or innocence of the charges shall be based solely on evidence presented at the hearing.

g. If a student requests at least 24 hours before the hearing a written transcript of the hearing record, it shall be made available after the Board has reached a decision with the cost of said transcript to be borne by the Board of Education.

h. Every student shall be free from forced self-incrimination.

i. Any student may file a written waiver with the school of any rights under this Section.

j. All hearings where the ultimate result could lead to expulsion must be held before the Board of Education.

3. Short-term suspension (three days or less) may be imposed by the administration of the school only in cases where school rules (as printed) have been violated beyond a reasonable doubt and the stated punishment for violation of these rules is suspension. A copy of the letter addressed to parents describing the reason for suspension will be filed with the building principal and the Area Director. Appeals pertaining to suspensions shall be directed to the building principal and a copy filed with the Area Director. Work missed during the period of suspension may be made up through a student's own initiative. Work includes

homework, classwork, tests, and time missed in courses such as physical education. The absence from school during a suspension shall be considered an excused absence.

4. Opportunity for conferences must be extended to the parents of a suspended student following each suspension.

B. The school shall not collect or keep in its files any information which is not necessary for and directly relevant to a student's academic work and the school's educational purpose.

1. A student and his/her parents shall have the right to examine his/her files by appointment. Students' records shall be under the supervision of school personnel while being examined. A counselor may be requested to aid in interpreting test scores and related material.

2. Files shall not be made available to persons other than those with primary interest without the written consent of the student and/or parent.

3. Students and their parents shall have the right to write and insert in their files comments or responses to anything contained in the file.

4. Personal behavior files shall not be used as a method of evaluation of academic performance.

C. Students shall be free from the use of police by the school as an adjunct to its authority, in absence of crime or any threat of crime.

D. Decisions concerning students' rights made by local school personnel are subject to review and may be appealed to the Area Director, Superintendent of Schools, the Board of Education, and then the courts.

E. Students shall be free from the school's jurisdiction in all non-school activities, be it their conduct, their movements, their dress, or expression of ideas. No disciplinary action may be taken by the school for non-school activities provided the student does not claim without authorization to speak or act as a representative of the school. When a non-school activity results in police action, it is an infringement on the student's liberty for the school to punish that activity, or to enter it on the school record, or report it to prospective employers or other agencies, unless authorized by the student.

## V. PERSONAL COUNSELING

A. All students shall have the right to receive information in school on matters of personal concern pursuant to Board of Education policy and statutory limitation.

## VI. RIGHT TO A QUALITY EDUCATION

A. Students shall be afforded the opportunity of representation on curriculum planning committees and to the widest extent possible be included in other decision-making bodies affecting the quality of education.

B. Students shall have the right to evaluate the performances of administrators, faculty, and courses, to improve the quality of education. These evaluations will be available only to the person or course being evaluated.

C. Each student will have the right and responsibility for planning his/her education although students under 18 will require the consent of their parents. The interest, desires, and capabilities of each individual student shall be considered in the planning of his/her academic program. The advice of the school professional staff is available to each student in his planning.

D. Students shall have the privilege of open campus where the program presently exists. When determining whether the open campus privilege will be accorded in a particular school, the views of the surrounding community, the administration, the teachers, and the students of the school should be considered. If a program of open campus is adopted by the school, a student shall have the privilege of open campus if a parent permit form is filed with the building principal. The principal or parent has the right to revoke the open campus privilege of any individual.